Writings and Relics

Writings and Relics

1990–1995

Michael Almereyda

Sticking Place Books
New York

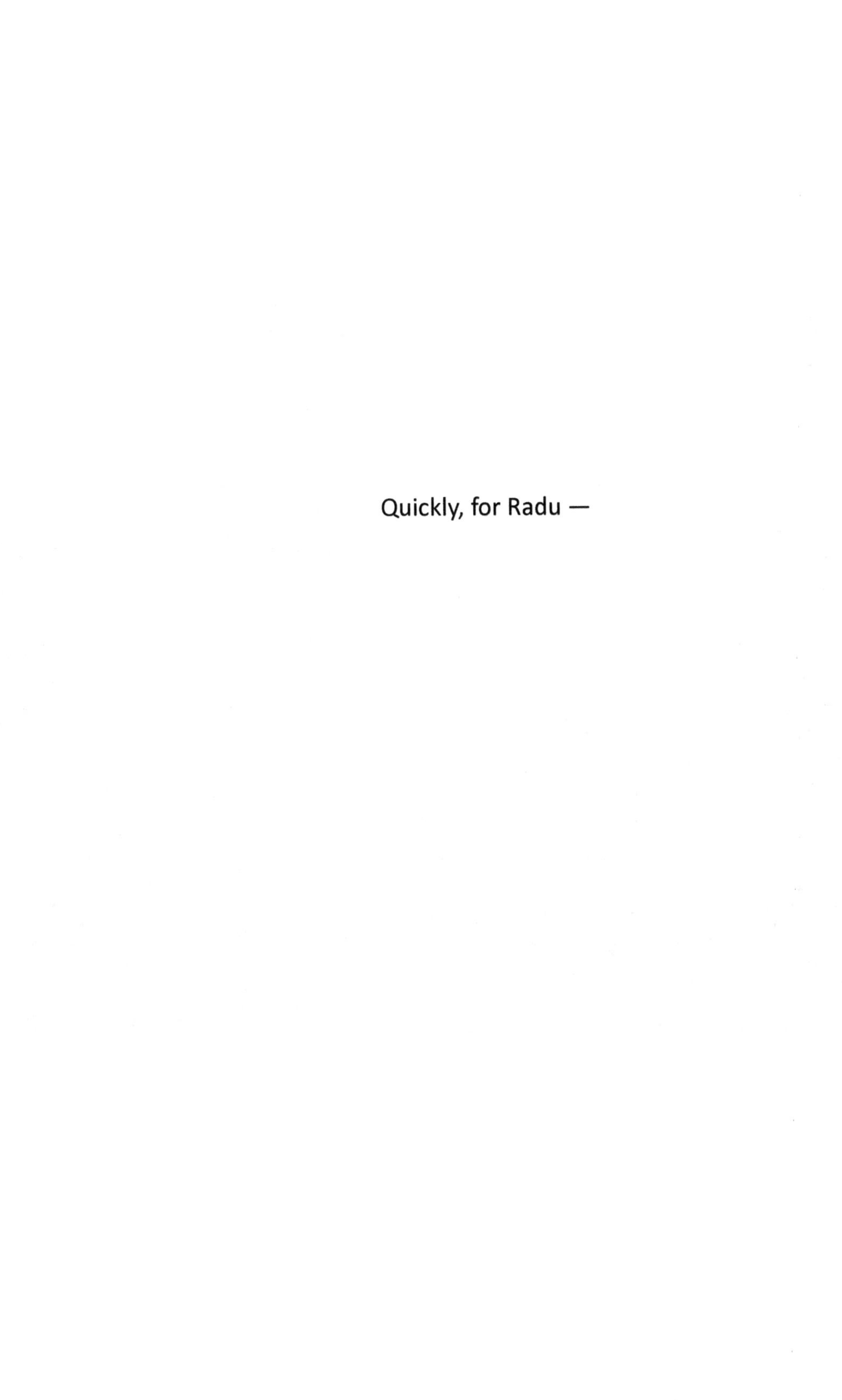

Quickly, for Radu —

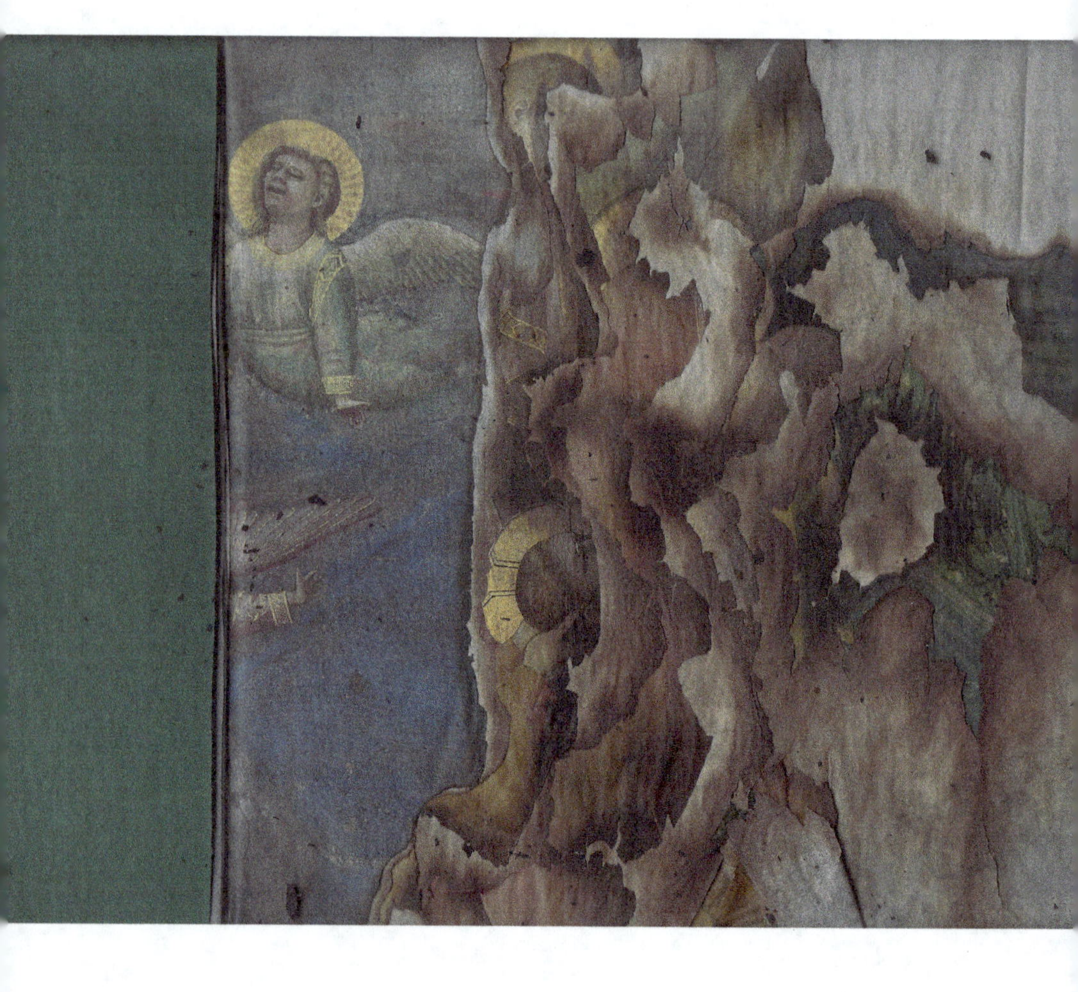

Contents

How did you know where to go?
By playing my memory like a roulette wheel.

— Susan Sontag, *Unguided Tour*

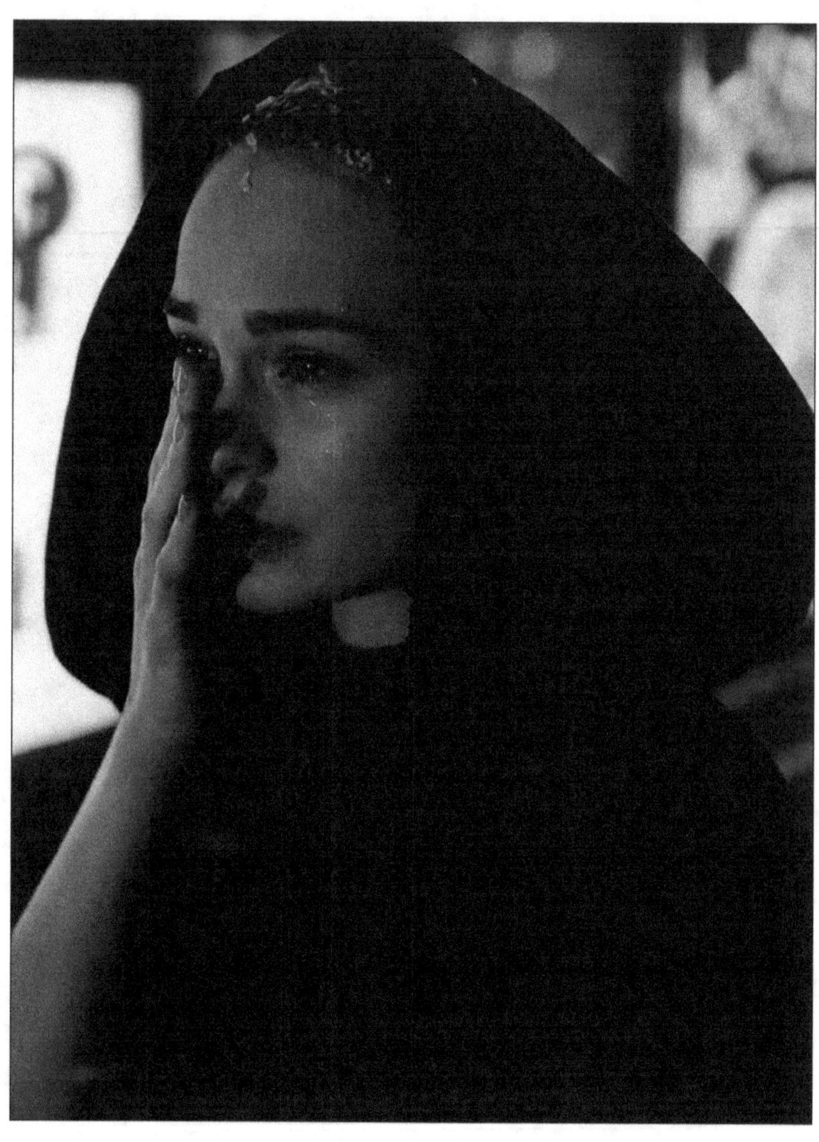

The vampire as wandering soul:
Elina Löwensohn in *Nadja*, 1994.

Introduction

> *She carried her head high, unlike everyone else on the sidewalk. And she seemed so delicate, she scarcely seemed to touch the ground as she walked... I had never seen such eyes.*
>
> — André Breton, *Nadja*, 1928

How do you find your way into a life unconstrained by complacency and routine? How to dissolve the boundaries separating waking life from the untamable world of dreams? How to live—and write—attuned to a state of wonderment, as if transported back to childhood, while remaining alert to the jagged cross-hatchings of anxiety and desire? André Breton, in his late twenties and early thirties, was preoccupied by such questions, and his first novel, *Nadja,* explicitly confronts them. The nominal plot kicks in on page 63, when the title character appears, a young woman calling herself Nadja ("because in Russian it's the beginning of the word hope, and it's only the beginning"), after meeting André, the narrator, by chance on a Paris street. There ensues a sequence of revelatory encounters; the woman embodies the principles of charmed coincidence, rapturous intuition, offhand clairvoyance and willful nonconformity that Breton shaped into a major aesthetic movement, if not quite a coherent philosophy. The André/Nadja relationship hinges, of course, on the tension and excitement of erotic possibility, and collapses once they share a hotel bed, though Nadja's wobbly mental health is unmistakably a factor in this dissolution. She ends up in a mental ward; André is unwilling to follow her inside.

Scholarship has revealed that episodes in the book were extrapolated from what we can warily call real life, with passages transcribed from letters Breton wrote to his wife at the time, tracking events as they were taking place over a concentrated nine days. In the introduction for his new translation, published in 2025, Mark Polizzotti distills contemporary detective work to provide thorough background on the real Nadja—Léona-Camille-Ghislaine Delcourt—and documents the tormented circumstances whereby Breton abandoned his muse while managing to mythologize her.

Nonetheless, *Nadja* is at its core a love story: two lost souls—or *wandering* souls, as Nadja describes herself—converge, however briefly, in the enchanted city. Forty-four full-page illustrations confirm the sense of enchantment, and amplify the book's originality: photos, napkin sketches, an array of amateurish and raw pictures that punctuate the text and yield the impression that the images have resulted from a haphazard but precise treasure hunt, and that Breton has recalled and recombined true experiences with an exacting sense of play.

I still value my 1960 Grove Press paperback, an Evergreen Original translated by Richard Howard. I remember being drawn in by the stark, jaunty orange-yellow-white cover, the stacked hand-written names: NADJA/ANDRÉ/BRETON. A band of yellow tape holds the spine of my copy intact, and the flyleaf reveals that the book was permanently borrowed, decades ago, from my friend Susan Tarr, who acquired it in 1967. (Susan, once an executive at Embassy Pictures, was largely responsible for giving me my first studio job, rewriting the screenplay for *Mandrake the Magician*, a fittingly surrealist project that was never produced.)

For Breton and his official cohort of poets, painters, photographers and filmmakers, Surrealism (yes, he capitalized it) was never imagined as an evasion of ordinary life, a fantastic replacement or escape, but a means for decanting a sense of delirium, mystery and magic—the unpredictable, alluring, exalted collision of images, feelings and thoughts that are otherwise hidden or forbidden behind conventional consciousness. The movement, of course, fostered conventions of its own, and for all its confrontational fury can appear more smoothly adaptable than any other modern art movement—the proof being its easy appropriation in advertising and in a broad range of unnecessary movies made in the shadow of David Lynch, whose own work tends to feel unmistakably original and urgent.

When, in 1993, Lynch offered to help produce one of *my* movies, provided I could come up with something that fit into a low budget and a definable genre, my thoughts veered to vampires and to *Nadja*. I extracted a few of Breton's sentences, his heroine's name, and strategies for arriving at surrealist openness and daring, wit and surprise, as best I understood them, transfusing the mixture into the bloodstream of *Dracula's Daughter*, the not-

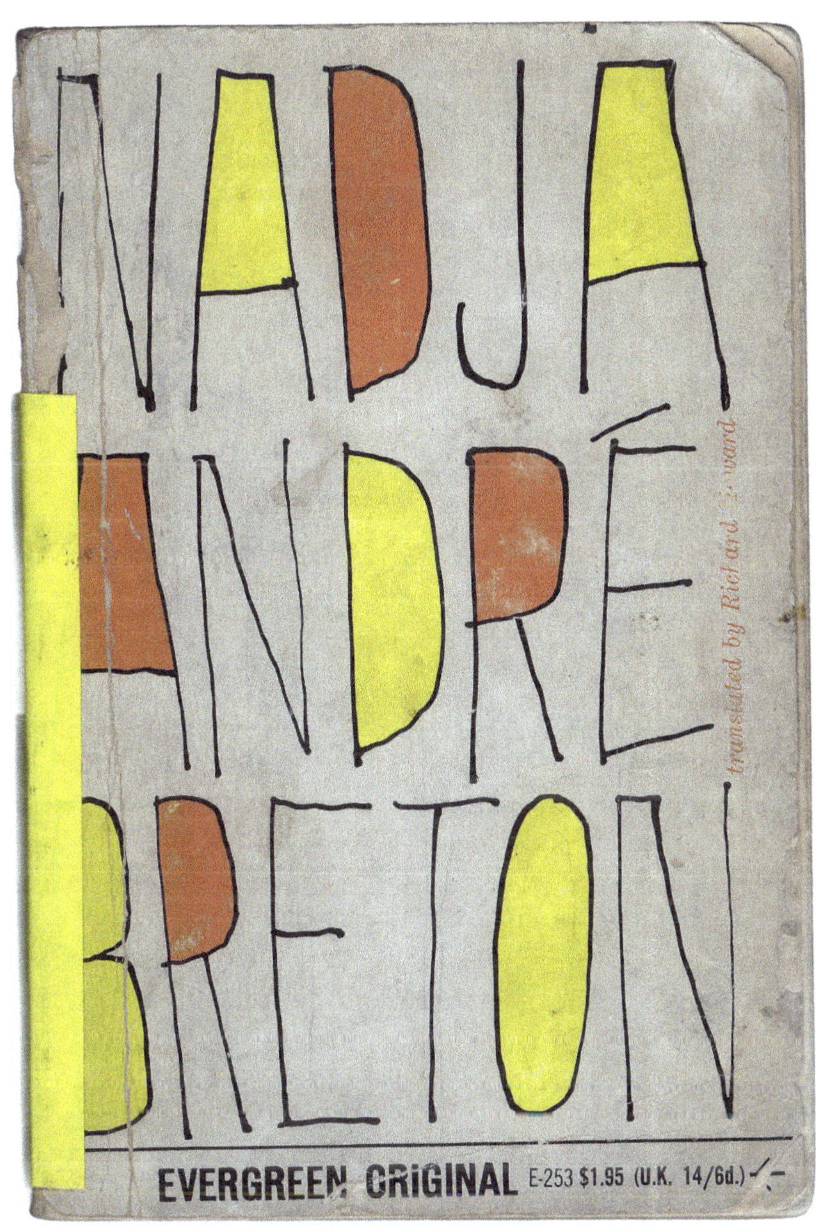

André Breton's unclassifiable *Nadja* had a more than incidental influence on my *Nadja*.

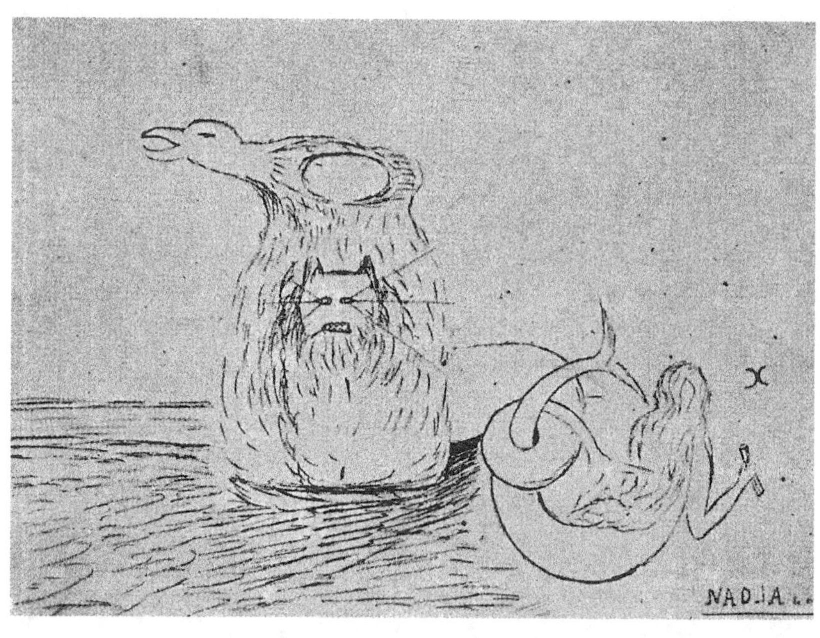

Nadja's self-portrait as a mermaid with a knotted tail.
She portrays André as a monster with radiant eyes,
an eagle straddling his head.

so-famous 1936 descendent of Tod Browning's *Dracula* from 1931. It was a rushed job, a giddy shotgun marriage.

It remains for me to circle around to the simple task of introducing the book at hand, a collection of published and unpublished writing bracketed by unearthed film stills, snapshots, sketches, postcards—people once sent *postcards*—and other random documentation from the early 1990s, specifically my 90s, reflecting a patch of personal history from a time when various projects were falling apart, or forced to the back burner, and I took up a plastic toy camera and managed to make an eccentric black-and-white vampire movie called *Nadja*, recently resurrected in a digitally remastered version, thirty-one years after its premiere at the Toronto International Film Festival.

The version of myself who wrote and directed the film feels far away, though he's not quite a stranger. I was younger, obviously, but not necessarily more hopeful. I was off balance with ambition and an unshakable sense of failure. I was only slightly more pretentious than I can currently be accused of being, though I was self-aware and self-mocking enough to project my heartfelt feelings into the spoofy story of a disconsolate vampire living in Manhattan, resolving to change her life. I offer up my films from that time, and these residual artifacts, with a mix of humility and pride, admitting from this distance that I'd experienced a measure of luck even as I was feeling unlucky, and sharing the evidence even if it's no more poignant and durable than footprints on a beach at low tide—assuming we're all heading toward the same horizon.

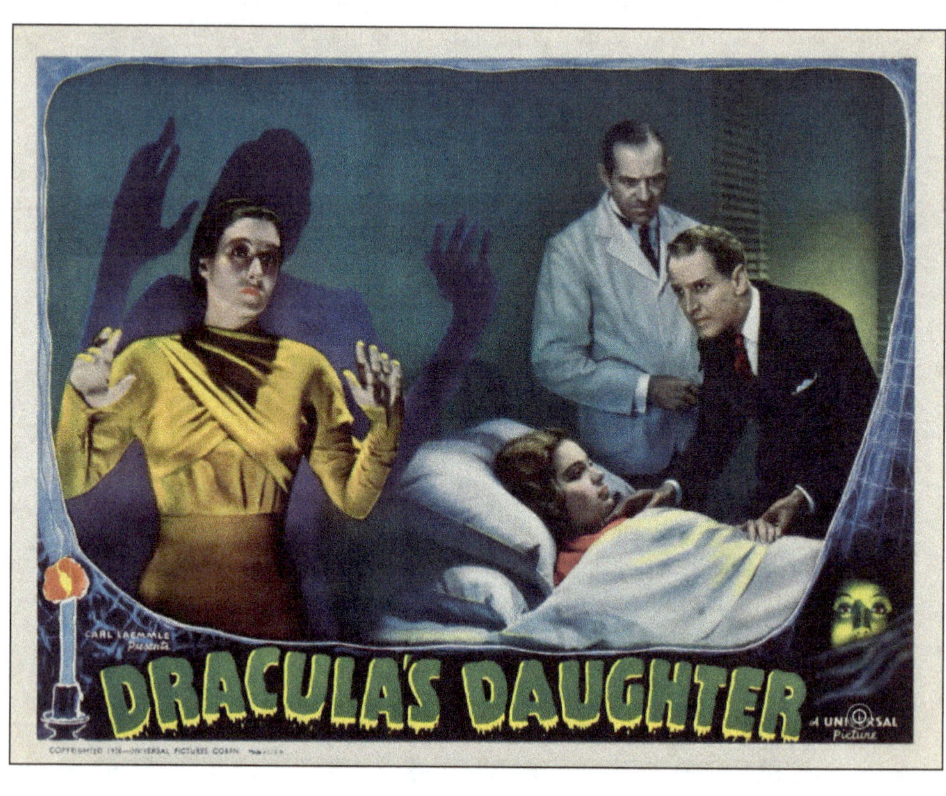

Poster for *Dracula's Daughter*, 1936.

Author's Note

This book was conceived of as a dossier or time capsule—not a memoir—
and can more accurately be described as a bird's nest, built out from documents and debris gathered from the defined five-year period. Inevitably,
a fair amount of autobiography has entered into the picture, like smoke
rising from a fire, making it fairly outrageous, for those acquainted with the
plain facts, that this account contains so many omissions and gaps. That's
the result of the almost instantaneous nature of the project—a process of
emptying boxes and folders, finding things I'd forgotten while looking for
others that are lost—as much as proof of vanity, memory loss, or discretion.
At any rate, most of the essays, photos, and drawings were produced by
yours truly between 1990 and 1995, unless otherwise captioned and credited, with a few retrospective spillovers thrown in for good measure. Previously published writing has been assigned dates but isn't always arranged
chronologically. More recent commentary, set in a different typeface, was
conjured in New York City in late December, 2025.

M.A.

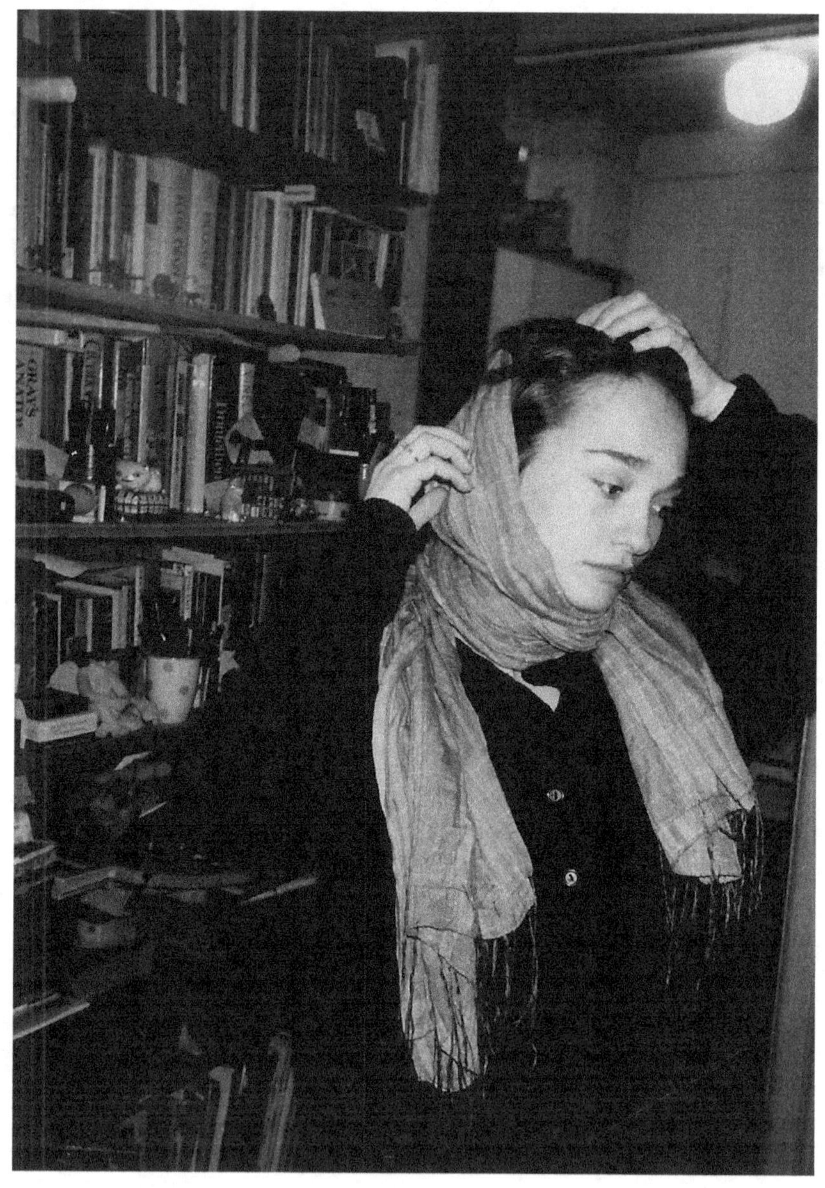

Elina Löwensohn in New York, 1990.

Heart Like a Dog

I first met Elina Löwensohn when she was a waitress at Around the Clock, a 24-hour place on East 9th St, December, 1989. Was it day or night? Elina assures me I came in for breakfast. I remember her zipping between tables with a wide smile, her incredible energy, her shiny cap of Louise Brooks hair, her cheekbones, her effusiveness. The Romanian revolution was frontpage news and she seemed giddy to acknowledge it and to relate her family history in and out of Romania. She was born in Bucharest. Her father had been a Holocaust survivor, eighteen years older than her mother, a dancer, and he'd had a role in the government, though his Jewishness hampered his career. He died when Elina was seven. Her mother, emigrating to the US, talked on Radio Free Europe and obtained a visa for Elina, her brother and grandmother by sleeping outside the Romanian embassy in Washington, DC.

She didn't reveal all this on our first encounter, but her basic and ongoing biography, breezily confided, was shared with matter-of-fact trust. *Nadja*, in due time, was written specifically for her, with personal details stitched into the screenplay. Yes, her father, valuing bodily strength, worrying about her thinness, forced her to eat sandwiches loaded with butter, and Elina, fleeing to the bathroom, scrubbed off the butter with a brush. Later, in the 90s in Massachusetts, her mother warded off diagnosis-resisting ailments with injections of shark plasma imported from Mexico. I didn't include these details to be mocking or weird; rather, I felt their weirdness anchored the character, giving access to a more poignant and specific human story, even if the original context was obscured.

Breakfasts at Around the Clock, at any rate, led me to offer Elina a role in a version of Dostoyevsky's *The Devils* played out among a gang of anarchist squatters. I've located some script pages and storyboards, reminding M.J. that was the inexplicable name given to the character I wanted Elina to play.

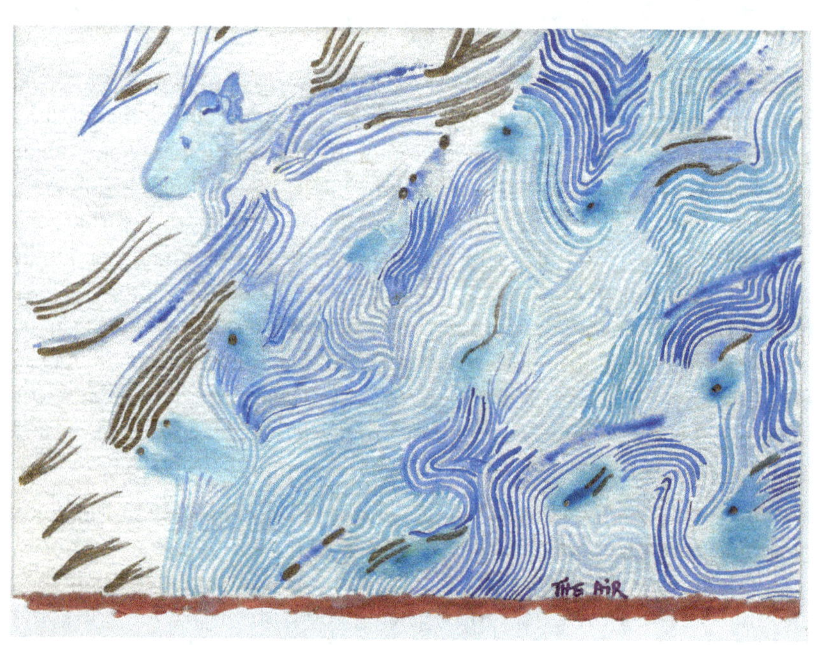

Watercolor and inscription by Elina Löwensohn. Circa 1992.

"... that the pains people endure would be less if only — if only they did not put so much imaginative energy into recalling the memory of past misfortune, rather than bear an 'indifferent' present with equanimity."

Goethe (and I think alike)

Elvira

I tossed elements of Conrad's *Secret Agent* into the script, and capped it with a title slanted from the Bulgakov novella *Heart of a Dog* (about a scientifically humanized dog trying to find decent housing in Soviet Russia). Yes, I was shameless/pretentious, but I don't remember advertising this source material, and I managed to attract a cast that included Lisa Bonet, Suzy Amis, Michael Rooker and Richard Brooks.

Elina agreed to do a test—a camera test, more than an audition—and wore a blue dress while sitting on the landing of my apartment's stairwell, setting fire to the tissue-thin pages of a book of Giotto paintings. (I still have this beautifully disfigured book.) We were echoing images in Derek Jarman's *The Last of England* and, like Jarman, we were shooting in Super 8, but the threshold of natural light was so low the images were unreadable. A fiasco.

Yet the project gathered steam. Roger Deakins read the script and was game to shoot the movie (decidedly *not* on Super 8) after I gave him a tour of the neighborhood, roving through the clotted encampment of plastic tents that had metastasized in Tompkins Square Park, devouring benches and fences and vast tracts of space. This would have been one of my few movies absorbing and reflecting the raw grit of local reality. I remember a lanky street hustler regaling us—me and Roger—as we passed his perch: *"Hey, it's Butch and Sundance!"*—which charmed me for half a minute before I realized this is what he'd call any pair of white guys who looked solvent enough to supply a handout.

But my efforts to raise financing for this adventure slammed into one wall after another. The fact that the script starts with a knot of young people swarming around a newly installed cash machine and lighting it on fire— that might go some distance toward accounting for this particular failure. I'm also willing to concede that, independent of market considerations, my take on Dostoevsky was probably too sweet-tempered, too inclined toward "lyricism," when the core of *The Devils* (the title is often translated as *Demons* or *The Possessed*) is more sinister and unsparing. I recognized something closer to its true spirit when, late in 1994, I attended a New York Film Festival screening of *Sátántangó* and watched it through, seven plus hours, fortified by complimentary coffee doled out at two fifteen minute breaks.

In telling the story of a fine-featured false prophet manipulating the wretched members of a collapsing farm collective, Bella Tarr and his co-screenwriter László Krasznahorkai delivered a wind-blasted mock-up of contemporary eastern Europe, even more trash-strewn than my East Village, making the tale as visceral as it is bleakly comic, anchoring it in mud while also dissolving it in mist and adding an element of metaphysical levitation, looping and elongating repeated scenes. From what I can tell, Tarr had zero patience for Dostoevsky's interest in love and mercy, but he captures the remorseless nihilism that slithers through Dostoevsky like a snake. I recognized Tarr's masterwork, in any case, as something more daring and far superior to the adaptation I had in mind. Besides, when New York City officially shut down Tompkins Square Park, dismantled Tent City and shoveled the homeless population into less scenic precincts—my desire to make *Heart Like a Dog* was effectively snuffed out.

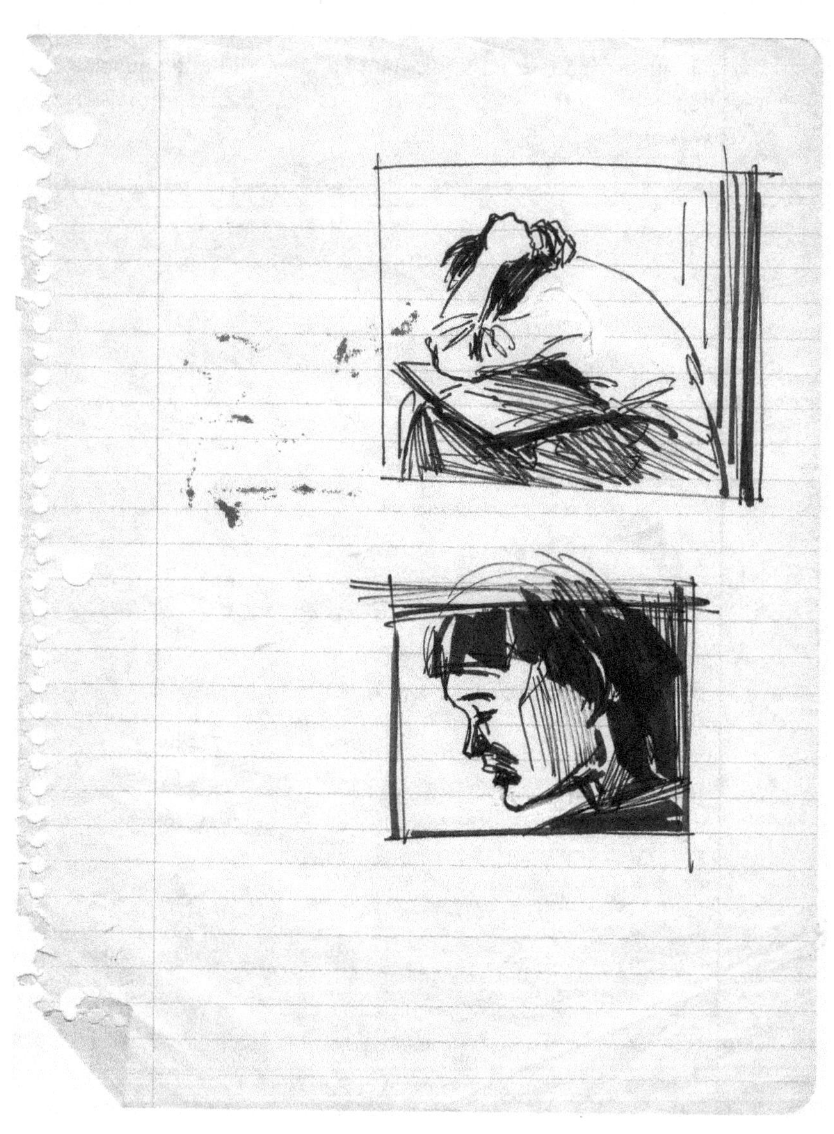

Above and over: samples of my storyboards for *Heart Like a Dog*, 1990.

B.

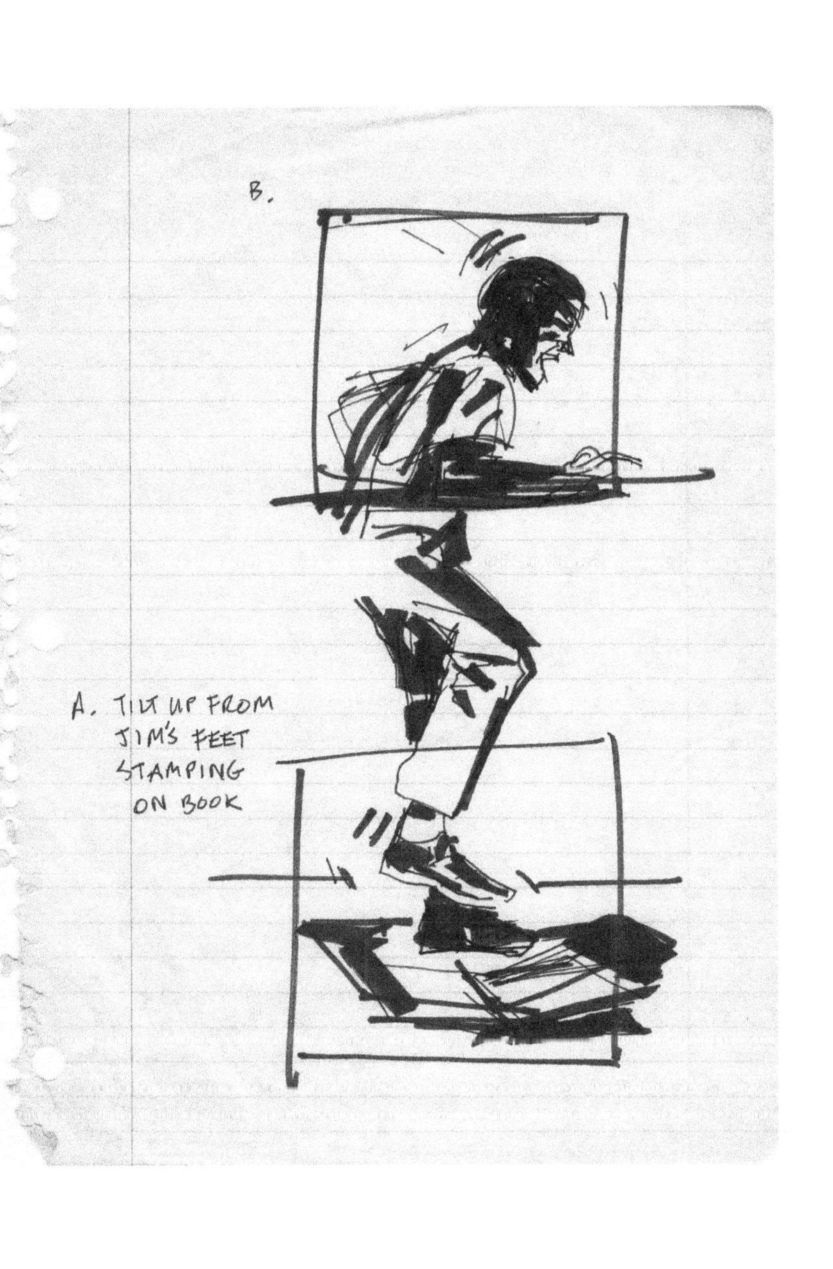

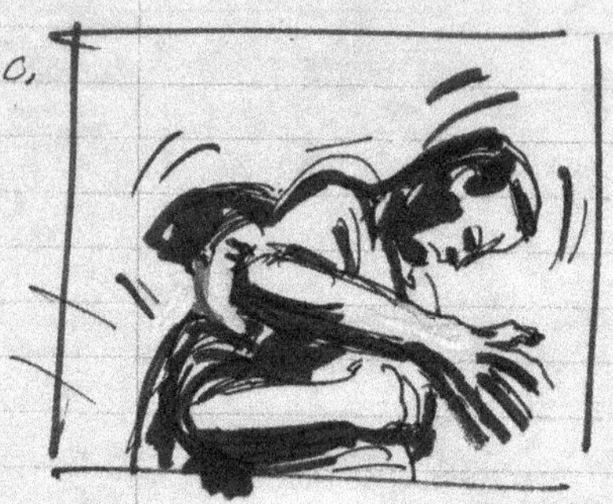

C.

M.J. GRABS HIM
FROM BEHIND

A SCUFFLE - SHE
SWINGS HIM AROUND (LEFT)
- HE ABRUPTLY
EMBRACES
HER   D.

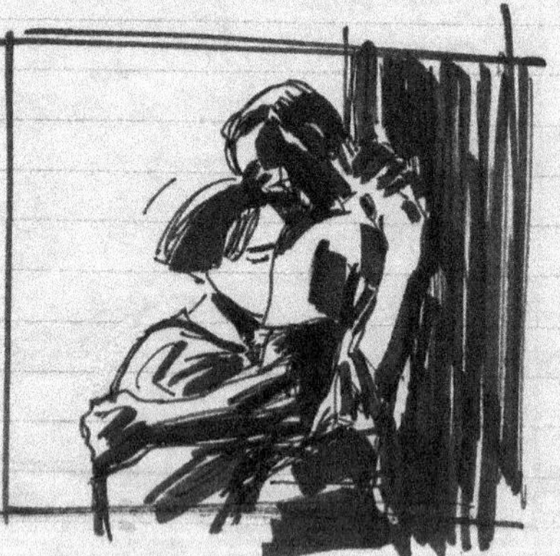

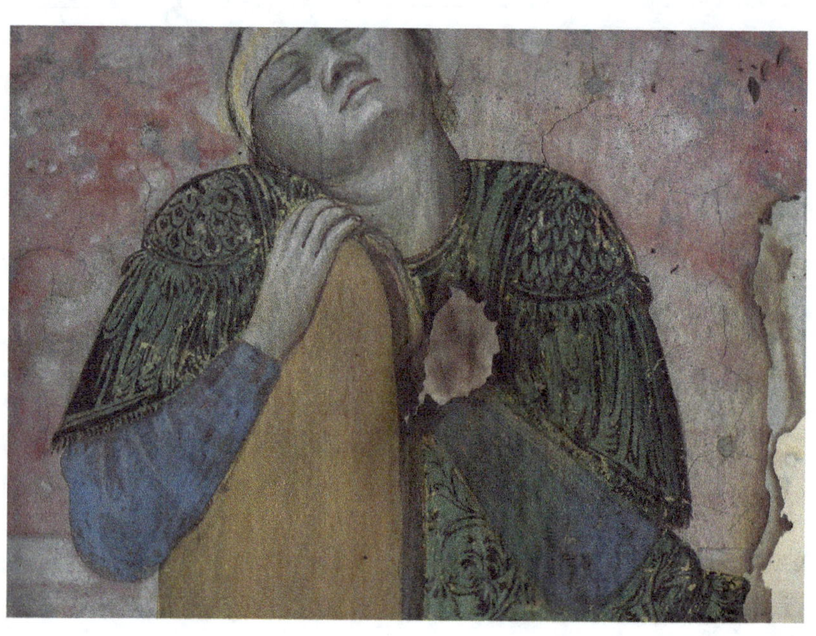

Surviving pages from a scorched Giotto book—artifacts from our failed test shoot.

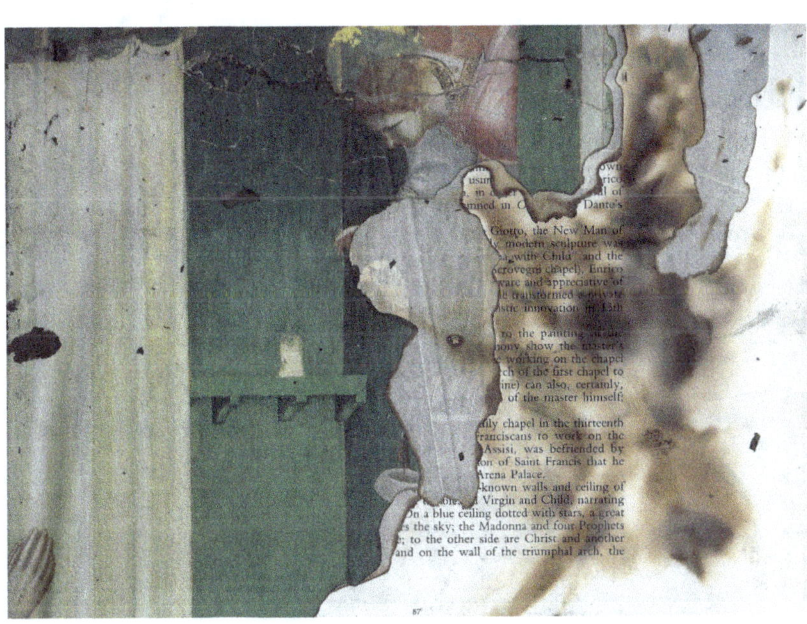
own
usin   rico
n, in   al of
mned in C   Dante's
Giotto, the New Man of
ly modern sculpture was
a with Child and the
crovegni chapel), Enrico
ware and appreciative of
le transformed a private
istic innovation in 13th
to the painting of the
nony show the master's
e working on the chapel
ch of the first chapel to
ine) can also, certainly,
of the master himself.
ily chapel in the thirteenth
ranciscans to work on the
Assisi, was befriended by
on of Saint Francis that he
Arena Palace.
known walls and ceiling of
Virgin and Child, narrating
ue ceiling dotted with stars, a great
y; the Madonna and four Prophets
other side are Christ and another
he wall of the triumphal arch, the

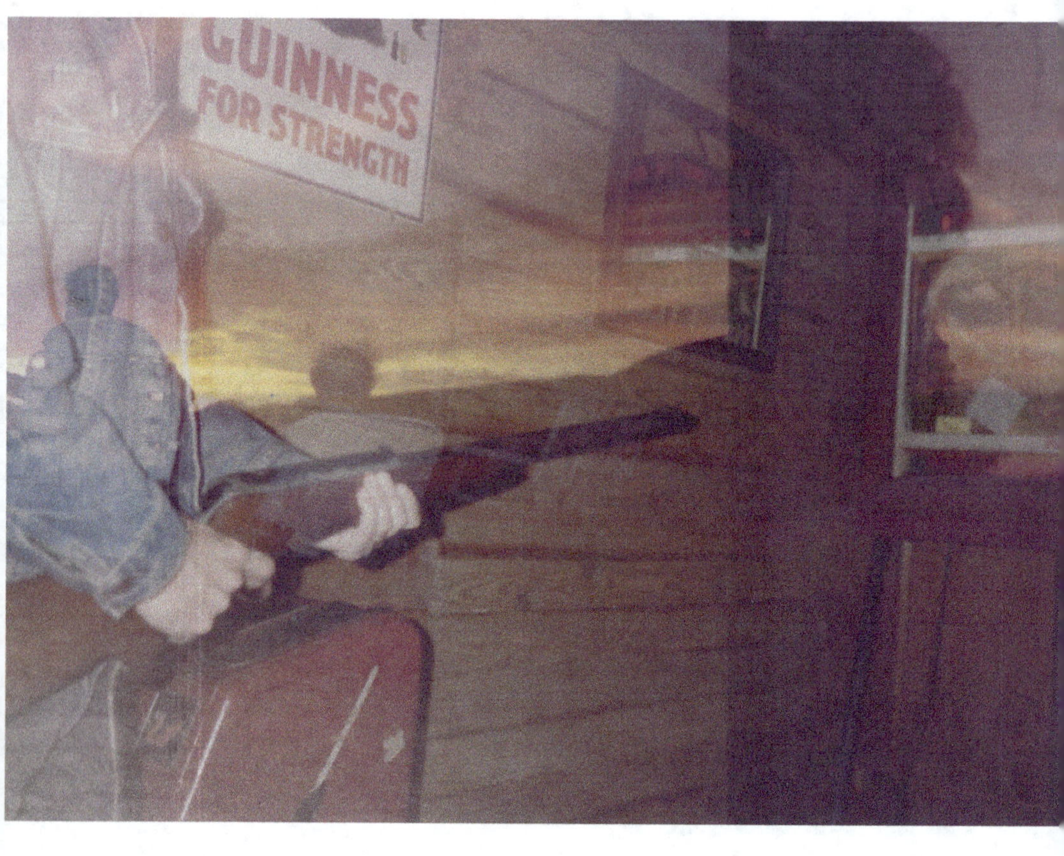

Jamie Bishop in New Orleans,
overlapping a sunset in Cabo San Lucas, Mexico, 1990.

The Fun of It

In the distant, pre-digital era, it was possible to shoot a roll of film, leave the cartridge in your camera, then shoot another run of pictures—to produce uncontrolled, accidental double exposures, only learning of the blunder when you picked up the results from the lab. A sunset in Cabo San Lucas, Mexico bleeds into a New Orleans bar, leaving just faint traces of the people in a fishing boat you were also trying to document. Looking at these photographs, I can regret that I didn't make this mistake more often.

The young man aiming the electronic gun is Jamie Bishop, my most reliable traveling companion from that time, a painter who had eased into movie art departments thanks to a lift from his brother Dan, an ace production designer. (They both worked on my first feature, *Twister*, shot in Wichita, Kansas in 1988. Dan was the art director; Jamie was in charge of props.) Given his aura of offhand physical assurance—you can glimpse it here, I think, in these photos—I'll always valorize Jamie for his mastery of *things*, his comfort with all the charmed and challenging objects and processes that can seem to define physical reality: furniture, firearms, barbecue grills, cars and trucks, machines of all kinds; electricity, for that matter, and *weather*; dogs and fish, plants and trees, and nearly anything, really, that you could keep in a tool shed or fit in your backyard. He was one of the most open-hearted people I'd ever met, and the world seemed to open up in his presence. In Wichita we'd undergone episodes of heartbreak that felt semi-symmetrical and we rode out the desolation with a shared instinct to look the other way and, given the opportunity, to light out for the territories. Over the next several months and, for that matter, years, I visited Jamie on relatively remote film sets when he took jobs out of town—in Kadoka, South Dakota and Eagle Pass, Texas, Lafayette, Louisiana and Jamestown, Virginia. Otherwise, I was content to play Tom Sawyer to his Huck Finn back in New York, floating through a circuit of East Village bars that operated within a few blocks of one another: the International, the Horseshoe Bar, Sophie's, Max Fish, the Chair Bar, the Cowboy Bar, the Tile Bar. We assigned our own names to half of these places. The Chair Bar, I remember, was below street level on Orchard, and it was where Jamie turned from his martini and decked a fellow customer with an agile punch when the guy tried to slam a chair on his head. (Jamie finished his martini; we were not invited back.)

I'd moved from Los Angeles to Manhattan in late 1989, in large part motivated by a need to escape the feeling, the fact, that my life had become circumscribed by the movie business, though I was darting around a lot and kept circling back to LA, kept trying, with various levels of ingenuity, to throw myself into other projects. *Twister* had been a troubled film that sank out of sight when the company that financed it went out of business. Its meager commercial release came about because Jonas Mekas happened to like it, tipped off by *New York Times* critic Vincent Canby. Anthology Film Archives screened it for a short spell, but that, and a few sympathetic reviews, didn't convince anyone to provide financing for my next picture.

I'd spent a great deal of time researching and writing a script about Amelia Earhart. My friend Jim Robison, a wonderful novelist and short story writer, co-authored the screenplay. He recently recalled our meeting, in 1990, in the Silver Lake home of producer Lynda Obst, the elfin, raspy-voiced producer of *Adventures in Babysitting,* who told us: "I am going to produce the fuck out of your movie." Lynda had just wrapped *The Fisher King* the day before and her conviction seemed unquestionable.

I had sifted through extensive archival material in the Natural History Museum in LA and Radcliffe's Schlesinger Library, but extra fuel for the fire was provided by a visit to Muriel Earhart Morrissey, who had outlived her older sister by several decades. When I learned Muriel was in Medford, Massachusetts, I simply called her up, introduced myself, and said I'd like to talk.

Muriel's voice was bright and clear. She said: "A lot of people call and ask me things, but first I want to ask *you* a question."

"Sure," I said, bracing myself.

"Which side of a bear has the most fur?"

I said, "I don't know."

Muriel said: "The *out*side."

The conversation picked up from that point on. She continued with: "What did one wall say to the other wall?"

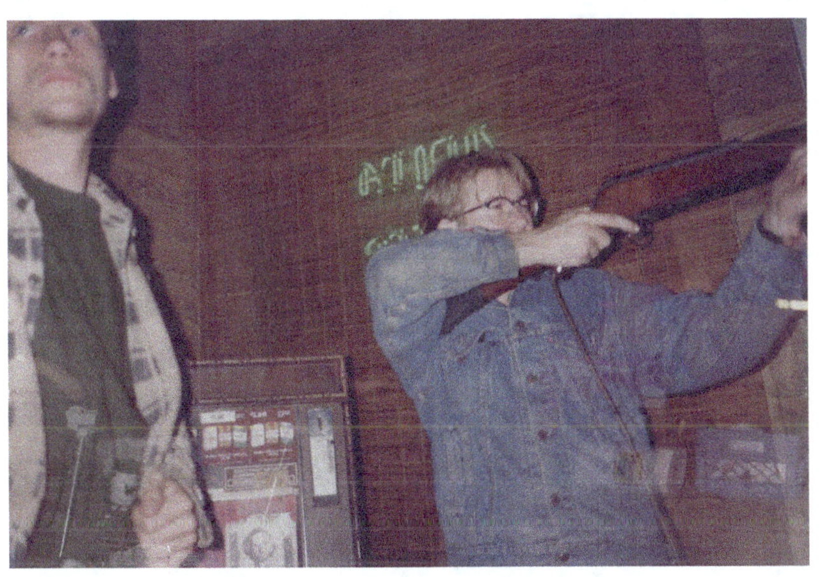

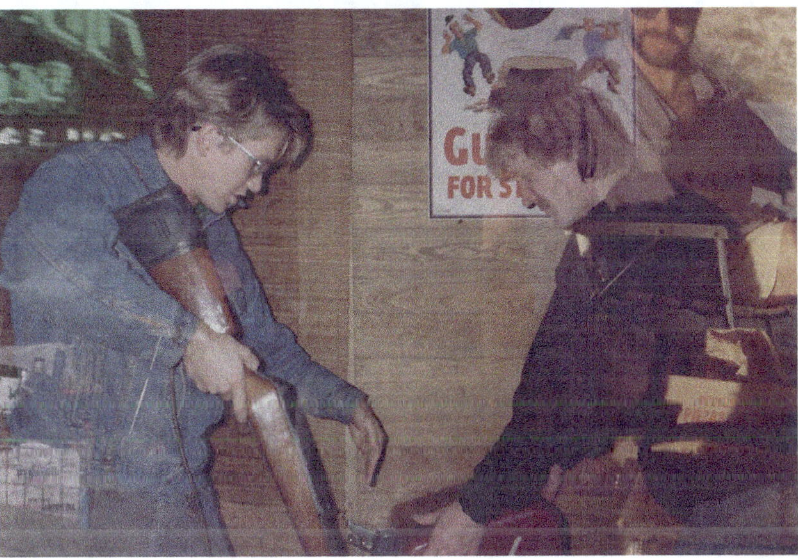

Michael Martin, Jamie Bishop, John Kofler in New Orleans,
overlapping John Hemmindinger on a boat in Mexico, 1990.

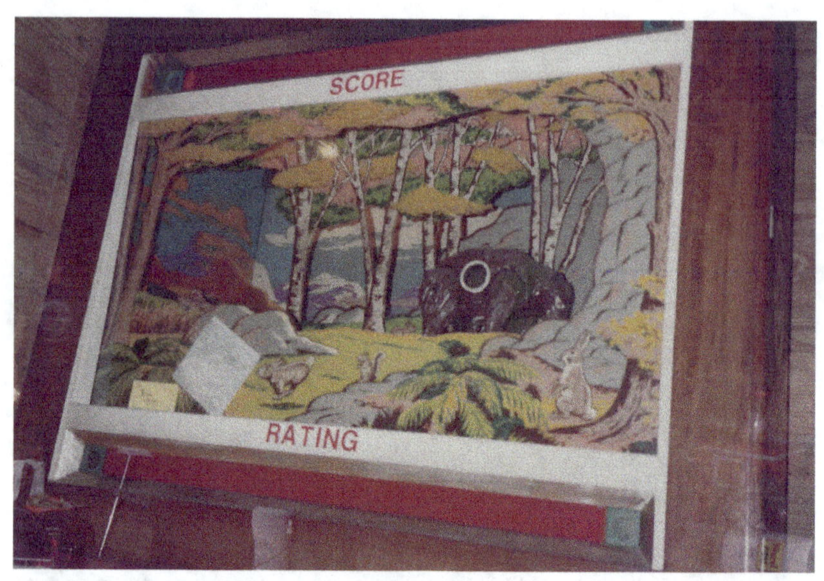

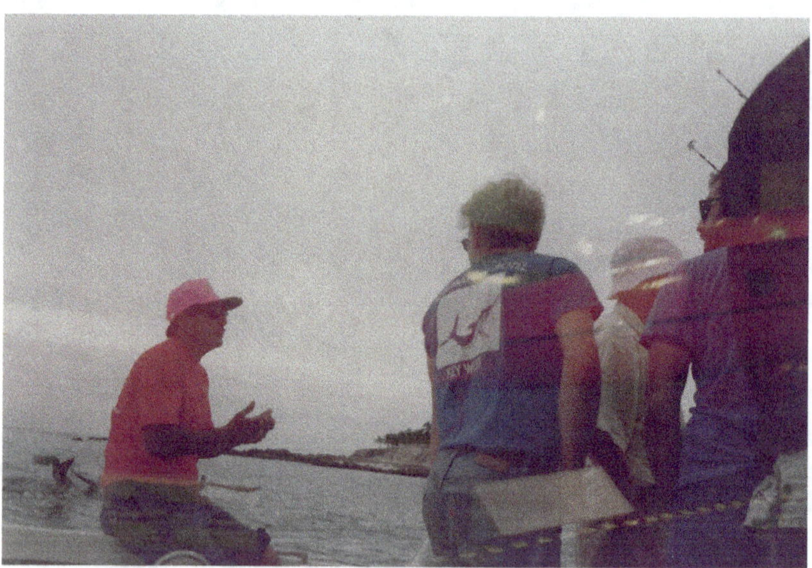

A bar in New Orleans fusing with Jamie Bishop,
Noel and John Hemmindinger in Cabo, 1990.

"I don't know."

"Meet you at the corner."

"What's the best way," I said, "to catch a rabbit?" A pause, then I told her: "Hide in the bushes and make a noise like a carrot."

This was enough to provoke an invitation to visit Muriel at her home. Ahead of the meeting, Muriel's daughter cautioned that her mother was about to turn ninety and she, the daughter, felt a need to be there with us. I remember feeling shy and slow, once the three of us gathered in her living room. The out-of-focus photo I managed to take, and keep, confirms that Muriel had a radiant smile and was wearing a nifty candy-striped dress. Her resemblance to her vanished sister was, of course, thrilling to me.

But I didn't know how to coax her into saying or revealing anything that hadn't already been said or revealed, anything that wasn't pre-rehearsed and settled. I began to wish I knew more dumb jokes. Finally, I asked: "When you think of Amelia, what's the thing you remember most?"

And Muriel said, "She was a lot of fun to be around."

What else would you want someone to say about you, I thought.

Jim and I focused our script on four years in Amelia Earhart's life, centering on her relationship with publisher and promoter George Palmer Putnam, who had plucked her from a crowd of candidates to be the first woman to fly across the Atlantic Ocean. She agreed to marry him after he proposed seven times. The script ends before Amelia's final flight, her disappearance, but events are shadowed by the anticipation of it. We imagined the film to have the quick bantering energy of a Howard Hawks movie, with the characters impelled by a similar element of existential daring, risking it all while maintaining an air of brazen good cheer. I took a clue from the title of Amelia's autobiography, *The Fun of It*, understanding her definition of "fun" to include what Yeats called "a lonely impulse of delight" in the face of foreseeable death. We aimed to track that impulse riding inside the story of an imbalanced marriage. I loved Amelia, and love her still, for her contradictions, for how her gray eyed Midwestern coolness didn't quite conceal an essential wildness.

Casting, I remember, presented a major hitch. I was angling to cast Suzy Amis, the forthright, flawless lead in *Twister* and a striking Earhart lookalike, but of all the young actresses in existence, only Julia Roberts, Lynda Obst lamented, could launch a studio movie at that time. We agreed this was not the solution. (Lynda produced the fuck out of *Sleepless in Seattle* in 1993.)

Muriel signed a book of her poems for me, a thin pamphlet printed on blue paper, which I can't locate at the moment, and she mailed a note in receipt of roses I sent for her birthday. Wikipedia tells me she died, age 98, in 1998. Lynda Obst, approaching legendary status as a trailblazing hitmaker and unblushing memoirist, died in 2024, age 74. Between these two events, Mira Nair directed a low-flying Amelia Earhart biopic, released in 2009. I can't help but admit, despite the steep odds, that my desire to make my Earhart movie is undiminished.

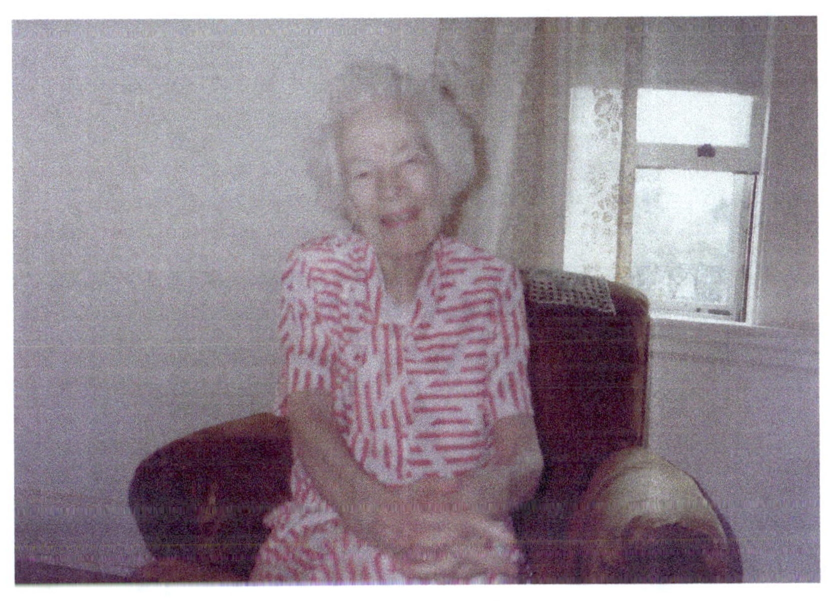

Muriel Earhart Morrissey at home in Medford, Massachusetts, 1989.

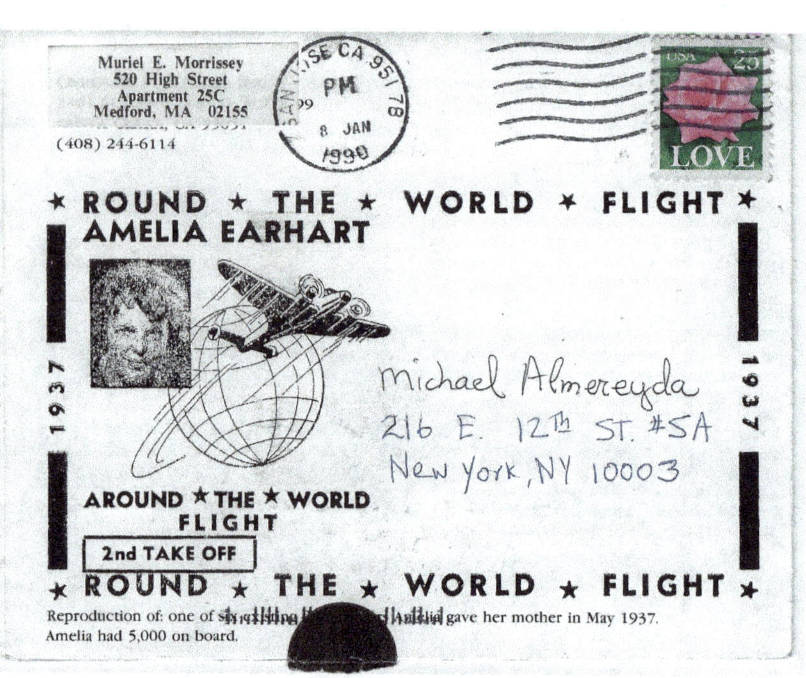

Greetings from Muriel Earhart Morrissey, 1990.

Throughout the story, we see a woman guided by a mix of ambition and selflessness, uncertainty and courage, gathering her inner resources to move beyond mere fame -- all the while insisting she's simply doing things "for the fun of it."

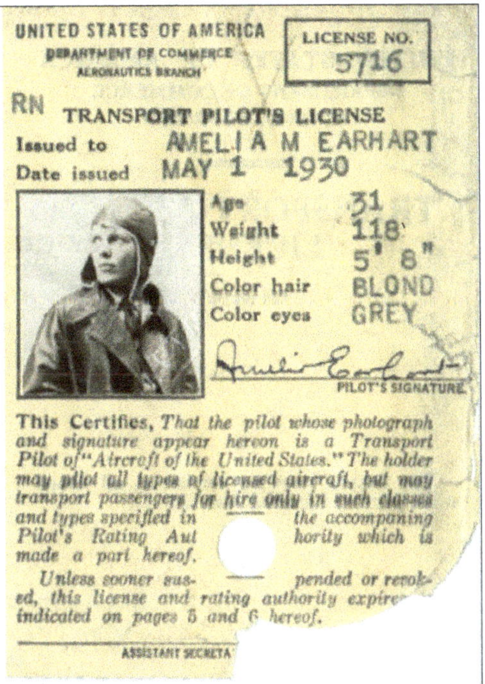

UNITED STATES OF AMERICA
DEPARTMENT OF COMMERCE
AERONAUTICS BRANCH

LICENSE NO.
5716

RN TRANSPORT PILOT'S LICENSE

Issued to   AMELIA M EARHART
Date issued MAY 1 1930

Age   31
Weight   118
Height   5' 8"
Color hair   BLOND
Color eyes   GREY

PILOT'S SIGNATURE

This Certifies, *That the pilot whose photograph and signature appear hereon is a Transport Pilot of "Aircraft of the United States." The holder may pilot all types of licensed aircraft, but may transport passengers for hire only in such classes and types specified in the accompaning Pilot's Rating Aut hority which is made a part hereof.*

Unless sooner sus- pended or revoked, this license and rating authority expire indicated on pages 5 and 6 hereof.

ASSISTANT SECRETA

A page from a lookbook intended to generate interest in *The Fun of It*, featuring Amelia Earhart's 1930 pilot's license.

                    JIM
          ~~It's about my dad. He's giving~~
          ~~us a lot of trouble now. We can't~~
          control him. He wants to get
          ~~married.~~

                    AMELIA
          He must be crazy.

Dorothy Putnam, in a black velvet dress, drunk, enters and
crosses to the refrigerator, opens it.

                    DOROTHY
          Sorry. I thought George might be in
          ~~here.~~

                    JIM
               (mutters)
          ~~He's pretty cold by now if he is.~~

Dorothy gets the rest of the pie and sits with Amelia. Jim
~~goes back to his whistling and scrubbing, occasionally~~
stealing glances at the two women.

                    DOROTHY
          ~~You aren't afraid of me.~~

                    AMELIA
          No. Why should I be?

Dorothy shakes her head.

                    ~~DOROTHY~~
          It's not that you're unobservant.

                    ~~AMELIA~~
          I hope not.

                    ~~DOROTHY~~
          You're just fearless.

                    -AMELIA
          - ~~What are you talking about?~~

Dorothy seems to have been talking to herself, but now
refocuses on Amelia, with a fierce, steady gaze.

                    DOROTHY
          Some people - most people - reach a
          ~~certain stage in their lives and~~
          they make deals with themselves not
          to feel things any more.
               (MORE)

                    DOROTHY (CONT'D)
          They decide it's too painful, they
          give up, they decide not to care.
          Do you know this?

                    AMELIA
          Yes.

                    DOROTHY
          Well - George isn't like that.

Amelia inclines her head, listening carefully, half
suspecting what she's getting at.

                    AMELIA
          And you're not like that.

                    DOROTHY
               (abruptly desolate)
           - I don't know any more.

EXT. POINT HARBOR AIRSTRIP (LONG ISLAND) - DAY

A pasture and a hangar. A Ford Trimotor skims down, touches
ground, skips, then goes into a sudden, uncontrolled skid.

INT. TRIMOTOR CABIN - DAY

Amelia is fighting the stick as the plane continues to skid
and jolt; CARL HARPER, 35, seated beside her, has his strong
arms wrapped over his head.

EXT. AIRSTRIP - DAY

The plans sheers off the planed runway, shoveling a trough in
the sod. It nearly noses over but settles upright, plowing to
a stop.

INT. CABIN - DAY

The windscreen is splintered. Amelia's rubbing her shoulder,
shaken and angry. Harper begins speaking, calmly, as if
picking up the thread of an earlier conversation.

                    HARPER
          You know what you did?

                    AMELIA
          Yeah. Again.

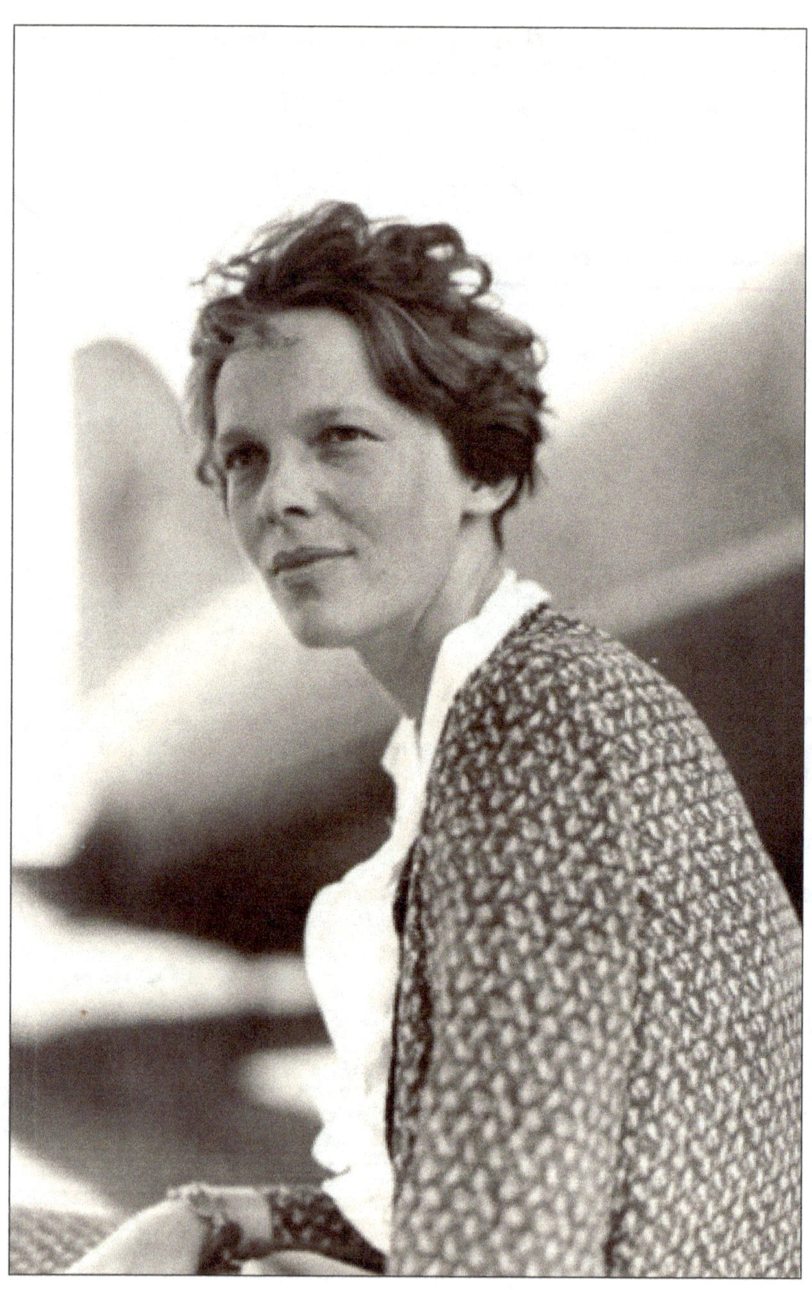

Amelia Earhart.

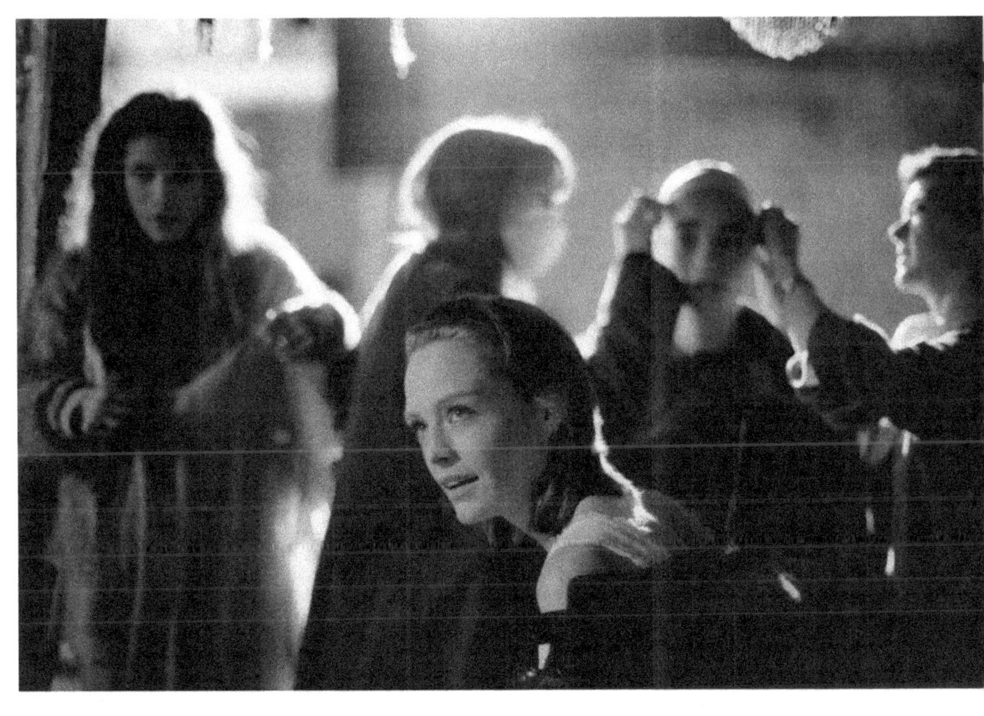

Suzy Amis on the set of *Nadja*. Behind her: Galaxy Craze on the left;
Libby Villanova and Prudence Moriarty secure a bald cap on
Elina Löwensohn. New York City, 1994.
Photograph by Susan Shacter.

Tips For Better Video

Holding Camcorder:

The handle area of the PXL2000 Camcorder is designed for a comfortable grip by either the right or left hand. Figure 10 shows the correct holding position for comfort and better video.

- Keep your hands and fingers away from the microphone to prevent recording any unwanted noise.

- Hold the camcorder steady by supporting your arms against your sides or a stationary object such as a tree or wall. Also brace the soft rubber eyecup against your face.

- If you want to move your field of view, move the camcorder slowly and steadily. If you are following a moving subject, try to move a little ahead to compensate for stop and go action.

- Use the mini bipod when you want to be in the video or when you simply need the steady support of a table or other flat surface.

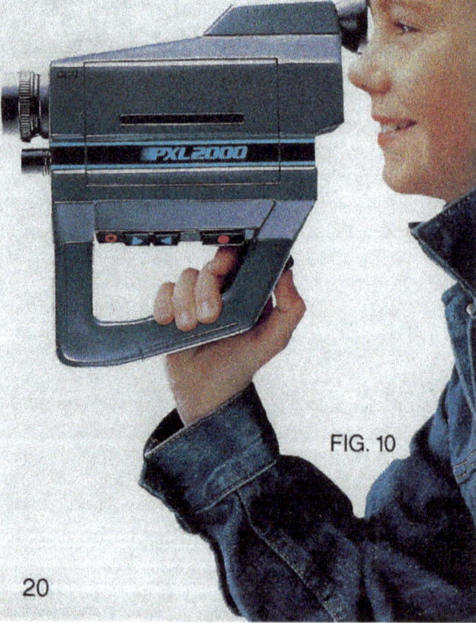

FIG. 10

From the brochure accompanying the Fisher-Price PXL 2000 camera, 1987.

My Stunning Future:
The Luxuries of Pixelvision

This is a testimonial for a technically defunct medium, an endorsement for a product you can't buy, and incidental proof that sometimes you can only be taken seriously when you choose to act like a child.

I'm talking about the Fisher-Price PXL 2000, a plastic video camera manufactured in 1987, marketed as a kid's toy, and discontinued three years later. Folklore has it that images produced by this camera—black-and-white, framed by a boxy internal border—are composed of a grid of two thousand square "pixels." This accounts for the camera's tacky, sci-fi name. The pixels shift and shimmer and seem to shed light as you watch, endowing everything the camera records with a distinct phys-icality, a lush trembling texture, a feel of floating weight and depth. In other words, the pixel image is alive—completely unlike the flat, cold quality of ordinary video.

In its customary use, the pixel camera records picture and sound on a standard audio cassette. You get about five minutes of imagery on one ninety-minute tape. Flip the cassette and you can record on the other side. This is swell, but the tape is crude and unstable and you have to contend with the cassette's considerable whirring noise which, inter-cepted by the camera's built-in mike, can resemble one of those machines used for polishing rocks.

Side-stepping the camera's clumsier habits, I made an hour-long pixelvision film. This involved a series of simple but apparently unprecedented technical adjustments,* but it hardly qualifies me as an expert. My introduction to the medium came through Sadie Benning, the one accredited pixelvision whiz-kid, fifteen when her father James Benning, a tremendous filmmaker, gave her the camera for Christmas. Late in 1991 (three Christmases later) a friend showed me about forty minutes' worth of Sadie's work up to that time.

These justly famous tapes are basically video diaries, raw, urgent and funny. The camera (occasionally whirring demoniacally) crawls over tabloid headlines or a TV screen, or ribbons of Sadie's sharp, block-lettered writing accompanied by bursts of deftly chosen music. The main spectacle is Sadie's tow-headed face, intently outstaring the camera while her dry, low voice says stuff like: "My arm is made of ham."

She also says: "I've been waiting for the day to come when I could walk down the streets and people would look at me and say, 'That's a dyke!' And if they didn't like it, they would fall into the center of the earth and deal with themselves."

I remember thinking of Linda Manz, wistful and tough in *Days of Heaven*. And of the megawatt space embryo in *2001*. Sadie Benning seemed as vulnerable and all-knowing and, under the scrutiny of this particular camera, she seemed to radiate light. But mainly I didn't think of other movies because Sadie Benning was addressing the world on her own terms, and those terms—the honesty and grit and intimacy of her voice—seemed inseparable from the effects achieved through this strange cheap camera.

I mean, there's no mistaking Sadie's out-of-the-gate brilliance, but I also got the impression that anything shot in pixelvision might be riveting, even though (or because) the image appears in danger of disintegrating as you watch. Or rather, it is disintegrating, and continuously reconstituting itself, each picture sifted through a fine but distinctly perceptible sieve of white/gray/black pixels. It's as if the camera is prospecting for light. You have the sense that you're watching something intensely fragile and secret, on the threshold of visibility. You think of all sorts of images from lost or low-grade mediums: black-and-white Polaroids, third-generation photocopies, pulpy newspaper photos. Given a dose of art history, you might also think of Degas monotypes and Seurat drawings and coarsely beautiful photographs made by Bill Brandt and Robert Frank. If you happen to love movies, you can't help thinking of silent films, the Lumière brothers, incunabular nitrate. For

---

* We channeled the pixelvision output onto a Beta SP deck; offlined on ¾¼" tape, then onlined the Beta to a one-inch master; transferred that to 16mm film.

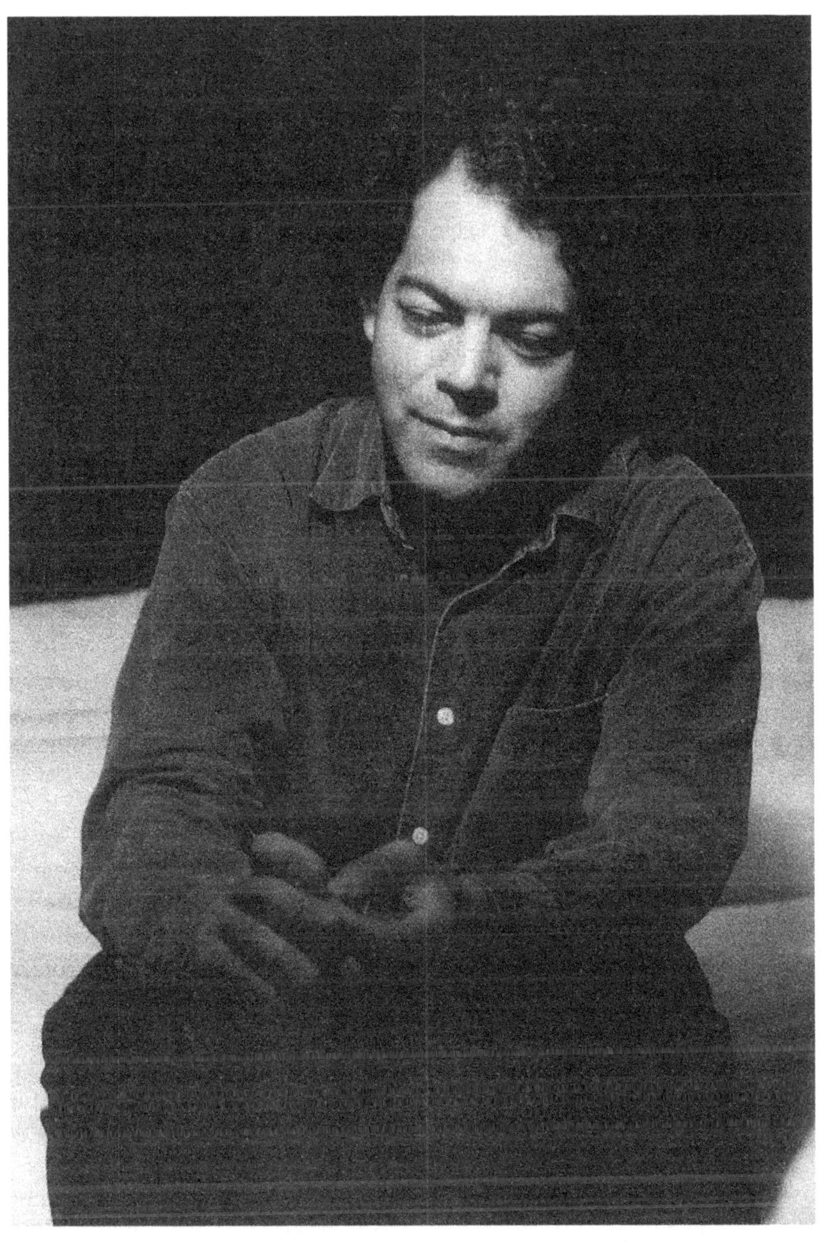

A Greg Henry prevailed upon me to be photographed for a book of portraits of film directors—a book that never materialized. New York City, 1992.

that matter, you think of dreams, cave paintings in candlelight, the Shroud of Turin, breath on glass.

I was smitten, raving like this to a friend on the street, when a young woman, hovering near, pulled a pixel camera out of her purse. She said Fisher-Price was selling them, used and repaired, for $45 apiece, and she provided an 800 number linked to operators in Ohio.

The cameras—I ordered four; three actually worked—arrived in a single box, nestled among Styrofoam peanuts, coiled power cords, Xeroxed instruction booklets. Director of photography Jim Denault, dissecting one camera to see how it worked, discovered that there's no lens to speak of, just a plastic disk shielding a 'photo receptor' attached to a small circuit board. "The business end of the camera," Jim explained, "is no bigger than the button on your shirt."

I shot whatever was at hand, every day for the next few weeks. Clouds out the window, pictures in books, anyone who strayed into my apartment. You can kill a lot of time in this way.

I should give this some context by confessing that in the spring of 1988 I had directed a feature film called *Twister*. It was my first feature, brought in on budget ($3 million) and on time, but it was hardly a happy experience. Arguments between me and the producer, a former friend, escalated throughout post-production. By the time editing was completed, the film seemed tainted; I was furious and heartsick and couldn't bear to look at it. But the film, of course, had a life of its own— a decidedly peculiar life, as time rolled on.

Vestron, the company that financed the picture, declared bankruptcy before releasing it, and all prints (only three were struck, I later learned) were pre-emptively withdrawn from circulation. But there had been two press screenings, and *Rolling Stone* magazine printed a premature review in which Peter Travers, the appointed critic, breezily summarized the film's plot before concluding on a feverish, upbeat note: "Almereyda's debut augurs a stunning future… *Twister* emerges as outrageous, original entertainment."

On a good day I might read such stuff with perfect scorn, but the whole year had been bleak and I found myself clinging to each word like wreckage in a storm. Other approving reviews trickled in—notably from the *New York Times*, *Village Voice*, *LA Times*—but these arrived about nine months later, because Vestron sold *Twister* to video before allowing an intrepid independent distributor to book the film in art houses, where it reliably generated business as an offbeat oddity, a cursed cult film.

While awaiting the arrival of my stunning future, I proceeded to write one or two new scripts per year, attaching actors, drawing up budgets—and getting routinely dangled, rejected and refused by every imaginable source of film financing.

So by Christmas of 1991, watching Sadie's vivid tapes, I was primed for a change. By mid-January I'd written a script, about forty pages, specifically for the pixel camera. The story of two messed-up young men and their involvement with perhaps too many young women. The action was confined to two apartments, a stairwell, a roof. You wouldn't be overly literal-minded to call it a home movie. It's possible that an element of dizzy desperation, specific to downtown New York and to my life at the time, found its way into the story. My downstairs neighbor Nic Ratner consented to play a version of himself, supplying his apartment, his music collection and the better part of his own dialogue ("Michael," he will tell you, "has the humanity of a tape recorder"). Otherwise, professional actors were recruited. (In this I was aided by the unerring eye of Billy Hopkins, who took time out from casting the latest Oliver Stone movie.) I also enlisted a few obliging friends and a fourteen-year-old Indian elephant named Daisy. Everyone except the elephant worked without pay.

The actors, confronted with what one of them called a "pixie camera," were all exceptional and selfless and the merest thanks I can offer is to name and commend them here in one quick gush: Isabel Gillies, Bob Gosse, Elina Löwensohn, Paula Malcomson, Liza Pariseau, Tom Roma, Maggie Rush, Barry Sherman, Mary Ward.

Tom Roma (a great photographer) also crafted aluminum brackets that allowed us to mount the camera on a tripod and dolly. There was a minimal lighting package (the guy at the rental house actually laughed when he took the order) and a crew of five. Everything was storyboarded and scripted, but I like to think we went at it with a kind of inspired amateurism. The pixel camera practically forces you to be reckless and original. If you're shooting something at a distance, with a crowded background, detail goes out of the window, so it's necessary to compose shots with an eye towards compressed space, to stage action with an awareness of how silhouettes register and relate to one another, and to favor close-ups. The crude little photo receptor homes in on the exact

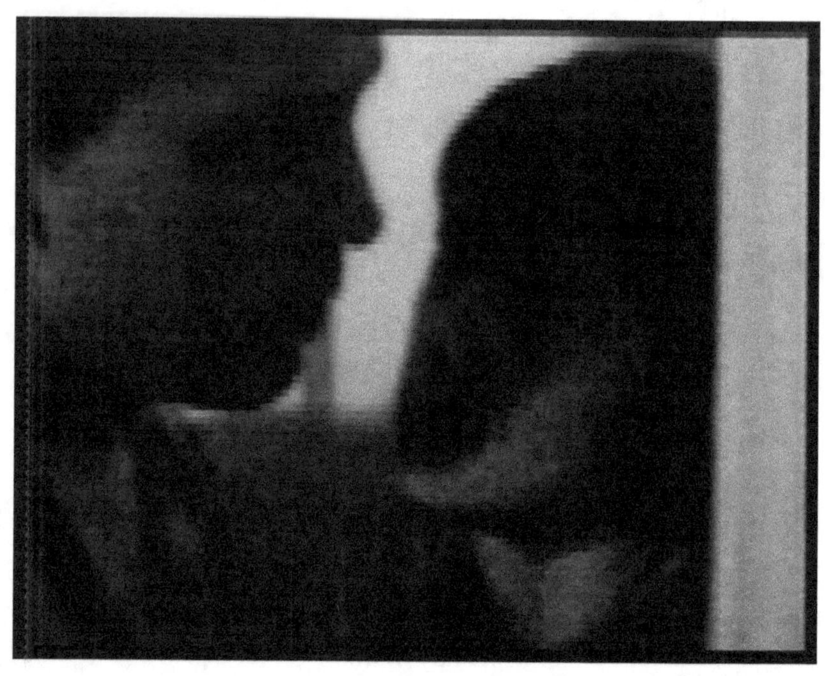

Barry Sherman with Mary Ward and (right) Elina Löwensohn
in *Another Girl Another Planet*, 1992.

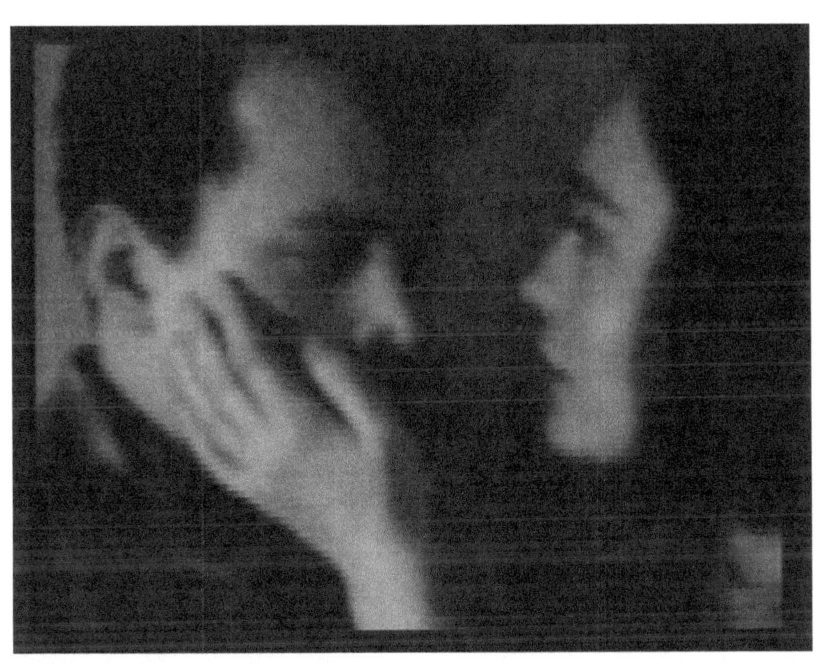

grain of any surface, a face, an eye down to individual lashes, reflected glints in the pupil.

All of which makes pixelvision inherently ghostly and graphic and fun to watch, but also qualifies it as a medium particularly sensitive to actors and to their essential business: the transmission of moments of true feeling.

We shot for one week. Two newly written bar scenes and a rooftop scenes were picked up over another weekend. There was an effort to create the moment-to-moment impression that the story was being cooked from scratch, as if recorded in a notebook with things pasted in, scribbled over, ripped out. But nearly all the jump cuts and discontinuous sound cues were specified in the script, and editor David Leonard and I worked hard to keep the rhythm rough and open. (As a stranger to video editing, I took a while to get used to the Mission Control aspect of monitors and buttons and unaccountable electronic mayhem. Occasionally David would make an edit, hit playback and be rewarded with a blizzard of red, gray and green squiggles. We were routinely thrilled, however, when we moved to the Calaway room to conjure up slow-motion shots, reversals, dissolves.)

The resulting film, *Another Girl Another Planet*, with its conspicuously odd look and sub-feature length, has found a life at festivals, where I'm always asked how we fit an elephant into the apartment. It's the first thing that comes up. Over time, the answers vary. I once insisted, "That wasn't an elephant. That was a guy in an elephant suit." Jim Denault, eschewing difficult technical talk, provided the best explication to a woman writing an article for *American Cinematographer*. "It was challenging to shoot the elephant," Jim said, "because the elephant was very big, and the camera is very small." This article, for some reason, has yet to appear.

But reviewers have been more than generous, their enthusiasm matched by an underlying amazement that anyone would be foolhardy enough to make a movie with a $45 toy. All the same, the most flattering adjectives thrown at the film – "haunting," "romantic," "dreamlike," "hypnotic" —are direct descriptions of the innate properties of the pixel image.

I must conclude, regretfully, with the dim news that Fisher-Price discontinued their used camera service shortly after I got wind of it. Pixel cameras are floating around but remain scarce. A hopeful rumor: the camera's inventor, James Wickstead, is alive and well in New Jersey. The camera's patent has reverted to him, and he intends to retool and market the device—as a toy for teenagers! He's also working on a color version.

A final confession. I still harbor vast hopes to direct big-budget films. Films with lavish sets, spectacular action sequences, actors everybody knows. Films that feed and reflect the immensity of pop culture. Basically, I want Tim Burton's job. But what is cinema, anyway? "Love. Hate. Action. Death. In one word: emotion." Sam Fuller's blunt inventory makes sense to me, and pixel-vision can cover those bases as well as the usual high-priced machinery. So there are days when I'm content. Days when I can pick up a pixel camera and leave my stunning future behind. Filmmakers, after all, are born free, but are everywhere in chains. The PXL 2000, if you can get your hands on one, remains liberating, spellbinding and inexhaustible.

From *Projections* 3, 1994.

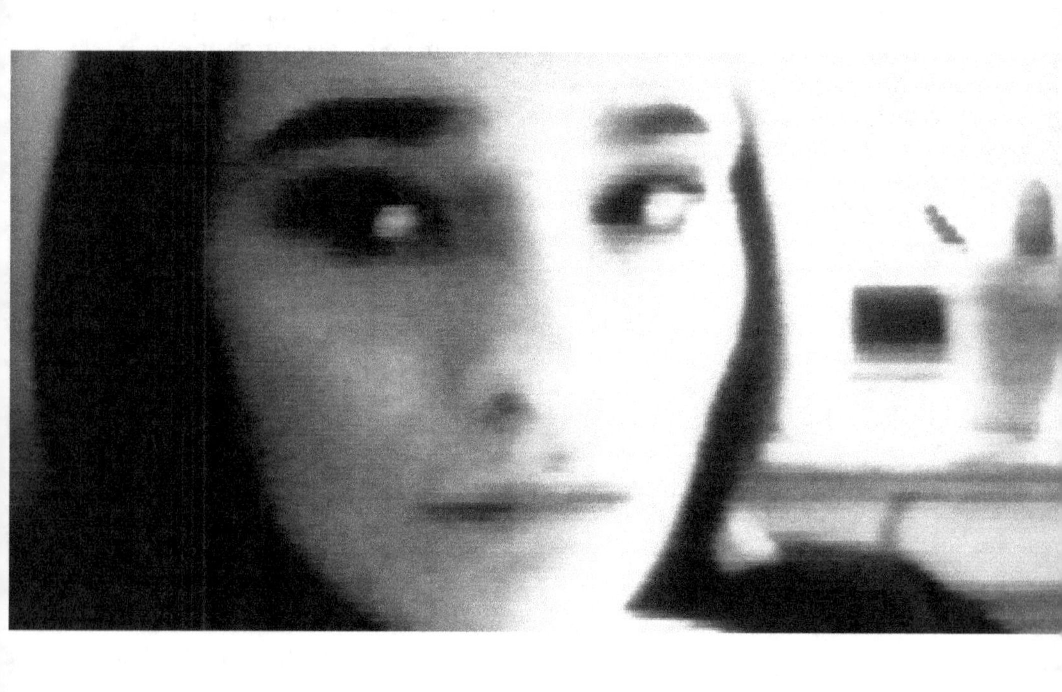

ANOTHER GIRL ANOTHER PLANET (1992)

Pixelvision video transferred to 16mm / 56 minutes
Cast: Isabel Gillies, Bob Gosse, Elina Löwensohn, Paula Malcomson, Lisa Pariseau, Nic Ratner, Tom Roma, Maggie Rush, Barry Sherman, Mary Ward
Camera: Jim Denault; Editor: David Leonard

The following is excerpted from *Paradise & Back*, a conversation commissioned by Ballroom Marfa to accompany an Almereyda retrospective in Marfa, Texas, the summer of 2009. Later sections from the interview cover two successive films.

Ramin Bahrani: "Fate versus free will" again seems a central theme. Characters who are stuck, doomed to repeat themselves, or kiss beyond their control. A "pinball machine" existence if you will allow me that. When talking about *Twister*, you commented about "how longing and need, responsibility and freedom, are not always on equal footing." Is this true for Bill? Does he change?

Michael Almereyda: I'm not sure Bill changes (and I'm not convinced characters have to change for a movie to mean something). The last scene shows him tuning a radio, and that's how I tend to think of him, trying to change stations but caught in a bad frequency.

RB: In fact, death permeates the film: from the initial voiceover on the rooftop, to nearly all the backstories of the women. Even the Lama had to yell at one dead man, "Andrew, you are dead now!" Do most of us need to be reminded if we are dead or alive? Are we living?

MA: I take your question to be rhetorical. My answers: Of course. And: Of course. I'll also toss in two quotes that were threaded into my thinking. "Not to be in love is to be dying" — this is in the movie, and it's from a John Updike essay. It runs parallel, I think, with a familiar Dylan lyric: "He not busy being born is busy dying." All the characters in the movie, you could say, are very busy.

RB: Were there cinematic influences or literary influences for this film? And had you seen Wong Kar-Wai's first two films (*As Tears Go By* and *Days of Being Wild*) — and I wish I could ask him if he saw *Another Girl Another Planet* before making *Chungking Express, Fallen Angels* and *Happy Together.*

MA: Godard's *Masculine/Feminine* and Scorsese's *Who's That Knocking* were two key influences. *Another Girl* was shot in one week in January, 1992. Wong Kar-Wai wasn't on my horizon then. By 1996, however, he was an international star and I was flattered to find *The Rocking Horse Winner* showing before *Fallen Angels* at a midnight screening in the New York Film Festival. (Both films happen to feature the same song by Mad Professor.) Wong was wearing his customary sunglasses at night; we were introduced, but I couldn't say we had a conversation. It's nice to imagine that, in your head at least, our films have been talking to one another.

RB: Elina Löwensohn has a stunning appearance here and later stars in *Nadja.* Can you discuss the casting of your lead Barry Sherman, Mary Ward as Ramona, who haunts the film, and Ms. Löwensohn?

MA: Even though there were no salaries for the actors and the entire production was threadbare, I worked with an excellent casting director, Billy Hopkins, who recommended Barry and Mary. I'd met Elina in 1989 when she was a wonderfully unrestrained waitress at a restaurant near Astor Place. I'd wanted to cast her at that time in an East Village version of Dostoyevsky's *The Devils* — anarchists squatting and squabbling — but I couldn't get the money. Ethan Hawke, who was going to be in a later incarnation of that movie, introduced me to Isabel Gillies — I think some of her scenes are the strongest in the picture. She's an underrated actress who just won a degree of fame by writing a best-selling memoir about the breakup of her marriage.

RB: I have never seen the film *Hello Elephant* (1952, directed by Gianni Franciolini and starring Vittorio De Sica) that Bill and Mia discuss. In the film, De Sica's character is given an elephant named Nabu (also the production company credited on your film) and De Sica is forced to find a home for it. Towards the end of the film after Mia has left Bill and he is alone, your camera finds him petting an elephant and he narrates, "Not to be in love was to be dying." Then, in an amazing sequence, the elephant enters Bill's apartment! Bill narrates, "The main thing is not to be bitter." It is a startling sequence that I hope you will help me understand.

MA: There are a number of animals in the movie, referred to and occasionally seen – a goat, axolotl salamanders, and the cartoon menagerie in *Dancing on the Moon*. Of course, the elephant has the most presence and impact. As in *Hello Elephant*—which is a miraculously good movie, by the way—Nabu is an oversized embodiment of the idea of happiness, of a sweet innocent life that doesn't actually fit into your real life. And this is a fairly flexible or ambiguous metaphor—the happy elephant. After all, even when young, elephants can look world-weary and sorrowful.

FADE IN:

2   EXT.   APARTMENT HALLWAY - NIGHT

We hear slack-key guitar music -- old country-and-western -- from
behind the door.

                    BILL (V.O.)
               Nic lives with his wife Prudence on
               the fourth floor of a five-story walk-
               up in the east village.

A phone rings o.s.

3   INT. NIC'S APARTMENT - NIGHT

ON BILL

He has disorganized hair, cloudy eyes, a certain slow, lost,
laconic manner which somehow passes for boyish charm.   C&W music
continues.

                    BILL
               I live upstairs, directly above. If,
               for instance, you shot a gun through
               the ceiling --

He's talking to RAMONA, who sits beside him, lighting a
cigarette. She's in her late twenties and has a fine-featured
face, a look of angelic purity playing against a wry, tomboyish
directness. She's wearing a pullover, cut-off jeans, striped
tights, Doc Martens.

                    BILL
               -- it would go through my floor and
               hit...
                         (he aims a finger, sights
                          up it)
               A chair I found on the street two years
               ago.

                    NIC
               Bill! Hey Bill!

                    BILL
               What?

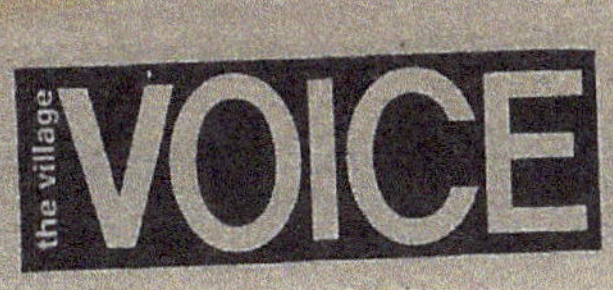

ANOTHER GIRL, ANOTHER PLANET:
What does an impatient filmmaker do when he can't raise a few million for a feature?

Michael Almereyda, director of the under-sung *Twister*, used five toy pixelvision cameras to make *Another Girl, Another Planet*, the most elegant Downtown love story since *Stranger Than Paradise*. It runs with two other delirious pixel visions: Sadie Benning's *It Wasn't Love* and Michael O'Reilly's *Glass Jaw*. April 5, 12, 19, and 26, the Kitchen, 512 West 19th Street, 255-5793. (Taubin)

Un Film de Fisher-Price
by J. Hoberman

"Film will only become an art when its materials are as inexpensive as pencil and paper," prophesied the poet turned moviemaker Jean Cocteau. Since then, each successive amateur format (16mm, Super-8, the camcorder) has brought filmmaking closer to the corner stationery store. But the ultimate example of cinematic pencil and paper is surely the Fisher-Price Pixelvision video camera, a molded plastic child's toy that listed for under $200 (TV monitor included) and uses an audiotape cassette on which to record an image.

Although the Fisher-Price PXL 2000 went on the market in the late 1980s, the fruits of this bargain-basement means of production (the precise "technological and ideological adversary" of high-definition TV, as Manohla Dargis termed it a few years ago in *The Village Voice*) have only recently been acknowledged. This past winter, the Los Angeles Film Critics Association voted a special award to "Pixelvisionary" Sadie Benning while, a few weeks later, the National Society of Film Critics gave special recognition to Michael Almereyda's 56-minute pixel feature, *Another Girl Another Planet*, for "expanding the possibilities of experimental filmmaking."

Although *Another Girl Another Planet* recently screened at the Museum of Modern Art/Film Society of Lincoln Center festival "New Directors/New Films," the 32-year-old, New York-based Almereyda is hardly a novice. His 1989 *Twister* was a Europeanized excursion into kitsch Americana, made on 35mm in color and populated by a number of well-known professional actors, including Lois Chiles, Crispin Glover, and Harry Dean Stanton. *Another Girl Another Planet*, by contrast, was shot mainly in Almereyda's tenement on New York's Lower East Side, using his apartment and that of his neighbor, Nic Ratner, who plays a character named Nic. The rest of the mainly professional cast was drawn from the neighborhood as well. Made in one week, *Another Girl Another Planet* cost something like $12,000 (including the 16mm blowup).

Twister was ironic and literate, two qualities that *Another Girl Another Planet* has in some abundance. The film concerns the symbiotic relationship between two neighbors—anxious, married Nic and smug, single Bill—and the series of interesting young women who wend their way from soirees at Nic's apartment upstairs to Bill's. ("It looks like you've just moved in" is a recurring comment, reflecting also the occupant's own sense of emptiness.) *Another Girl Another Planet* vividly evokes a particular form of youthful alienation. Each girl who visits planet Bill has been marked by an encounter with death; all are given to unanswerable musings. Even callow Bill suspects something is amiss, although the diffident seducer is chastened only when he falls for Mia, played by Elina Löwensohn, who made a memorable impression as the Romanian mystery woman in Hal Hartley's *Simple Men.*

Shot almost without exteriors (Pixelvision works best when plugged into a wall outlet), *Another Girl Another Planet* is both intimate and fluid. With close-ups de rigueur, Almereyda places the camera all but inside a pinball machine or a fish tank. The movie is as contrasty as a Balinese shadow play; the low-definition image, reinforced by the ubiquitous cigarette smoke of the twentysomething characters, creates a form of electronic pointillism. Taking advantage of the format's excellent sound quality, Almereyda employs all manner of creative voice-over (it's fortunate that he writes such strong dialogue) as well as musical accompaniment.

The music, drawn from Nic Ratner's personal collection, is an eclectic mix of nouveau flamenco, Hawaiian steel guitar, a postmodern chanteuse, West Indian singer Joseph Spence's fabulously garbled version of "Santa Claus Is Coming to Town, and the pre-Tina Ike Turner. ("This is the basis of rock 'n' roll," Nic pedantically announces.) Indeed, music is so intrinsic to *Another Girl Another Planet's* narrative economy that one immediately senses that Mia will break the mold when she makes a request of her own—Psychic TV's version of a melancholy anthem from the hippie era.

Almost a parody of hip, *Another Girl Another Planet* is rife with other examples of East Village connoisseurship: the most haunting leitmotif has Nic and, sometimes, Prudence (his aptly named wife) ritually showing their first-time visitors a 1935 Max Fleischer cartoon called *Dancing on the Moon*. The fantasy of a lunar nightclub patronized by zoo animals grows increasingly poignant as it punctuates Bill's amorous adventures; it also serves to establish a counterpart, formal no less than thematic, to the abstract quality of the pixel image.

Almereyda is currently planning a second pixel feature—a meditation on Edgar Allan Poe to be shot on location (and contemporized) in Poe's long-time home, Richmond, Virginia. Calling Pixelvision the ideal format for treating the famously tormented American writer, Almereyda says he'll be dealing with love, loss, death, and wayward behavior as well as documenting such prime pixel territory as "barbeque joints and jukeboxes."

Excerpted from Premiere magazine, April, 1993.

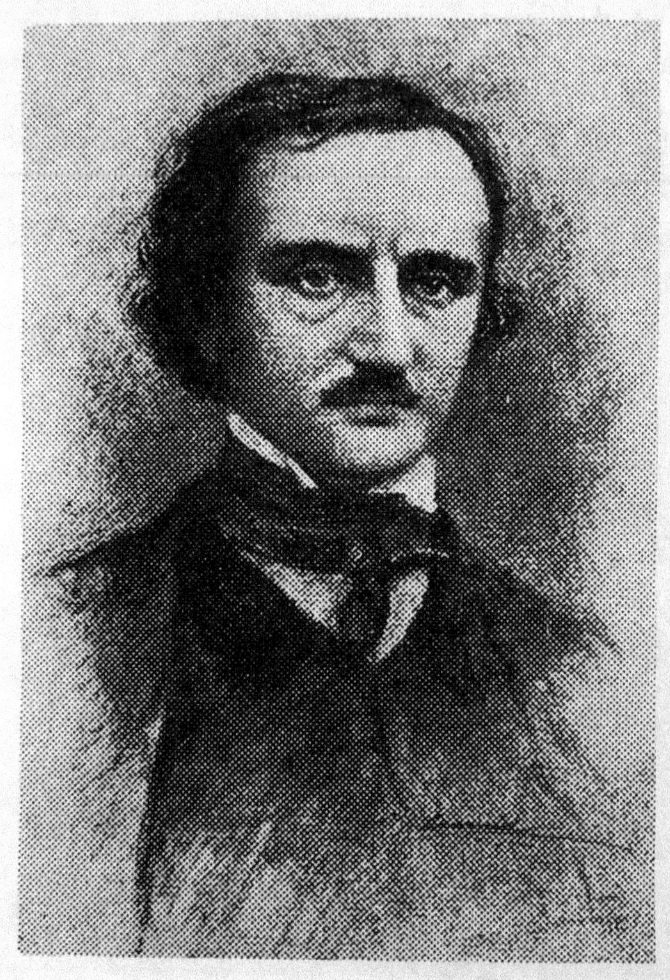

EDGAR ALLAN POE

Walking the Black Cat

Jim Denault was recommended to me, and recruited, as a gaffer for *Another Girl Another Planet*. I'd shot enough preliminary material to figure I could competently wield the Pixel camera while directing actors—but after lining up the first shot and unsteadily riding the improvised dolly, I abruptly realized I was in over my head and promoted Jim to take over. It was his first credit as cinematographer. Kelly Reichardt's *River of Grass* was his second. *Nadja* was his third.

In the fall of 1992, Jim packed his car with pixel equipment and other gear and drove with me to Richmond, Virginia, location scouting for the Poe project, imagining (incorrectly) that we'd soon be able to follow through with a full shoot. One idea behind the trip was to get footage of the last surviving Buffalo Soldier, Jones Morgan, while he was still alive. Born in 1882, Morgan had served in Cuba in the Spanish-American War, having enlisted when he was fifteen, wrangling horses for Teddy Roosevelt's Rough Rider regiment, cooking meals for fellow soldiers. Morgan was, at that time, the oldest living war veteran in the United States, but for decades he'd been deprived of government benefits due to a lack of documentation; it took a belated act of Congress to award him military payments only that year. I met him or, more accurately, I visited his bedroom, accompanying a freelance photographer assigned to get shots of Mr. Morgan on his 110th birthday.

In my memory, Morgan had a hairless sculpted head and looked like a whittled-down Woody Strode (the "Ethiopian" gladiator in *Spartacus*, the star of John Ford's *Sergeant Rutledge*). He was only semi-conscious, his eyes floating in and out of focus, but I registered a spark of amiability. My photographer friend had brought him a bag of potato chips and handed them to Morgan's daughter. "I know he likes his chips." The daughter was in her 70s, wearing glasses and a purple dress. We were allowed to step in and say Hi, but there was no question of photographing Mr. Morgan in his hazy condition.

Afterwards, my friend was nonplussed, recalling that the old man was sharp as a tack three months ago. "He remembered the names of his mules. But didn't want to have his picture taken. He said: 'Come back when I don't have so much on my mind.'"

I can report this not because I firmly remember it, but because it's planted in my Poe screenplay, fused with a retelling of "The Facts in the Case of M. Valdemar," a Poe short story about a hypnotist who puts a dying man in a suspended state at the moment of his death. Thirty years later, I question the cleverness, the decorum, of this mashup of fiction and fact, but I imagined I was recognizing a link between the undying sins of Jim Crow racism and the extended death rattle Poe describes in his story: "The voice seemed to reach our ears—at least mine—from a vast distance, or from some deep cavern within the earth. In the second place, it impressed me... as gelatinous or glutinous matters impress the touch."

When Jim and I landed in Richmond, we were regretfully informed that it was not a good time to pay a visit to the venerable old soldier. Jim, as I remember, was a bit disgruntled, and justifiably, as I'd applied more than a little wishful thinking to persuade him to undertake the trip, and he, once again, wasn't being paid. But we spent a mild October afternoon roaming around Hollywood Cemetery, a lush landscape studded with gravestones, statues and crypts, the final resting place for 18,000 Confederate soldiers. Despite the evidence of this book, I tend to be as camera-shy as Jones Morgan, but Diana Vicenti, part of Jamie Bishop's charmed circle, led us to her favorite spots, and I tried not to flinch when she turned her lens on me and Jim. Maybe, in fact, I was relatively relaxed. I'm one of those people who relax in graveyards.

Jones Morgan departed this world, Wikipedia tells us, August 29, 1993, two months shy of his 111th birthday, and was buried elsewhere.

Jim Denault (with camera) and Michael Almereyda in Hollywood Cemetery. Richmond, Virginia, 1993. Photographs by Diana Vicenti.

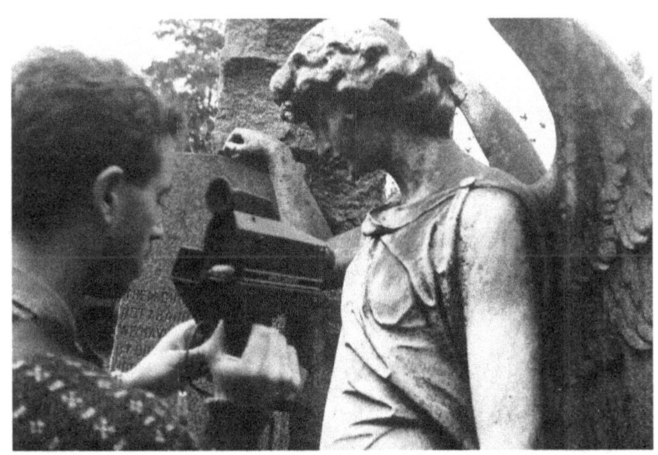

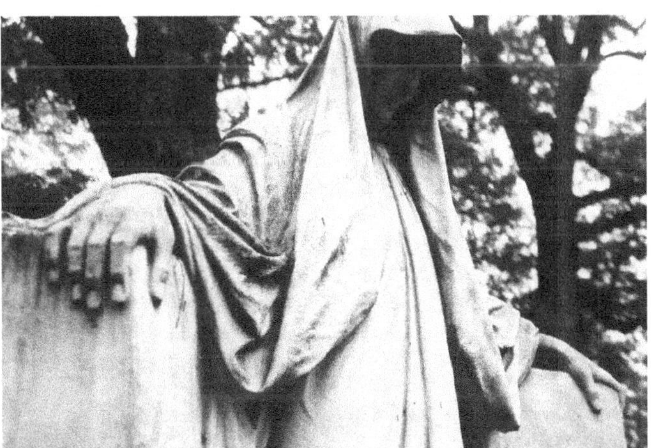

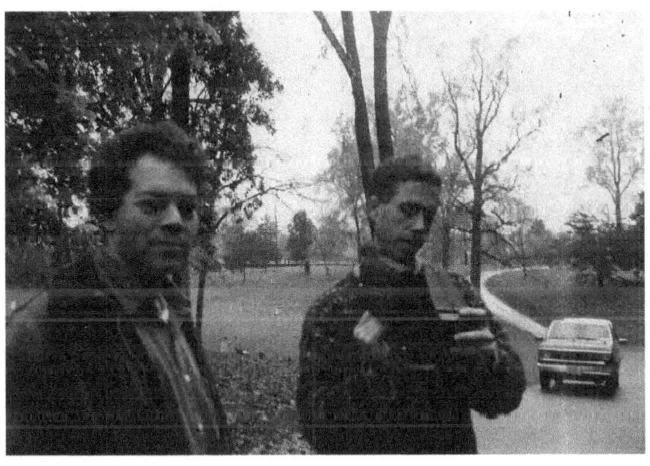

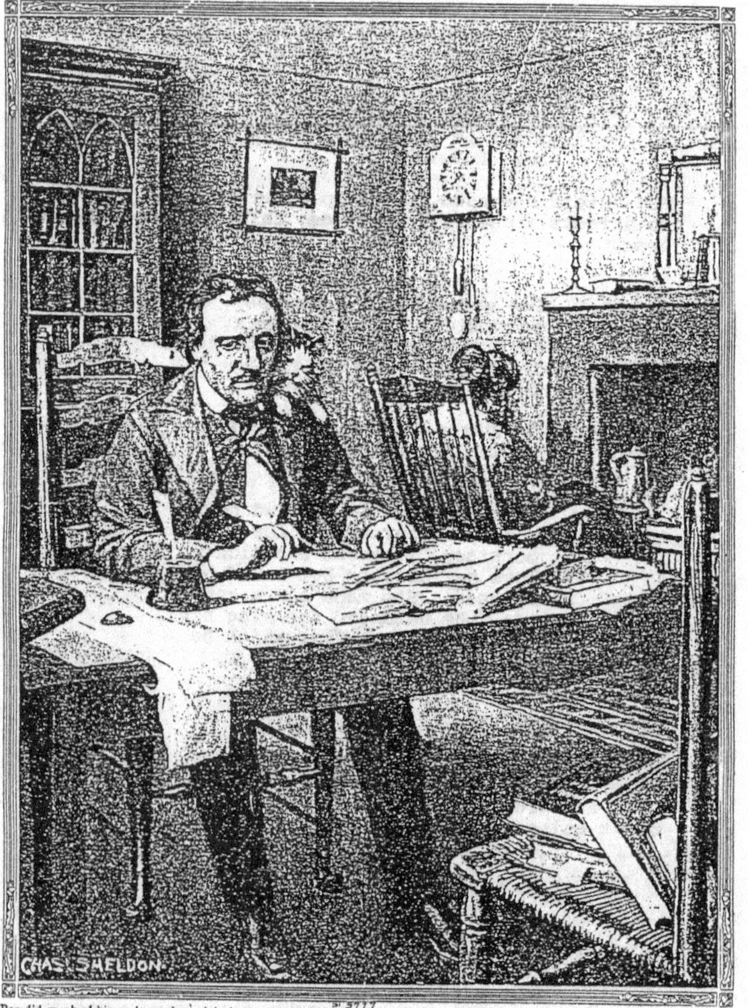

Poe did much of his early work at night in the simple living room of the cottage in which he lived with his aunt. At the plain wood table he would conjure up those tales of imagination or dream those musical poems on which his fame rests, while his pet cat Catalina perched on his shoulder. Mrs. Clemm, a woman in her sixties, would sit by the fire, and now and then would wake from her doze to warm Poe a cup of coffee.

INT. JOHNSON'S BEDROOM - DAY

MORGAN JOHNSON, 110 years old, lies motionless in bed. He
has a strong noble face, ancient, the skin a map of lines.
His eyes are closed. He looks dead.

DR. VOLDEMAR is in a chair beside the bed, holding a small
mirror to the old man's lips. Voldemar looks a bit like a
heavy-set, middle-aged version of Edgar Allen Poe: very pale,
with a high bulging forehead.

It's dim; the shades are drawn. Voldemar has to squint to
make out the faint breath-induced fog registering on the
mirror. He proceeds to ask questions in a low soothing
voice.

                    VOLDEMAR
          Mr. Johnson. Are you asleep?

No answer, but Johnson's lips tremor. In the background,
Iris, Tom and Jim quietly enter the room.

                    VOLDEMAR
          Are you asleep...?

A very slight shiver runs through Johnson's body.

ON IRIS, TOM AND JIM

They stand hovering near the door, the two men looking
puzzled, getting their bearings. Jim glances at pictures on
the wall: photos of Morgan Johnson shaking hands with a
succession of American presidents.

                    VOLDEMAR (O.S.)
          Mr. Johnson. Are you
          asleep?...Are you asleep...?

CLOSE ON JOHNSON'S FACE

His eyelids unclose enough to display pupil-less white slits.

His lips move sluggishly, producing a barely audible whisper:

                    JOHNSON
          Yes. -- Asleep now. Let me
          die.

                    VOLDEMAR
          Do you still feel pain?

The answer comes after a delay, less audible than before.

Screenplay page for *Walking the Black Cat*, 1992.

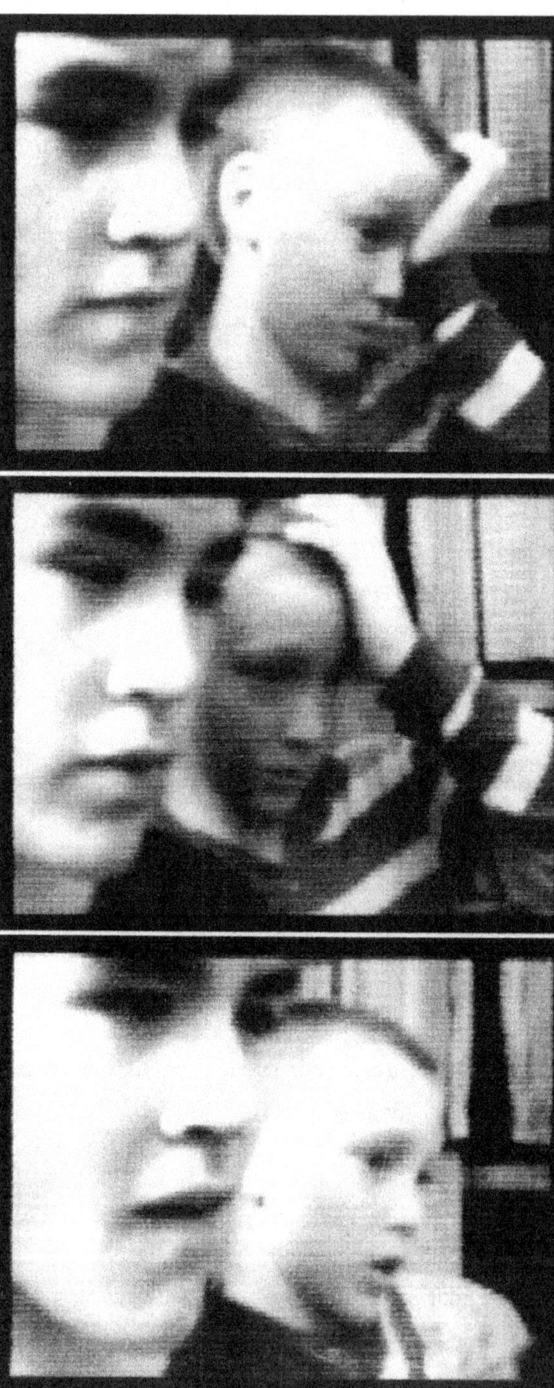

ALIENS (1993)

Pixelvision / B&W / 13 minutes
Cast: Christopher Norcross, Jonathan Norcross
Camera: Michael Almereyda; Editor: David Leonard

Two boys, brothers, discuss their favorite movies while playing a video game. Sigourney Weaver's animated avatar charges through flames and mows down her adversaries. The conversation rambles into a discussion of "passive resistance." The level of shared and contested misinformation tells a story, of sorts, about how history and pop culture can collapse into each other's arms and create an exquisite corpse. Or so I told myself in editing the footage and making it "a film." (*Aliens* premiered at the Institute of Contemporary Art in London, screening with *Another Girl Another Planet*.)

Given the ease of shooting video, I had the notion that it would be worthwhile to make at least one short a year, especially when bigger projects proved impossible. I've continued to work on unclassifiable portraits and sketches like this one, for the last three decades, even if I haven't always had the wherewithal to present them at film festivals.

Jonathan and Christopher Norcross in *Aliens*, 1993.

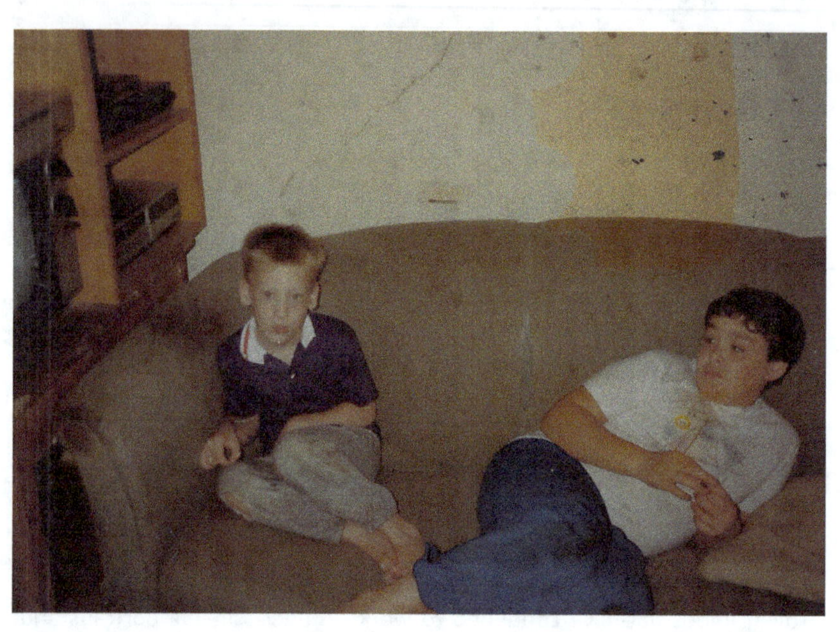

Christopher and Jonathan Norcross in Somerville, Massachusetts, 1993.

Hollywood Halloween

Last month a friend stopped by and started reading through reviews sent from a film festival in Rimini, Italy, Fellini's birthplace. "Michael Almereyda," she read, "has turned his back on Hollywood." She was translating from Italian, and we both burst out laughing. A year ago, having failed to raise money to make conventional movies, I resorted to using a plastic Pixelvision video camera, a gadget marketed as a toy for children. What most people might see as palpable proof of failure, an indulgent Italian journalist had taken as an act of defiance. I may be fatally provincial, nationalistic, narrow-minded, but in my book a film-maker turning his back on Hollywood is as preposterous as a fisherman turning his back on the sea.

I was there the other week. I flew in from New York for a Halloween wedding. (The invitation included a note at the bottom, in discreet red print: "Costumes okay.") The town seemed pretty much as I remembered—bright, cheerful, and apocalyptic. If I had turned my back on Hollywood, nobody there was holding it against me. Halloween afternoon I drove around with the car radio tuned to a station playing "the two hundred scariest songs of all time." I visited David Lynch, who was offering to help me make a new movie.

We talked beside a fountain in his back yard. Fellini had died that morning, and David, who shared Fellini's birthday, said he felt lucky to have seen him in the hospital in Rome, two days before he went into a coma. They had a good talk, a chance to say goodbye. He said Fellini seemed ready, at peace.

He recounted when he first met Fellini, in Cinecittà on the set of *Intervista*. He remembered the solid gold viewfinder Fellini wore around his neck. He had watched him direct a scene, and described how Fellini interrupted an actress and dabbed a spot of white paint on the tip of her nose. "It was fantastic. That spot of paint brought the scene to a whole new level."

I told him I'd watched *La Strada* two nights ago and couldn't think of anything better. And I remembered a recent interview with Fellini, which commenced with a description of the great man in a restaurant, sorting through his pills. "This pill," Fellini had said, "is for making me blond."

We also talked about River Phoenix. Early that morning another friend had called with the news of his death and this loss felt sharper—shocking and bitter. The sense of incompleteness and waste, of a life not only lost but destroyed, was piercing.

We were drinking coffee and smoking small black cigars. I don't smoke, but I was being sociable. The cigars were excellent, though the wind kept extinguishing them and I needed to lean in so David could re-light mine with his lighter. What I remember most from this afternoon is his 17-month-old son clattering around the patio, trying to work my still camera, and his mother, Mary Sweeney, an old friend, lifting him into her arms. I remember their matching blue eyes.

Two days later the winds that put out the cigars were sweeping fires through a few hundred houses in Malibu. Continuous TV news coverage called it *a firestorm*. As I drove into town from the Hollywood freeway, the light was low, soft, filtered—like dusk—"magic hour"—though it was ten in the morning.

I was given safe harbor in the offices of the new Tim Burton movie, *Ed Wood*, and treated to a tour of the sets, which included a beautiful unpainted spook house and an exact replica of the graveyard in *Plan 9 from Outer Space*. As the movie was being shot in black and white, all sets and props had been painted shades of gray and they looked at once spectacular and drab. I saw that the art department had begun to spiff things up with an occasional spot of color. In the classic, cluttered mad scientist's lab, bright green fluid shone from a single glass beaker.

The writer/director/producer of desperately low-budget pictures, sardonically cited among the worst movies ever made, Ed Wood died broke and broken in 1978. Hollywood, it's fair to say, had turned its back on him. So it was wild to see so much money and care expended on duplicating sets from movies that had been shot in a panic. (Wood had ten days for *Bride of the Monster*, four days for *Plan 9*. Tim Burton had something like three months for *Ed Wood*.) I had never been on a film set so relaxed. Here was Bela Lugosi, the humiliated heroin addict, played with lugubrious aplomb by Martin Landau. "I was classed as a madman, a charlatan… Now here in this forsaken jungle hell I have proven that I am all right!" These words were written, of course, by Wood, certified failure, now reincarnated by Johnny Depp as a giddy, glistening boy. I wanted to see the completed movie even as I was watching it being filmed.

Around six p.m., true magic hour, I climbed out of the production office window, onto the roof, and watched the sky go deep dark red. It was, I imagined, like Honolulu in volcano season. Failure, I reminded myself, is relative. We all fail, our bodies fail us, and time, an indiscriminate firestorm, sweeps over everything. Nothing to do but embrace these facts and, if you happen to be a filmmaker, to feel lucky. The idea being that your job affords you the chance, now and then, to leave something behind – a story, an image, a feeling – to be shared by anyone with open eyes.

Written for the London *Guardian,*
but never published; November, 1993.

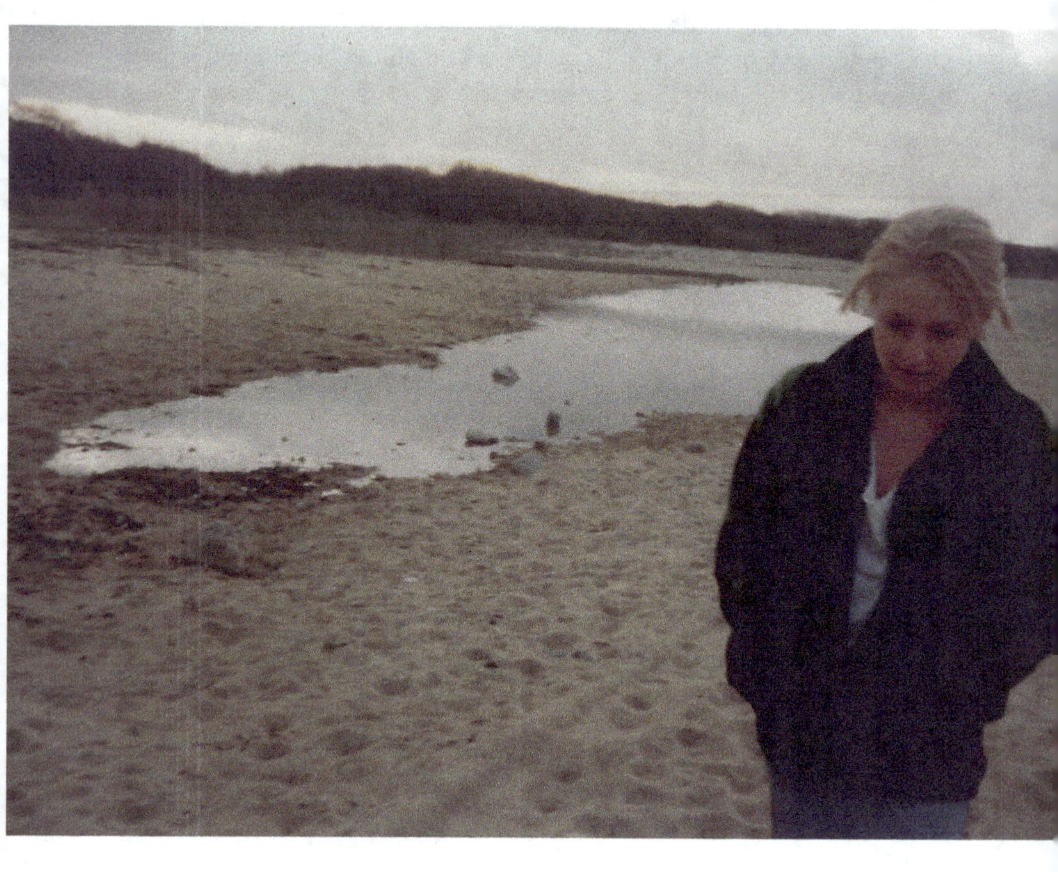

Paula Malcomson in Montauk, New York, 1992.

Hollywood Halloween: A FOOTNOTE

"Last month a friend stopped by and started reading through reviews…"

The friend was Paula Malcomson, whom I'd met roughly a year earlier in a bar on St. Marks, a place called EAT, where she was the bartender. I asked her, eventually If not immediately, if she'd like to be in a movie, and eventually if not immediately, she accepted.

She was a waif and a scamp, performatively fearless. She'd moved to New York from Belfast less than a year earlier, when she was twenty, trying to get out from under the pitch-black shadow of personal tragedy, not just the internecine violence of her native land but an electrical fire that had killed the boy who was the center of her life. In my memory, she revealed this to me with an absolute minimum of self-pity, but with an acknowledgment of how devastating it still was. So when she elected to appear in *Another Girl Another Planet*—her first acting gig ever—I didn't treat it as a casual walk-on. She had no dialogue, but was required to hold the camera's gaze with a kind of fierce nonchalance, her face and her mirrored reflection evoking the bartender in Manet's *A Bar at the Folies-Bergère*, in smoky black-and-white—or at least that was the idea.

These photographs tell you how I felt about her, and she knew without having to look at any photographs.

I texted Paula, just now, to get a fix on the blurry timeline: "Do you recall driving with me to Sundance at some point?"

She wrote back: "Yes. Probably Nineteen hundred and ninety three. I was depressed."

I texted that I remembered her, when we met, seeming bright, brash and feisty. She replied: "I was in fact surviving by acting as though I was OK and in control. That's the part you weren't able to see. You were attracted to damage. You were young too."

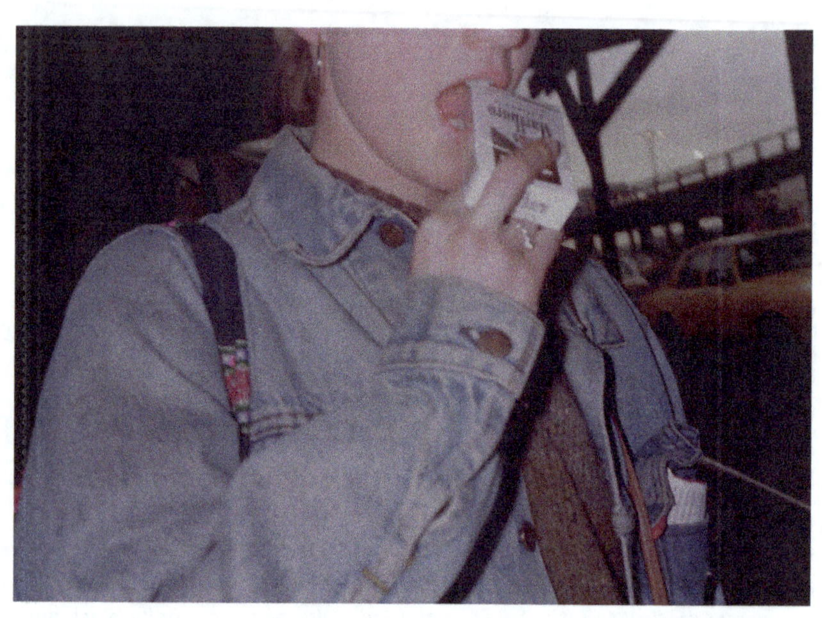

Paula Malcomson in the early 1990s.
The setting under the blue sky is identifiably Glassell Park, Los Angeles.

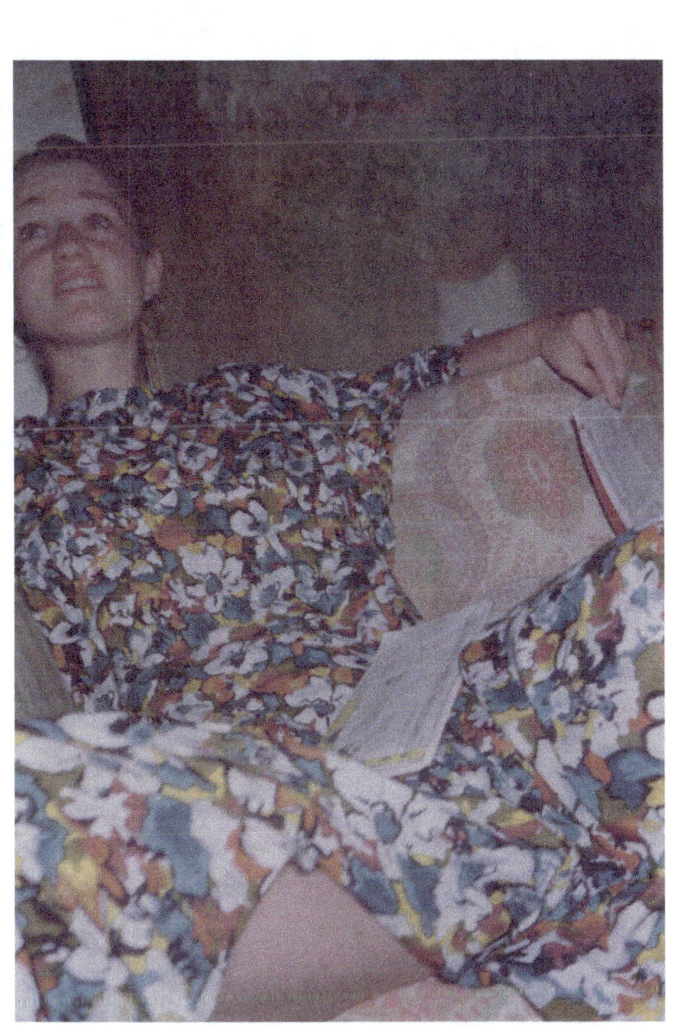

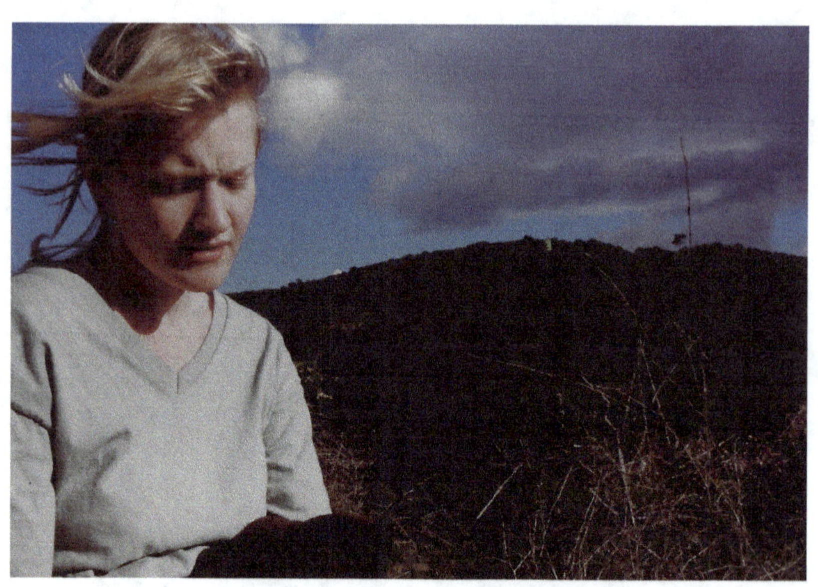

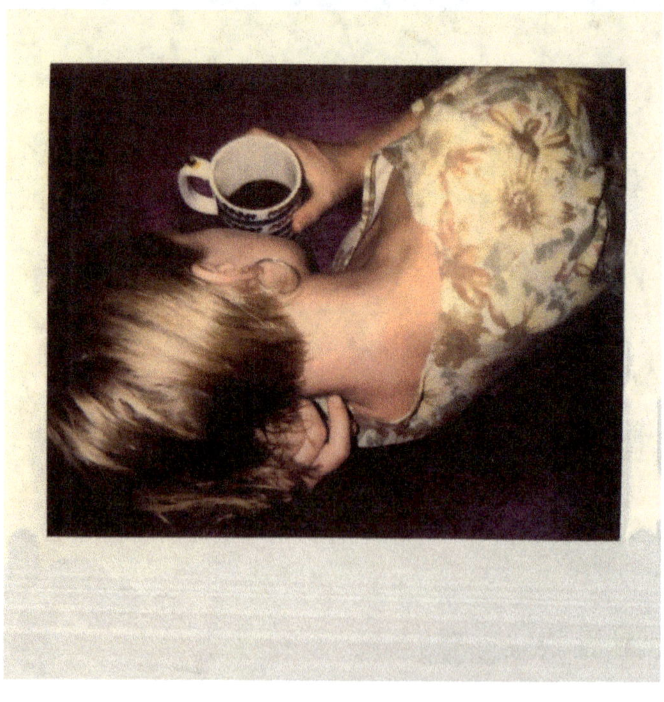

The 1993 Sundance Film Festival rejected *Another Girl Another Planet* while accepting, that same year, my first film, a 23-minute self-financed short completed in 1987, which my co-producer had submitted belatedly, as if acting on a stray afterthought. I couldn't have afforded to drive to Utah and book a room if I hadn't landed a job interviewing Sam Shepard for *Esquire* magazine. Paula can be glimpsed in the piece, described during a tangential stop at a gas station in Wyoming, though my memory doesn't place her at the festival itself.

But in truth my best memories from the early 90s involve Paula edging into the picture like a cat or a crow, sulking or squawking, gloomy or rhapsodic, in a succession of restaurants, rental cars and hotel rooms ranging from Saratoga Springs to Los Angeles.

She has appeared in five of my films, though she'll tell you—and I'll agree—that I barely scratched her surface, given the depths she's revealed elsewhere. In *Hamlet* (shot in 1998, beyond the bounds of this book, but allow me to flash forward) she was paired with Karl Geary's Horatio, and shown sleeping soundly while Sam Shepard, the ghost of Hamlet's father, watches over her. Maybe, in time, our interwoven futures can provide a more substantial display of her talents.

Karl is another close friend discovered—a grandiose term, but one that Breton might approve—in an East Village bar. As a teenage immigrant, fresh from Dublin, Karl was co-founder and manager of Sin-é, the tiny place where, one cold night in 1991, I witnessed twenty-four-year-old Sinead O'Connor sing "Summertime" *a cappella*, one of the most pure displays of unearthly talent I've ever experienced. I also noticed Karl, a shuffling, reticent Botticellian beauty, bussing tables. (Over time, other conspicuous traits sailed into view: his quick-witted intelligence, uncommon humility, irrepressible generosity.) As *Nadja* took shape, I thought it would be fitting to honor Bram Stoker's heritage by making Renfield, the vampire's loyal manservant, Irish—and what if he looked like... Karl? Karl took on the role, and (he later confessed) was terrified throughout the shoot. However, maintaining an air of vampiric detachment and, on occasion, offhand viciousness, proved to be well within his range. The movie, his first acting credit, led to others, and a career of sorts until he determined that writing novels is, in fact, what he was born to do. I'm happy to steer you to the evidence that midlife self-invention, finding one's true vocation, is truly possible. *Montpelier Parade* (2017) and *Juno Loves Legs* (2023).

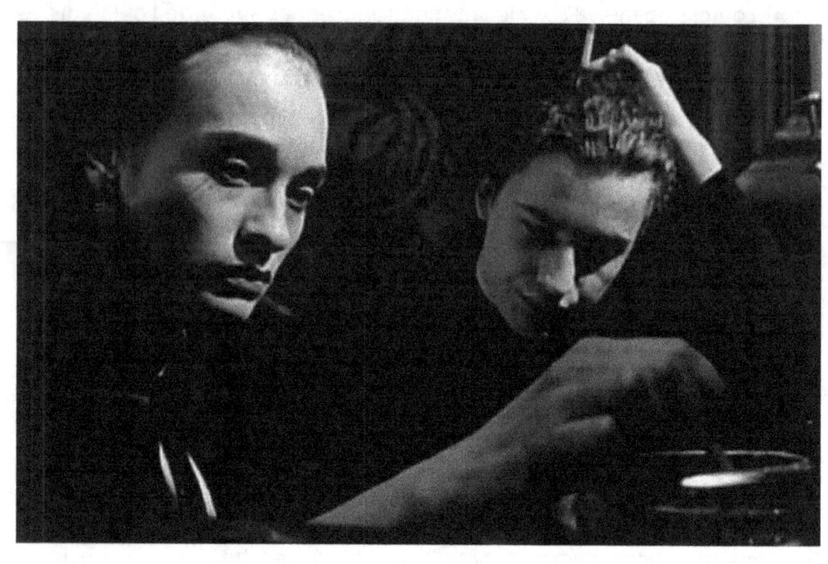

Elina Löwensohn and Karl Geary in *Nadja*.
Renfield's wardrobe Polaroid, most likely taken by Prudence Moriarty.

REDFIELD
CH # 2B
38 → 82
BROWN TN

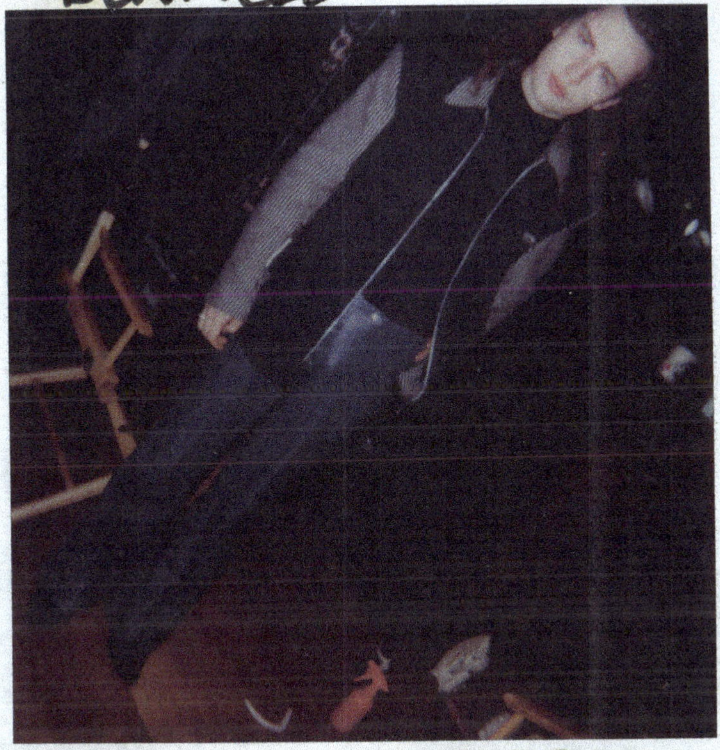

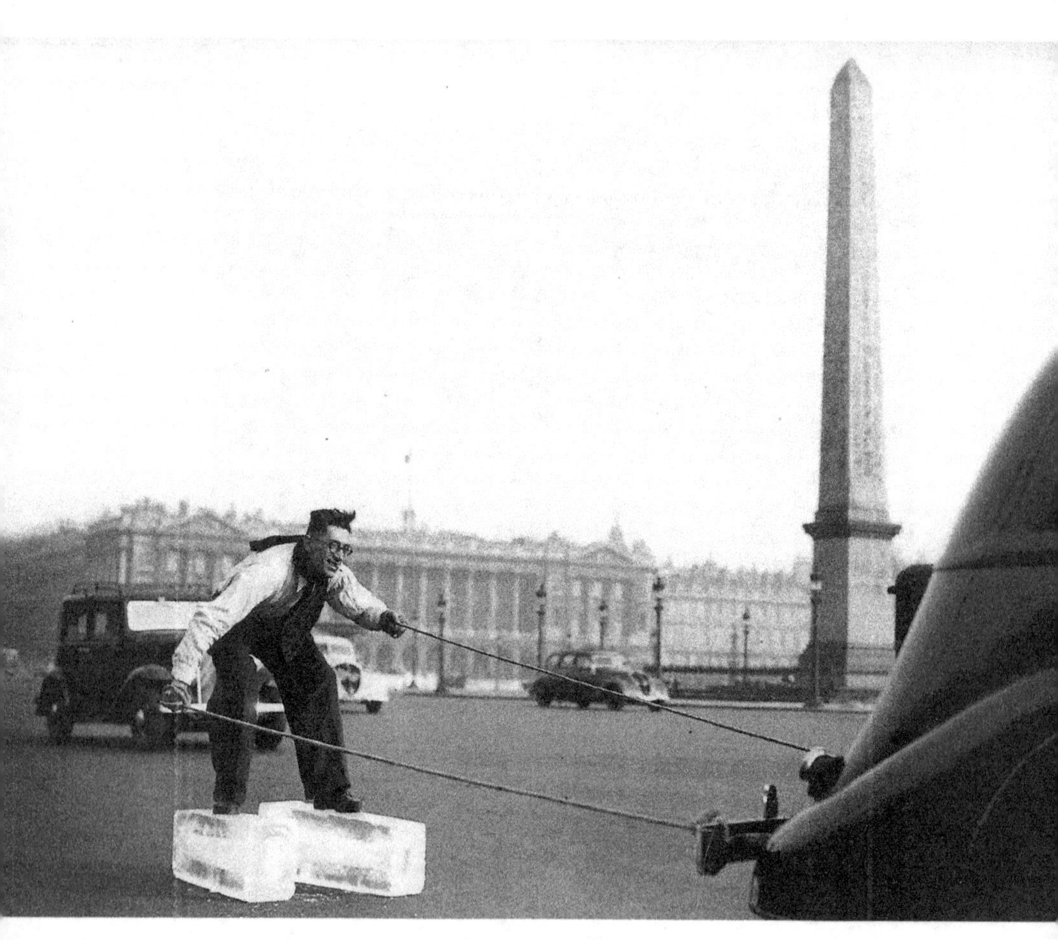

A birthday card from my mother, who has no memory of sending it.
Not sure of the year, though the man's activity seems to epitomize the
activity covered in this book.

Friends and Neighbors

There is not one talent for living and another for creating. The same suffices for both. And one could be sure that the talent that could not produce but an artificial work could not sustain but a frivolous life.

— Albert Camus
Notebooks 1951–1959

So the days pass and I ask myself sometimes whether one is not hypnotized, as a child by a silver globe, by life; and whether this is living. It's very quick, bright, exciting. But superficial perhaps. I should like to take the globe in my hands and feel it quietly, round, smooth, heavy, and so hold it, day after day. I will read Proust I think. I will go backwards and forwards.

— Virginia Woolf
Diary entry, November 28, 1928

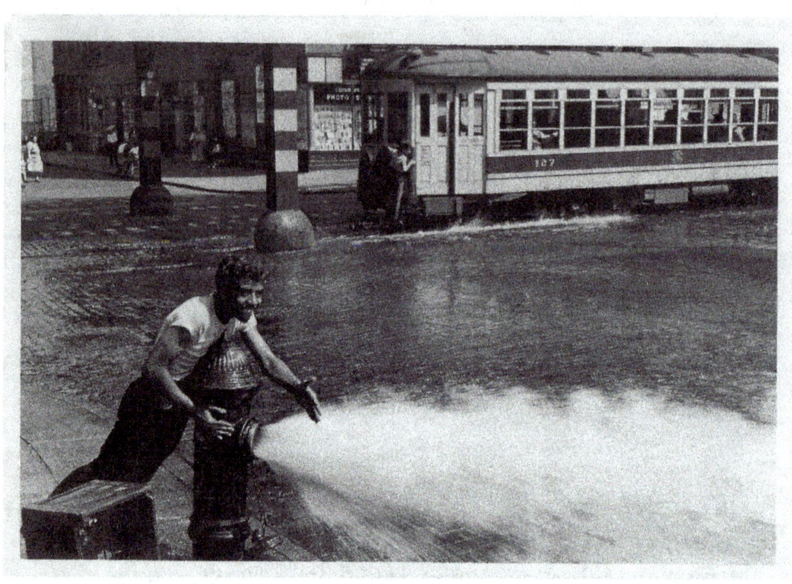

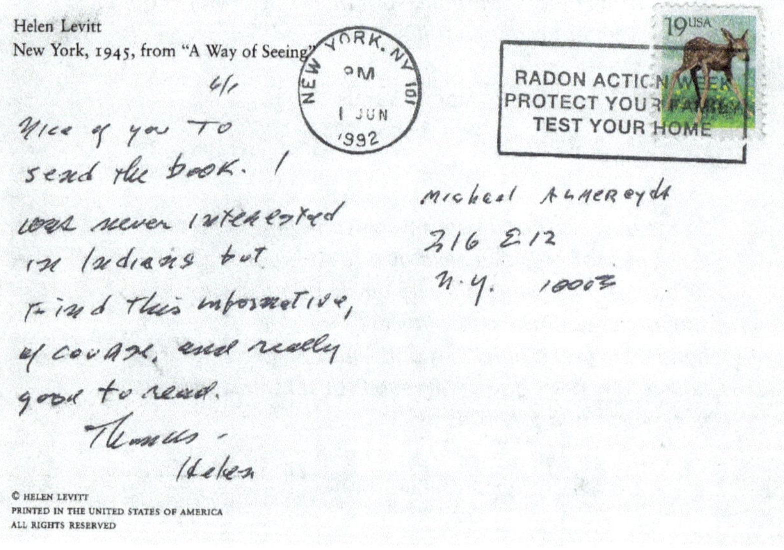

Two cards from Helen Levitt, who lived
three blocks down the street from me but
enjoyed communicating this way.

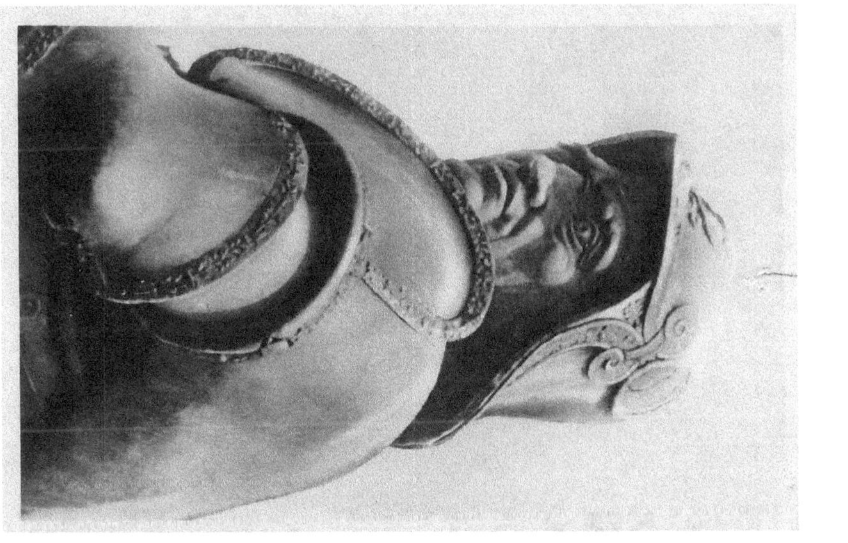

I hated to miss the
screening — got
hung up & exhausted
— Hope you let me
know if there is
another —
Helen (L.)

Michael Almereyda
216 E 12
N.Y. 10009

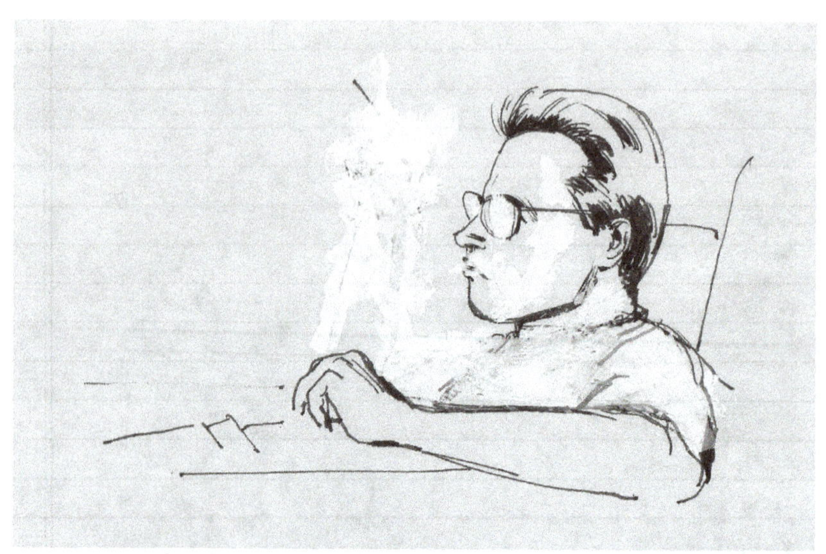

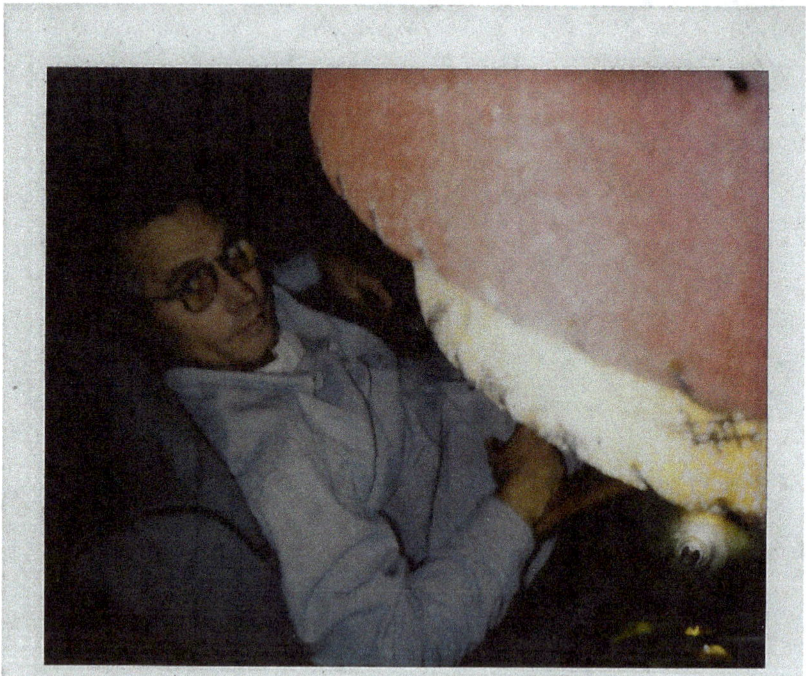

Hans Proppe, Val Verde, California.

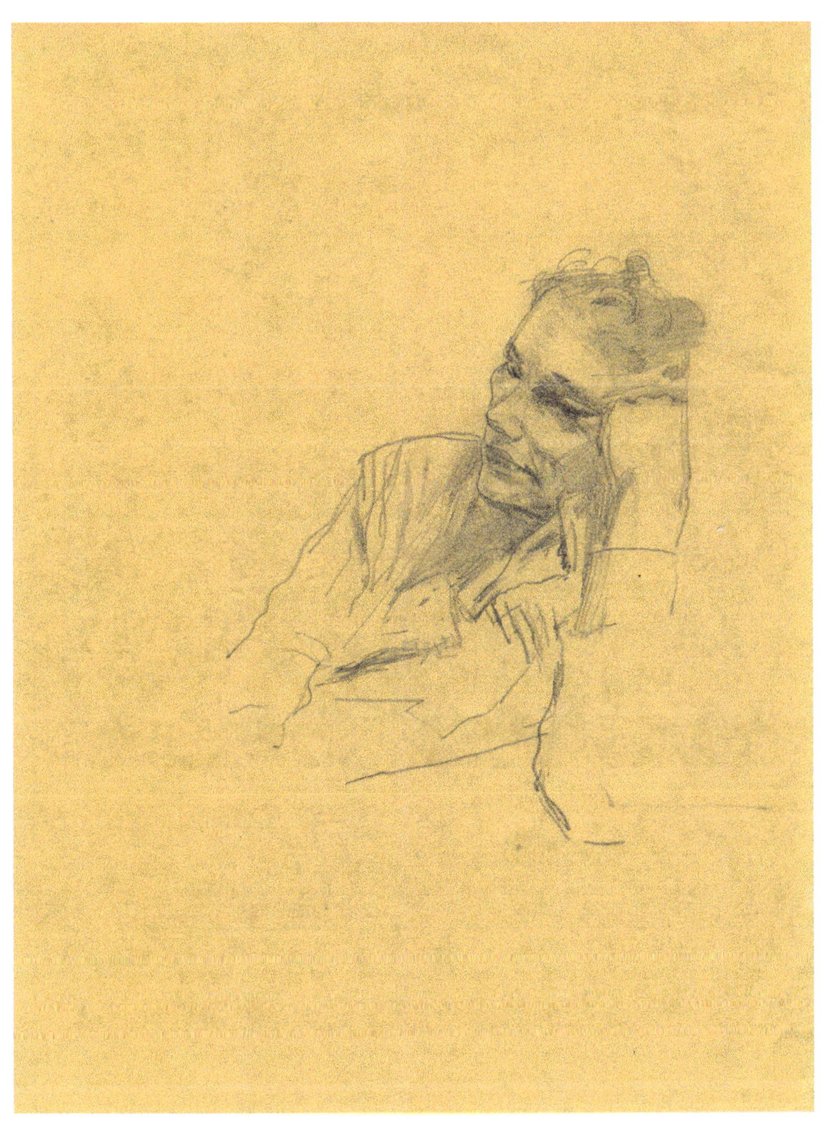

Susan Tarr, Val Verde, California.

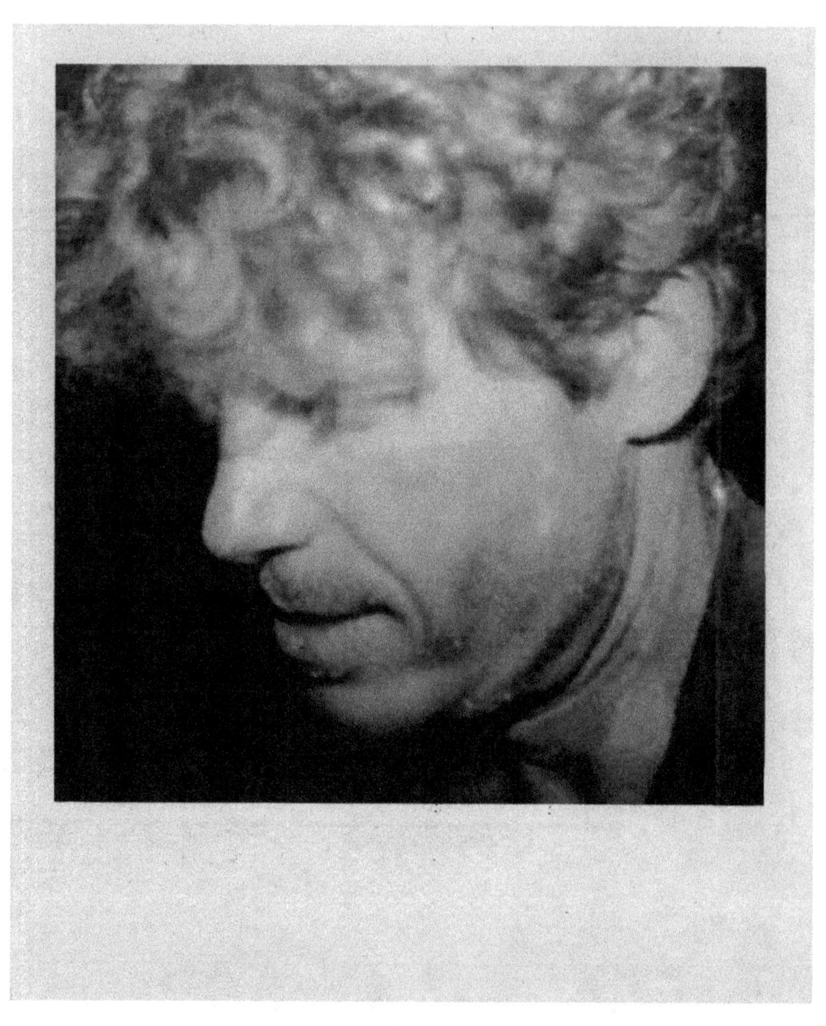

Jim Robison, Houston, TX, 1990.

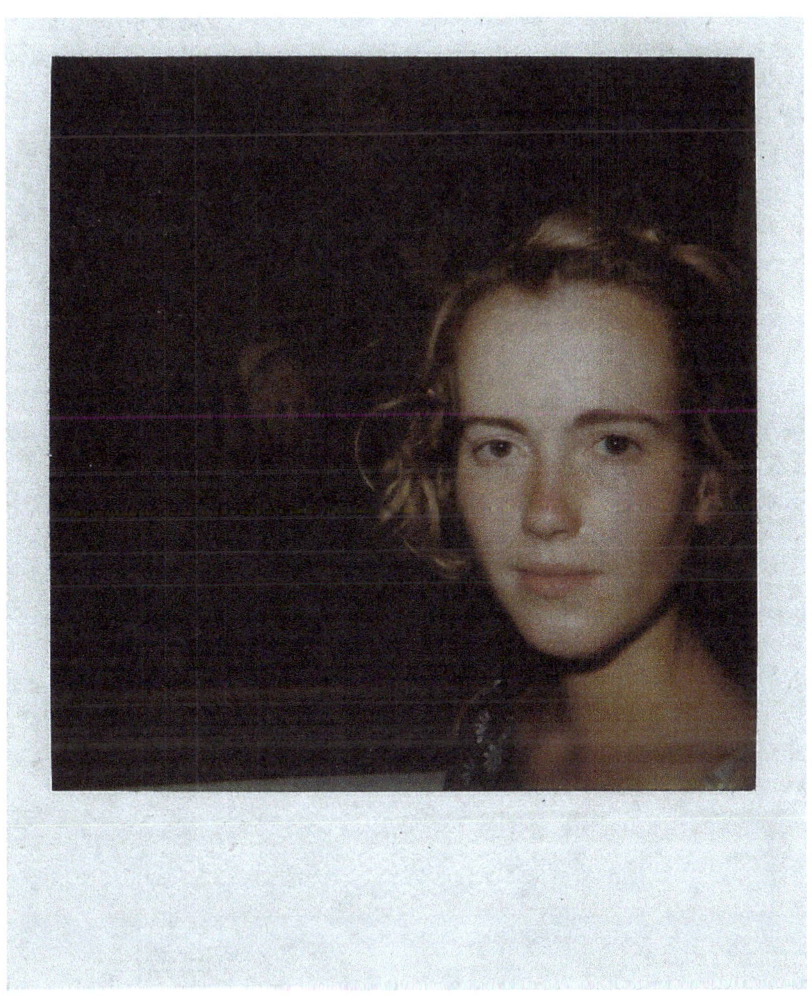

Daphne Beal, New Orleans, 1991.

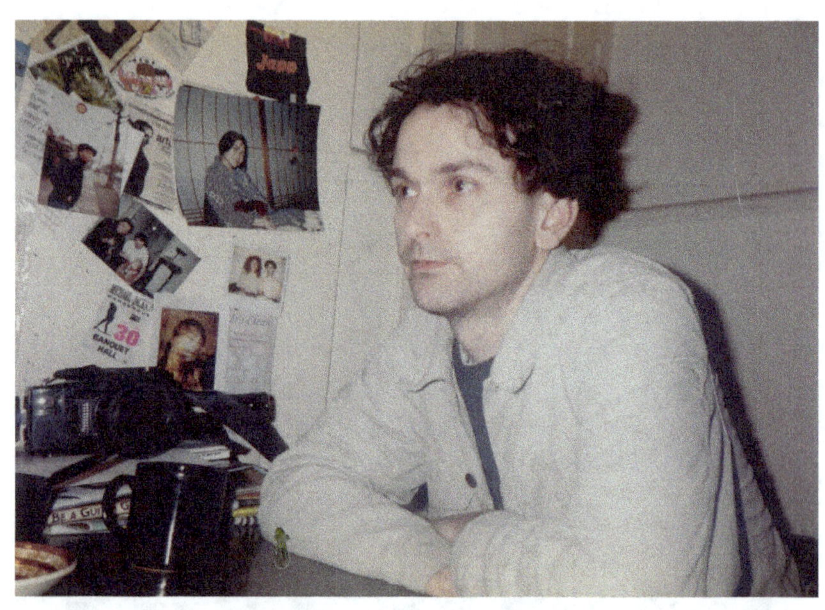

Paul Graham, London.

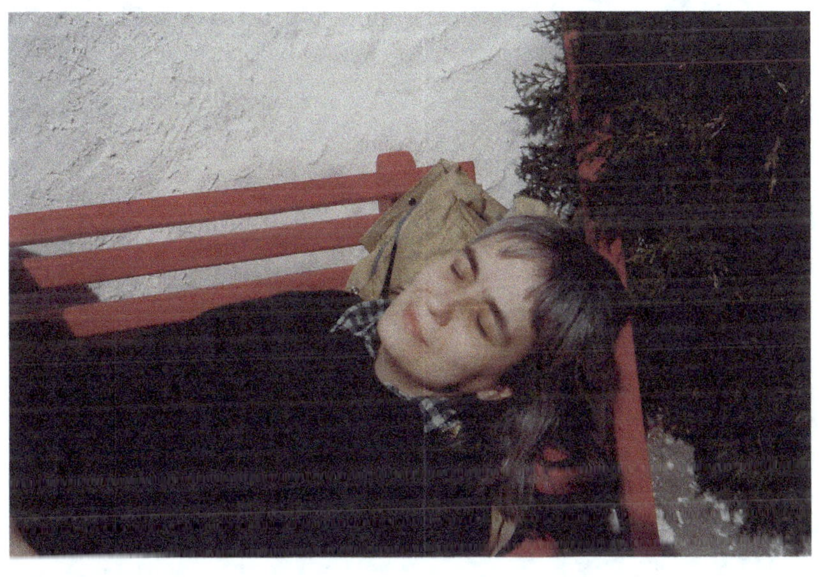

Susan Kismaric, Martin's Creek, Pennsylvania.

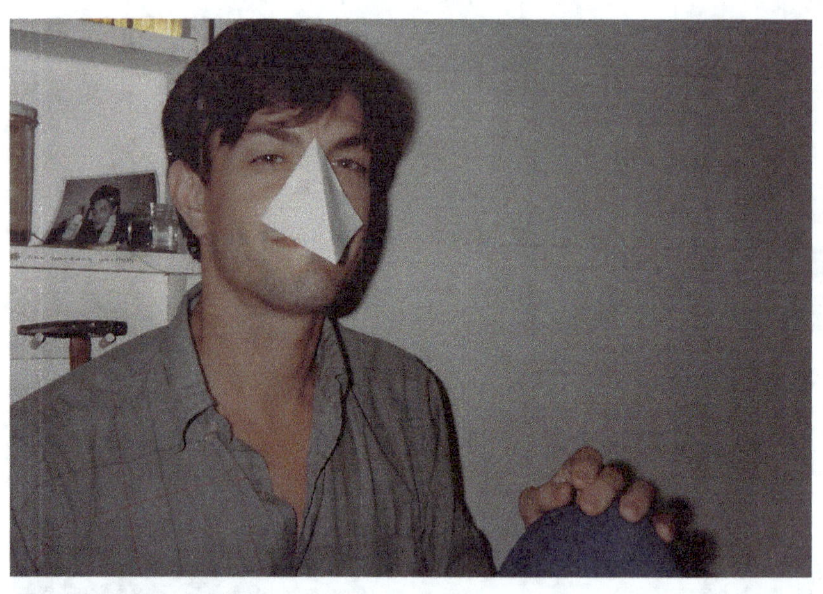

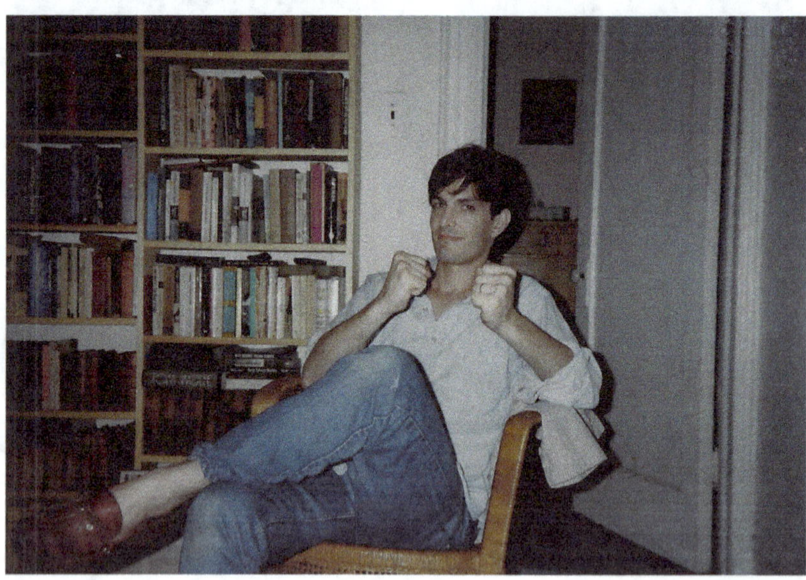

James Young, New York City.

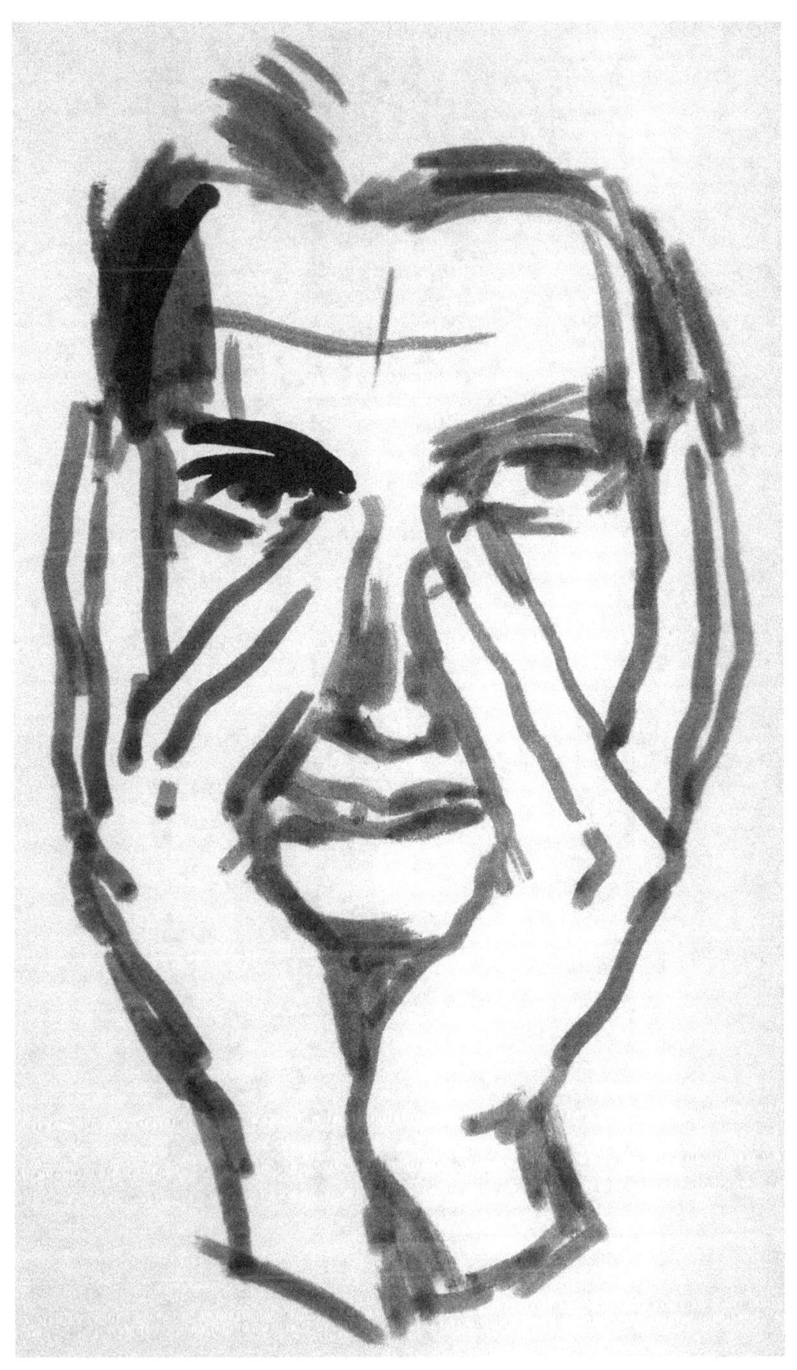

Dag Alveng, New York City.

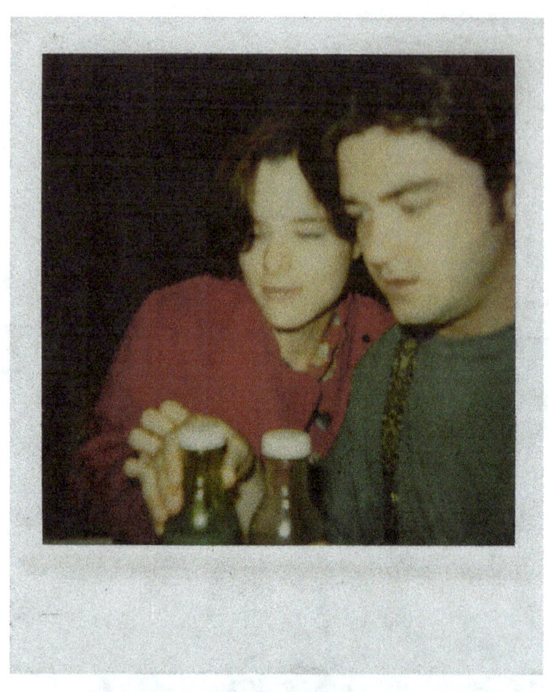

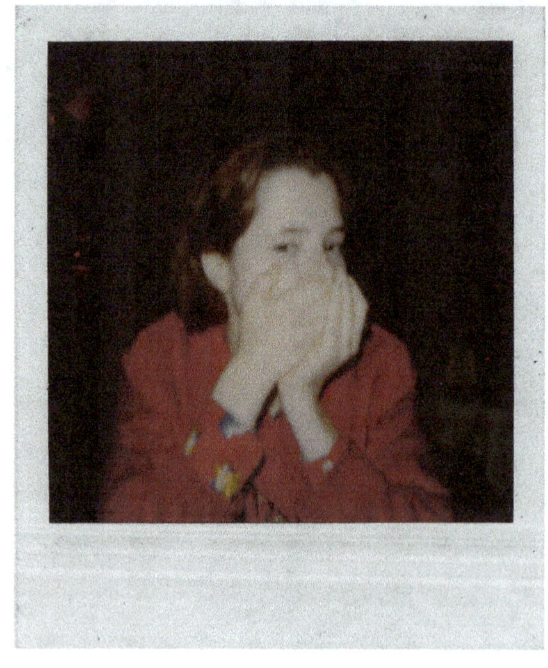

Parker Posey and Bob Gosse, New York City.

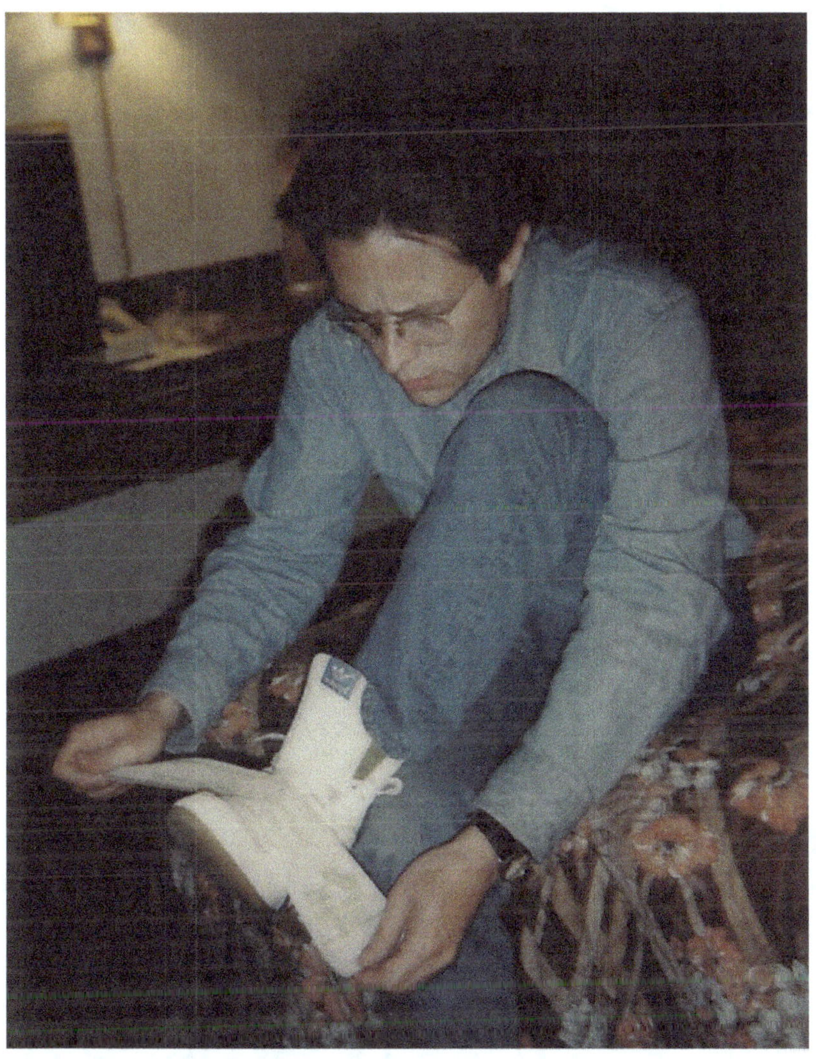

Lloyd Fonvielle in Hardin, Montana. Photograph by Toni Bentley.

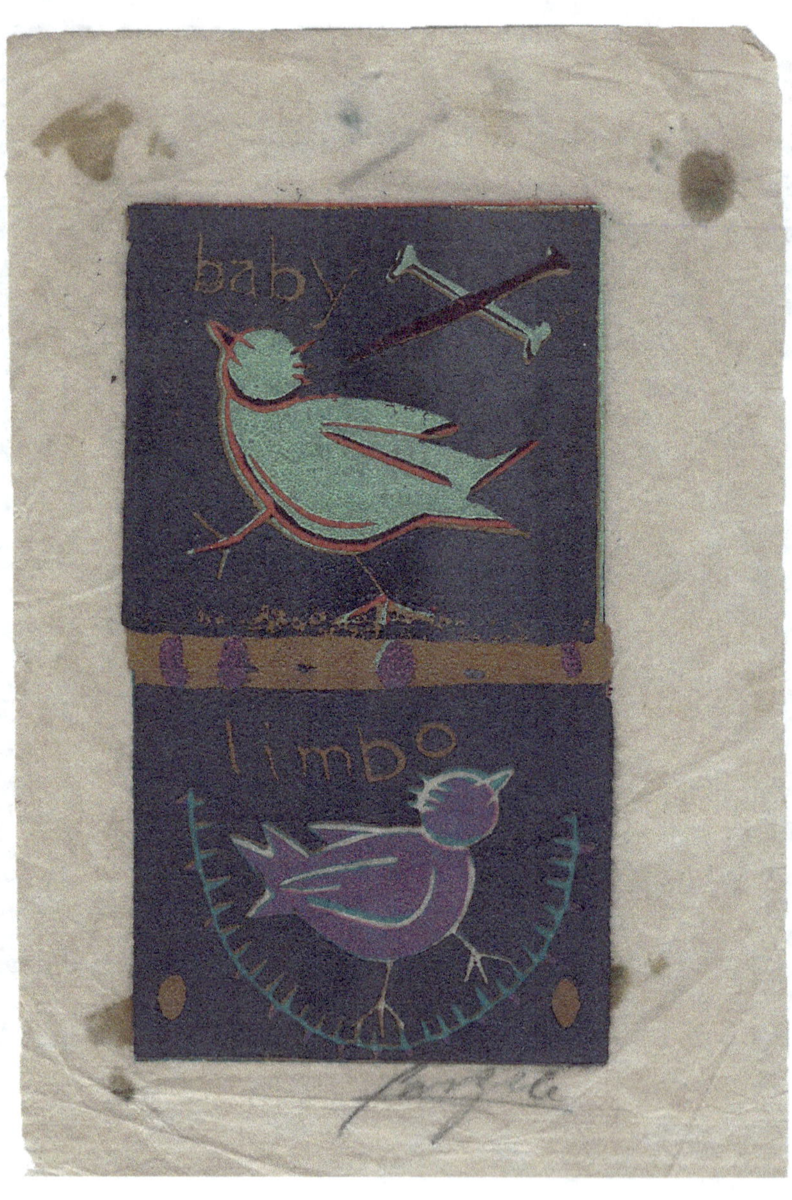

Baby Limbo, monotype by Carlysle Vicenti.

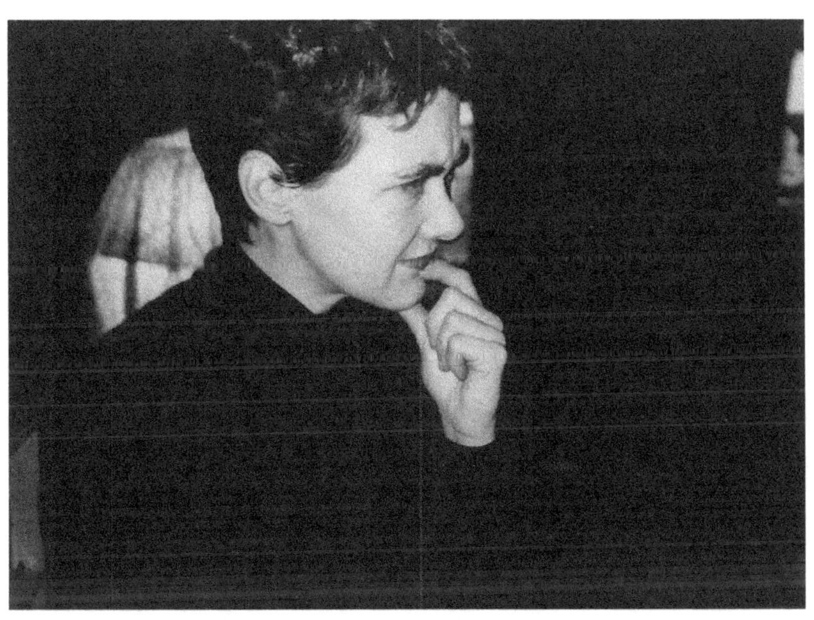

Prudence Moriarty, New York City.

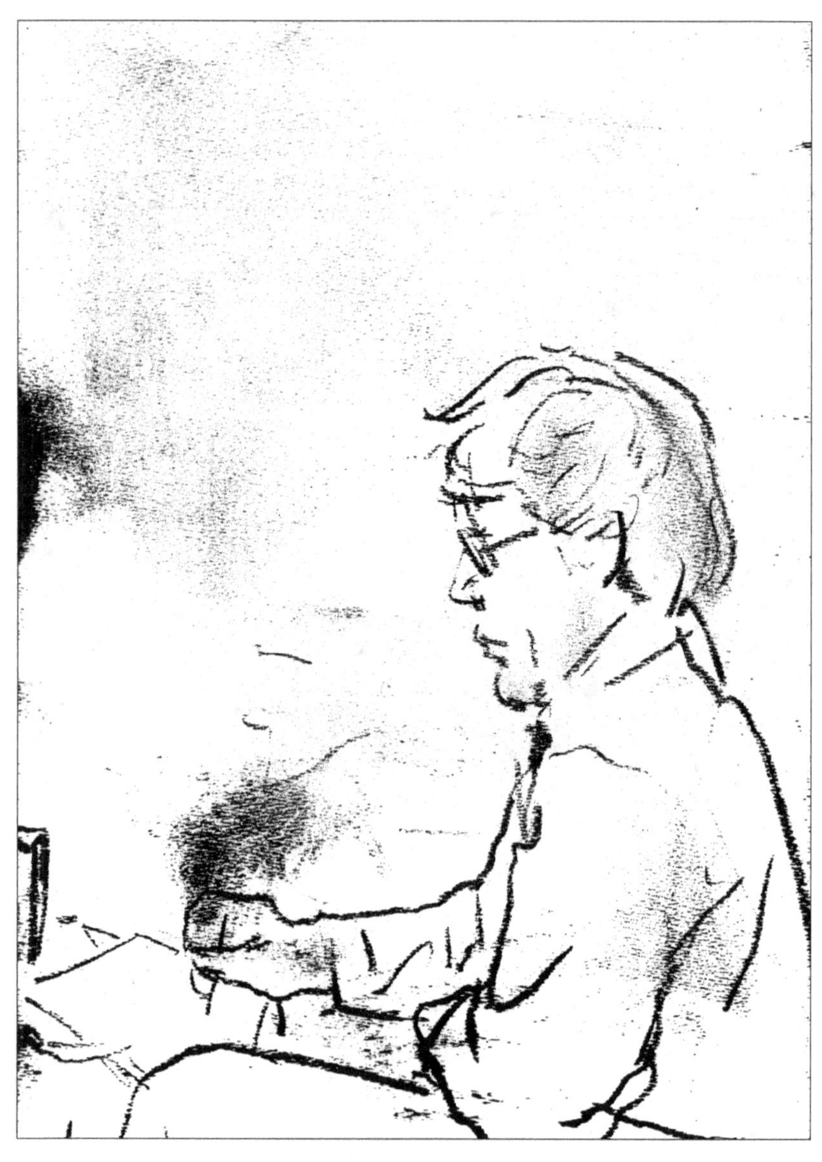

Jamie Bishop. Richmond, Virginia.

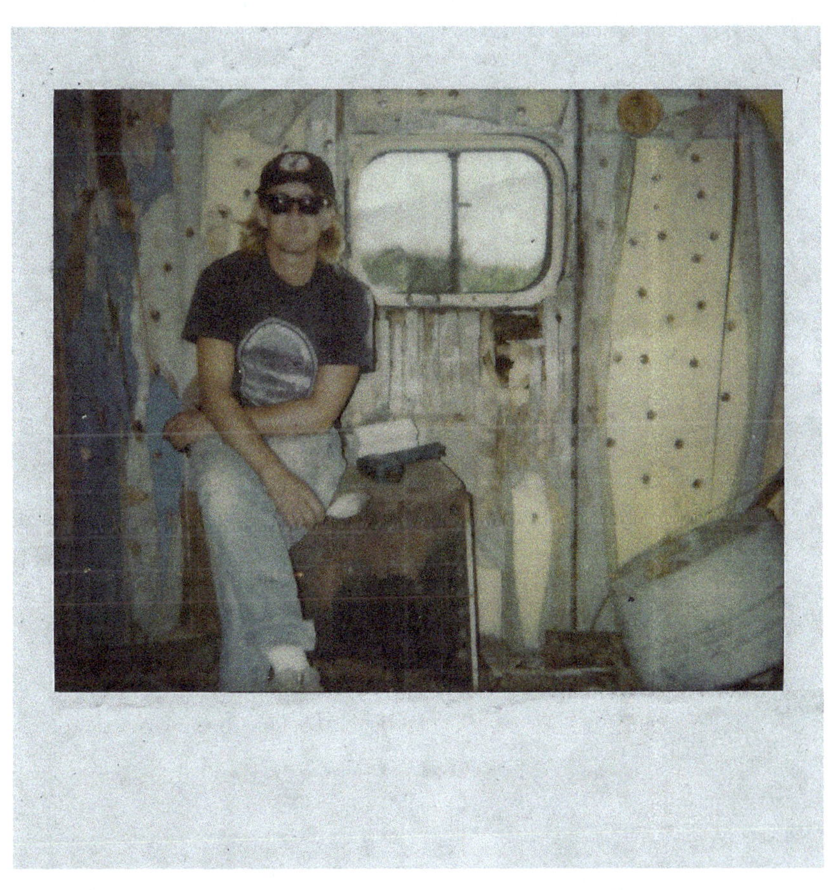

Jamie Bishop, Kadoka, South Dakota, 1991.

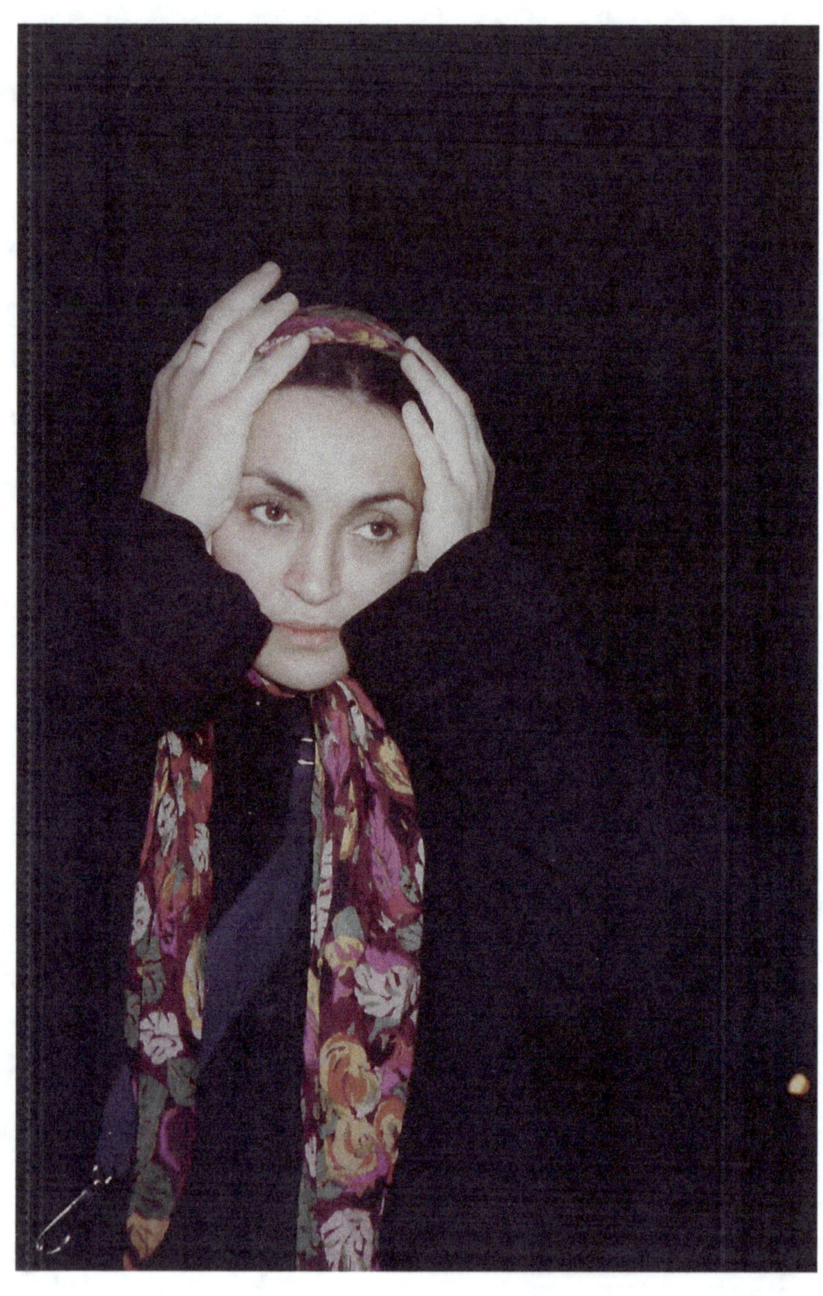

Michelle Charles in New York City, 1994.
Watercolor by Michelle Charles.

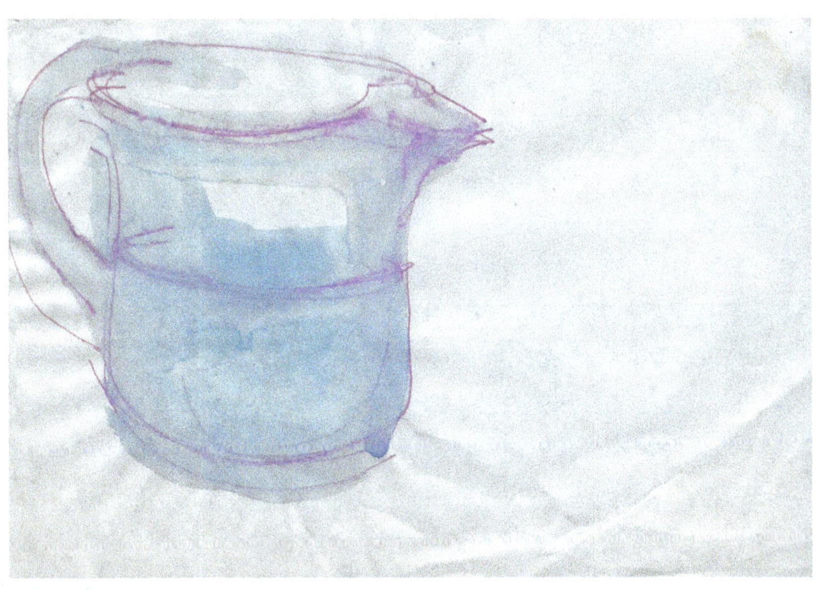

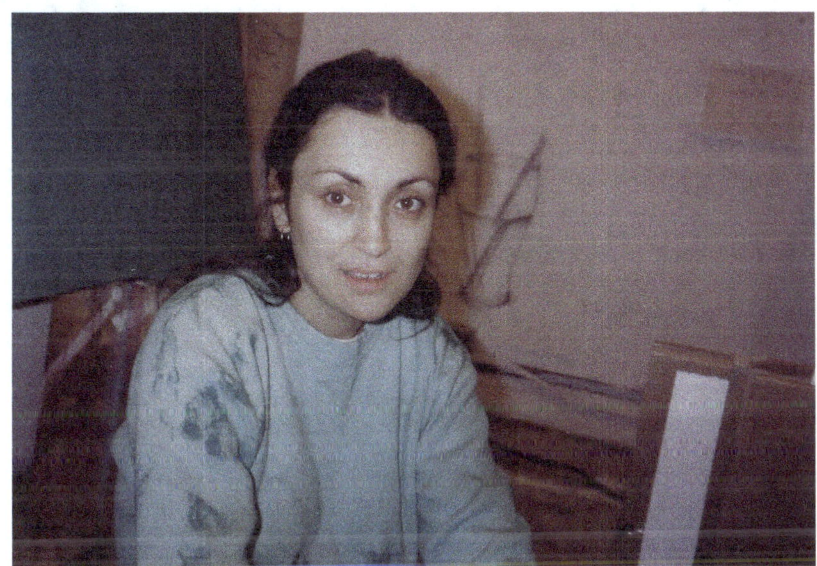

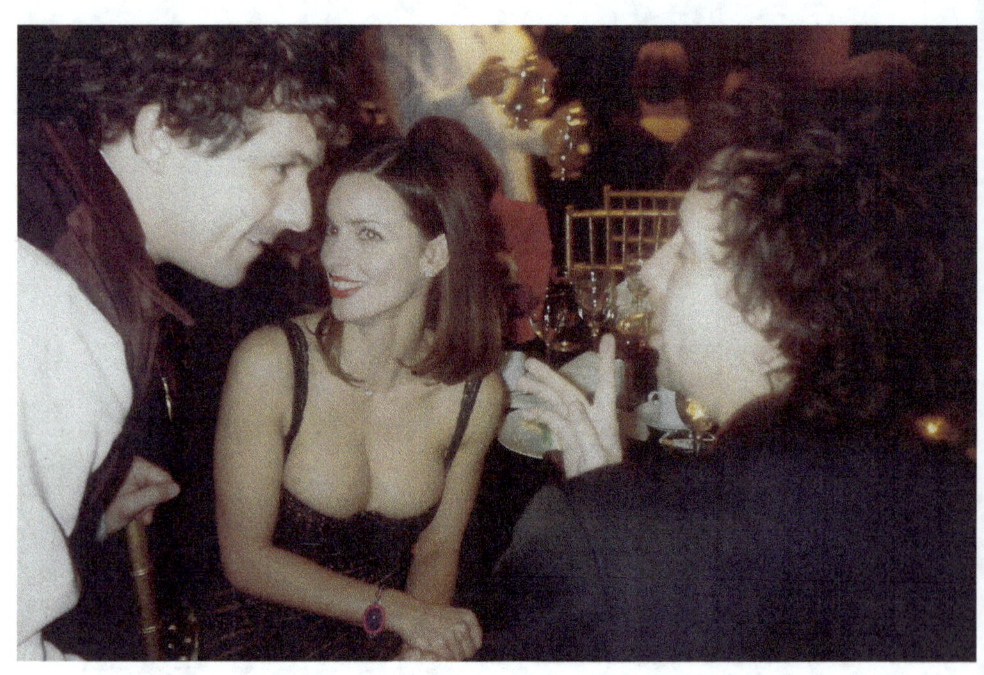

Billy Hopkins, Lisa Marie, and Tim Burton in New York City, 1995.

The Cult of One

Beauty must be CONVULSIVE, or will not be at all.

— André Breton, *Nadja*

A few years past the period covered in this book, I was courting an actor who had rather abruptly become well-known, having achieved a measure of notoriety by appearing in a number of impressive non-mainstream films. He'd just been paid a hefty sum to star in "a stupid action movie," but after reading my screenplay he said, "I'll work for you for nothing, if you can promise me one thing. Promise me that this movie will be somebody's favorite movie of all time."

Isn't that always the idea, I said, before admitting I just couldn't promise it.

I think of him fondly, still, for applying that impossible standard. A parallel thought, slanting in from a different angle, prompts me to think of *Nadja*'s self-declared number one fan, Guillermo Maytorena IV, a once young man from Phoenix, Arizona who wrote me a multi-page letter, penned in flowing purple ink on half sheets of fine paper, elegant paragraphs declaring his admiration for the film, his handwriting enhancing his words, as if the sentences had traveled through time, reaching me from a corner of Madrid or, indeed, Transylvania during a candle-lit era pre dating typewriters and laptops.

I've searched for this letter—I'm reluctant to merely summarize it; but I can confidently recount one detail: my correspondent let me know that he valued *Nadja* so highly he would test the suitability and potential of any of his romantic interests by inviting them to his home to watch the film in his company. Few of his potential paramours, he acknowledged, were as receptive to the movie as he wanted them to be, which inspired him to sign himself, at the missive's end, "Your Cult of One, Guillermo Maytorena IV."

Initially, I should explain, Guillermo had announced his love of my movie when he paid a visit to Manhattan in the stunned, tentative days following 9/11. He'd consulted the phonebook in his hotel room—remember phonebooks?—and called my now defunct landline. I invited him to the editing room, not far from Ground Zero, where I was working on another film. I remember next to nothing about this meeting, except that Guillermo had a round face, a tidy Baron Mordo goatee, and I found him personable, likeable. His fingernails were painted black—or were they green? I suspect I appeared disappointingly ordinary to him. He filled out his New York trip by visiting various *Nadja* locations: the Apollonia Coffee Shop, where Jim brings Van Helsing after he's been released from jail; the Village Copier, where Lucy, in her zombified state, stands over a flashing copy machine; and Max Fish, where Nadja and Lucy talk beside the jukebox and Lucy later flings Jim across the serpentine bar. I don't think I've ever had this kind of relationship with a movie.

I've located a later letter from Guillermo, in the same flowing purple script, dated 2003, in which he recommends I go after the rights to Lemony Snicket's *A Series of Unfortunate Events*, figuring I'd be simpatico with the orphaned children in those stories and could somehow afford to enter a bidding war for the film rights. A postcard from 2013 has also turned up, testifying to his stamina and good cheer.

The question occasionally arises: Who are you making these films for? Who is the ideal audience? Then there's the even more fatal question: What is the point? We can agree there's no point fishing for compliments, or fans, or trying to prefabricate reviews. All the same, I feel a swell of respect when I think of Robert Frank's compact declaration in a note addressed to the Guggenheim committee, when he was applying for a grant:

> When I first looked at Walker Evans' photographs, I thought of something Malraux wrote: "To transform destiny into awareness." One is embarrassed to want so much for oneself. But, how else are you going to justify your failure and your effort?

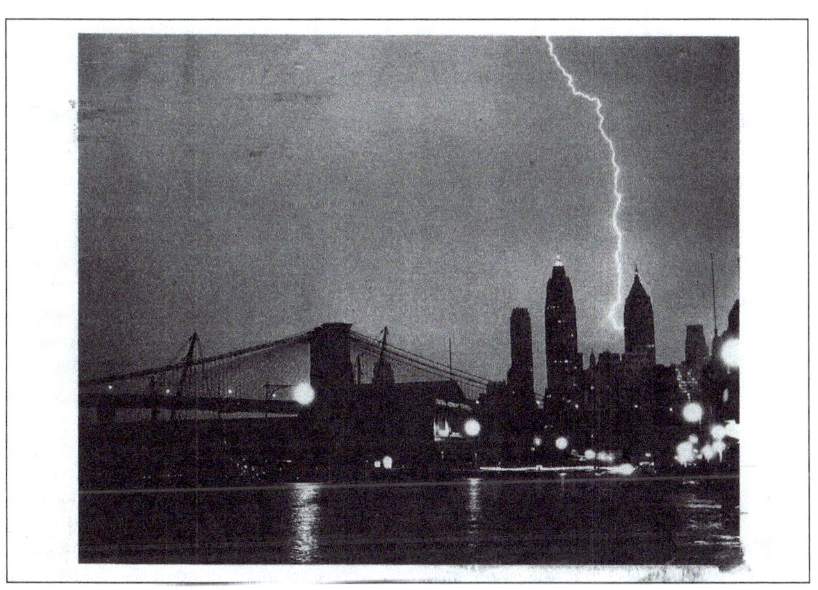

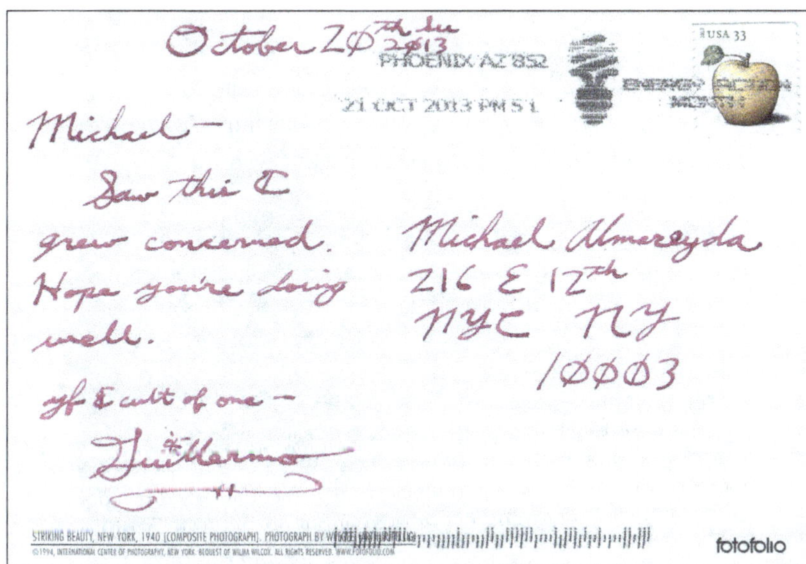

A postcard from Guillermo Maytoreno IV, 2013.

In Paris, in 2015, I was pleased to be introduced to Bertrand Mandico, and to learn that my Cult of One could stretch to include other cultists and wasn't necessarily limited to the continental U.S. Bertrand had seen *Nadja* despite the film never being released in France. His fascination with *Nadja*'s lead actress—his future wife—grew out from his appreciation of her performances in Hal Hartley films and in Philippe Grandrieux's extraordinary, crepuscular *Sombre* (1998). Bertrand wanted to ask Elina to be in his first feature film, yet, while waiting for financing to come through, asked her instead to be in a short, *Living Still Life*. As Bertrand recounts in a recent email:

> We spoke on the phone; she was in New York performing with Dafoe in a play by Richard Foreman. She was immediately enthusiastic. Then I asked her to star in another film, BORO IN THE BOX, even though we hadn't shot LIVING STILL LIFE yet. In this film, she had a double role, BORO (a filmmaker wearing a box on his head) and his mother. During the shoot, it was artistic love at first sight. And we've been collaborating ever since.

Bertrand's English is shaky; my French is worse. I feel we've been comfortably communicating, over the years, through Elina and through their films, though I can also recognize a kindred soul via opinions expressed in Bertrand's occasional interviews, as in these excerpts from a 2017 conversation with Nicholas Elliott:

> What I like about novels is that there are digressions, sudden shifts, changes in rhythm, new directions: in short, the unexpected.

> I really want the viewer to be swept away... The film becomes a river, with accelerations, rapids, occasional calmer pools of water, and, finally, a waterfall brings us somewhere else.

> I'm not making erotic films, but my films eroticize pretty much everything they touch, from nature and the setting to the characters; there's a constant erotic tension.

And, especially:

> I think that ultimately naturalism, so-called realism, in cinema is completely fake. Trying to make us believe that a famous actor is a factory worker is anything but realistic. On the other hand, making films that accept and present themselves as such, films that show their artifice and their own production, that's realism.

How many films have Bertrand and Elina made together? Bertrand's answer makes me smile:

> Since 2010:
>
> Four feature films.
>
> Thirty short and medium-length films completed.
>
> +
>
> Eight films in post-production...

Chase them down, by all means, if you care to see Breton's notion of convulsive beauty given credible delirious cinematic form.

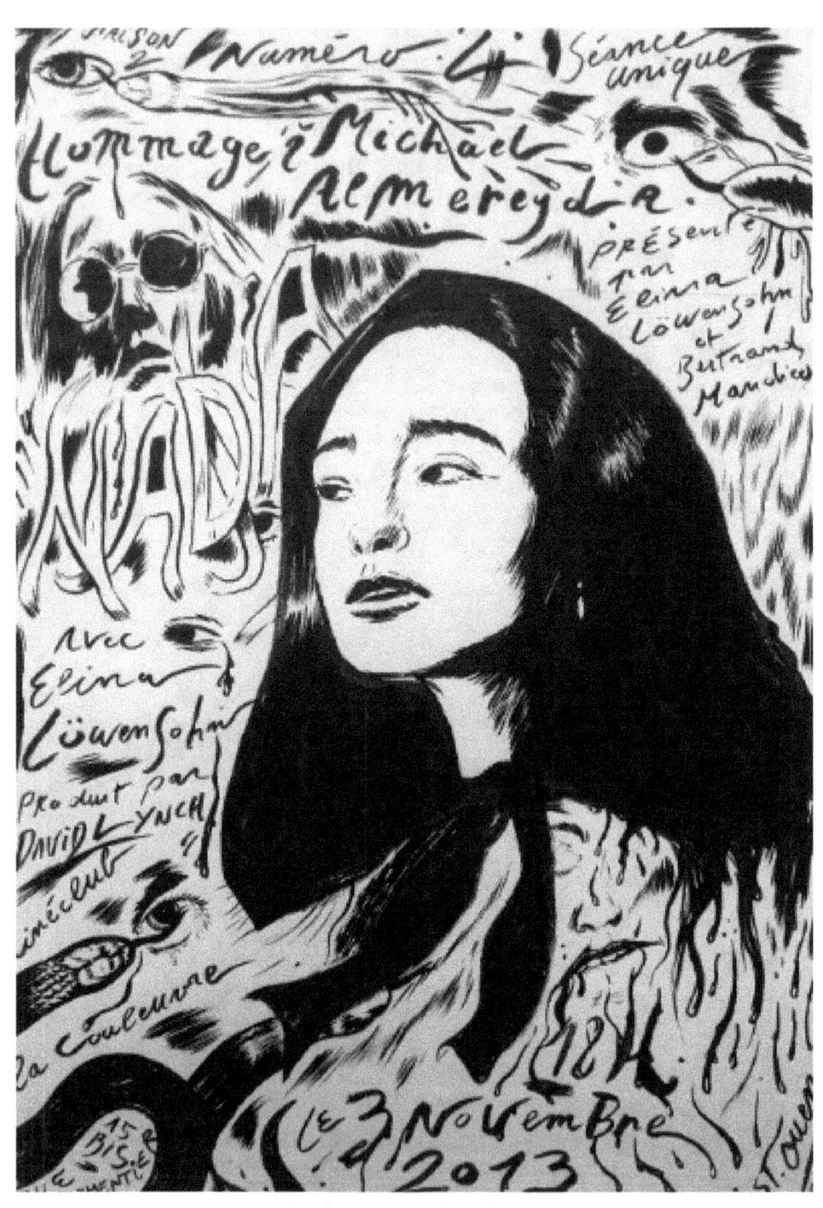

Drawing by Bertrand Mandico, 2013.

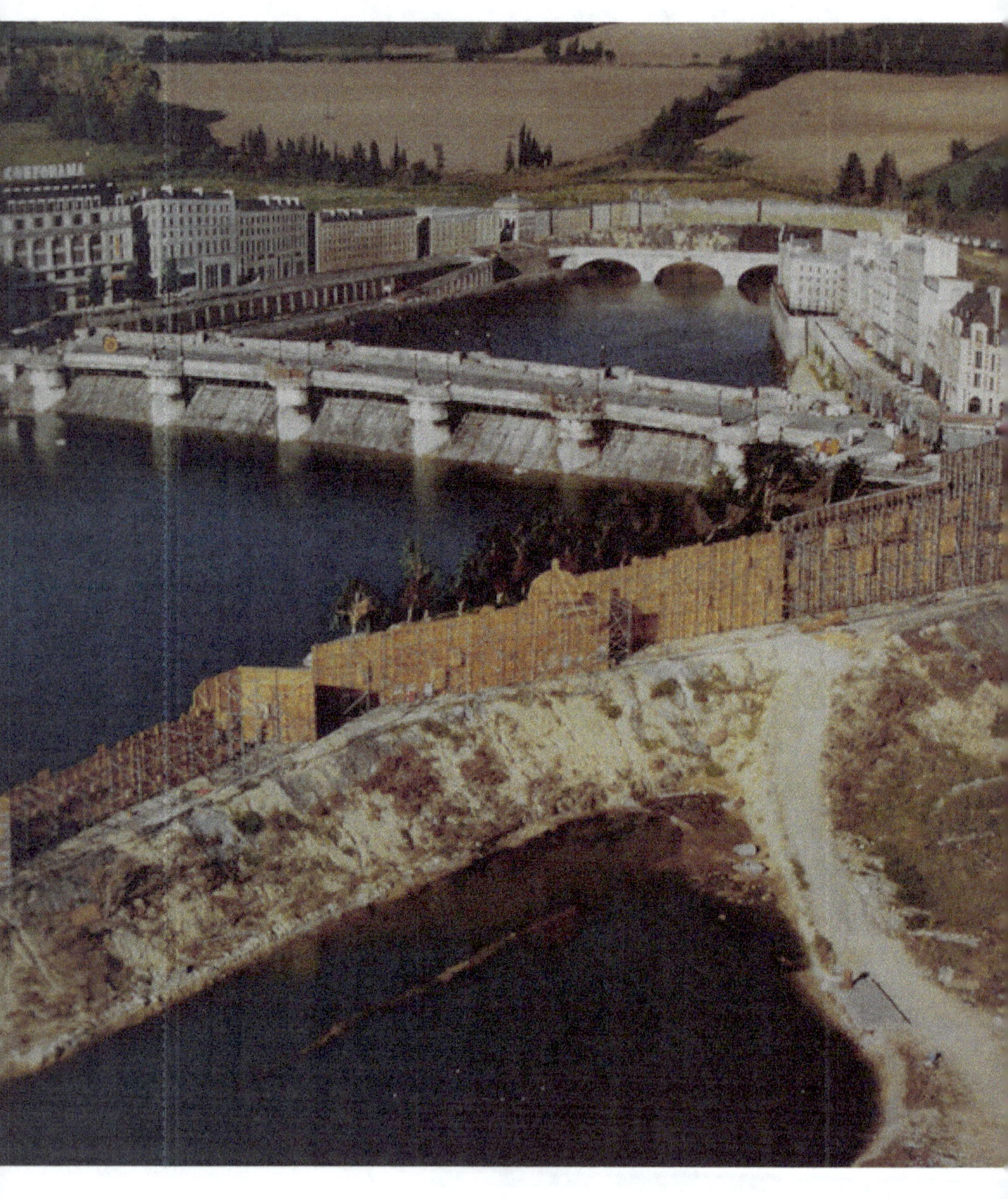

The set for Leos Carax's *Les Amants du Pont-Neuf* (*The Lovers on the Bridge*), built in the French countryside.

Leos on the Bridge

*His imagination sees the hidden connections between
conscious and unconscious substances with such assurance
that he hardly bothers with metaphors—he links them by
tying their hidden tails. He is a new kind of creature moving
about under the surface of everything.*

— Robert Bly on Pablo Neruda

I felt an immediate kinship with Leos Carax when we met in Los Angeles in late 1986, maybe early 1987, after a screening of *Mauvais Sang* at UCLA. We had a friend in common, and I think our love of certain filmmakers (Vigo, Welles, Lang, Godard) allowed us to instantly like and trust one another—it was almost that simple, even if inevitable widening distances have opened up over time. Juliette Binoche was with him then, they were a couple, and I was enough of a romantic to be immensely affected when they explained that many of her closeups in the movie were filmed while Leos, off camera, was holding her hand.

Perhaps because I was an American who didn't speak French but who had read, and could recommend, a fair bit of contemporary fiction, it was possible for Leos, a self-conscious loner, to consider me a helpful, neutral, non-competitive colleague. He shared screenplays with me and I helped him rummage for writers who might provide source material for future films. When I moved to New York and Leos and Juliette passed through, together or (after they split up) separately, I could expect to hear from them, to catch up in hotel rooms and restaurants. Until the belated release of his third feature, in 1999, Leos's work was largely unknown or neglected in the U.S. I could have qualified, at that time, as his devoted *Cult of One*. (As for Juliette, in my experience, it wasn't until the release of *The English Patient*, in 1996, that New Yorkers started really staring.)

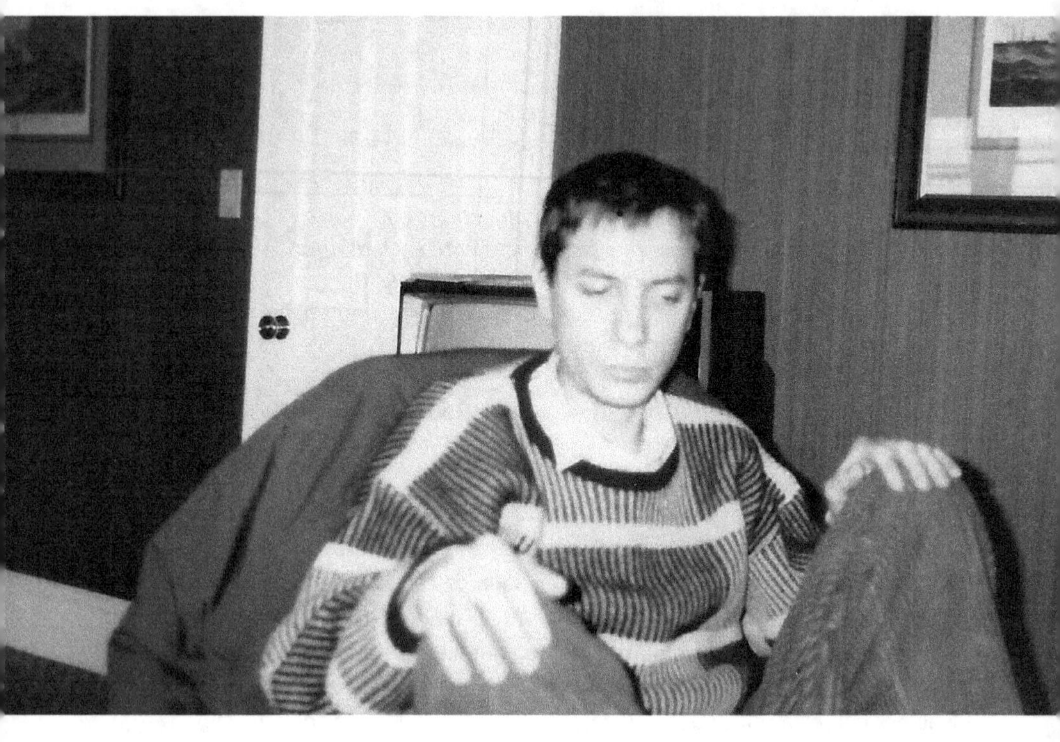

Leos Carax, New York City.

This is all by way of saying I don't remember how I landed in Montpellier in March of 1990 during the extended filming of *The Lovers of the Bridge*, a movie that had become imperiled when Denis Lavant's minor injury required a delay in shooting, followed by more serious postponements, with the production losing permission to continue on the real bridge. They'd relocated to a massive set constructed in the French countryside, replicating the Pont-Neuf, a section of the Seine with circulating water, and "Paris" seen on either end in diminishing perspective.

In a sharp and thorough mid-career assessment of Carax's accomplishment, Jonathan Rosenbaum quotes Jean Epstein, with resounding aptness: "The cinema is an anti-universe where reality is born out of a sum of unrealities."

Roaming the set, I could appreciate the audacity, the Napoleonic assertion of will, the sheer defiance of the odds, Leos reframing reality to suit the demands of his imagination, with budget costs climbing past any "reasonable" scale. (The movie, conceived as an intimate story about three isolated characters, acquired a negative fame for being one of the most expensive French films ever made.) This, I could consciously recognize, was not a workable model for myself, even if my own obsessiveness was weighing heavily on me. For better or worse, I was surviving, and survive still, on the other side of the financial spectrum, where money and make-believe do a more subdued dance.

When I saw him again in New York, a year or so later, I loaned Leos a spare Pixelvision camera. I'm fairly sure he never used it, and I haven't asked for it back.

I've uncovered a roll of film from my time in Montpellier, and three loose pages of incomplete typewritten notes—I've had to guess at their order.

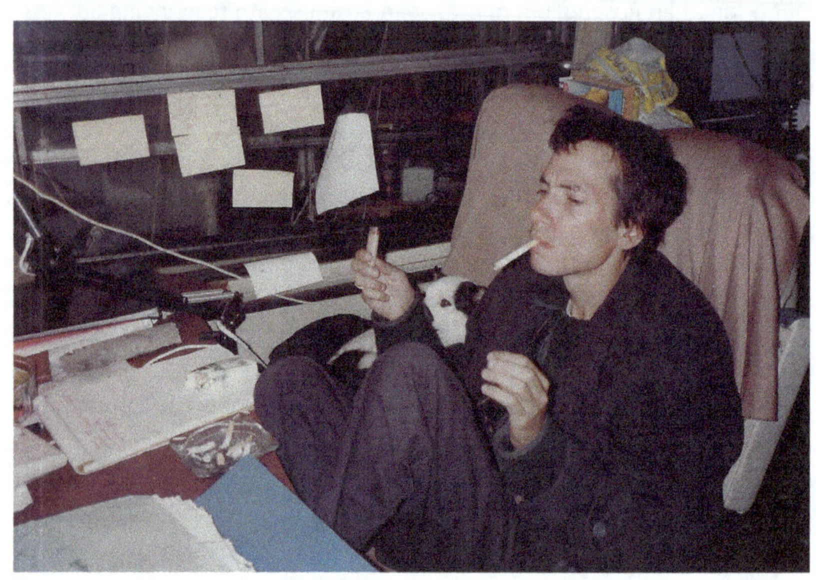

Leos Carax with Theo. Montpellier, France, 1990.

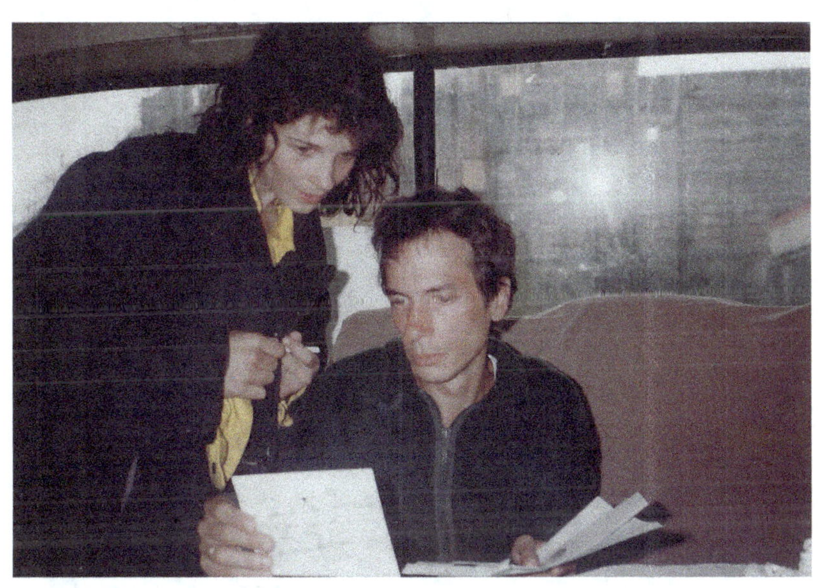

Juliette Binoche and Leos Carax.

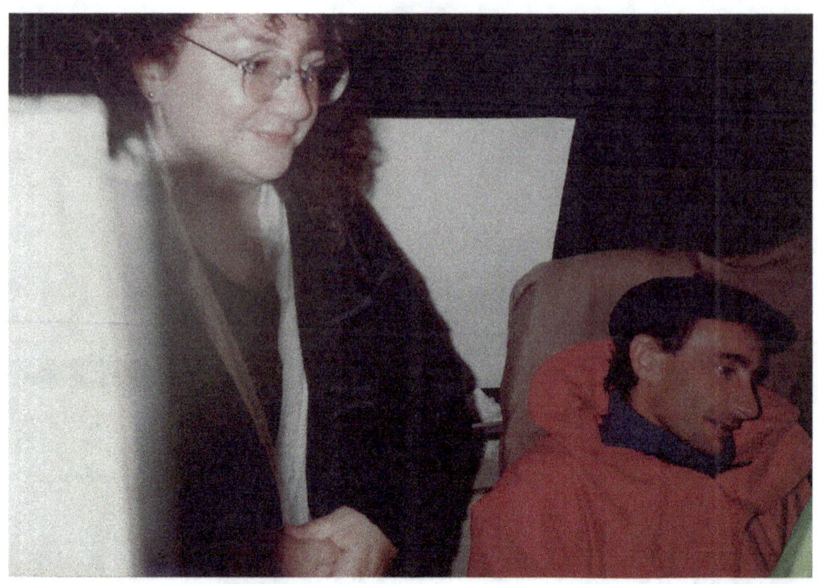

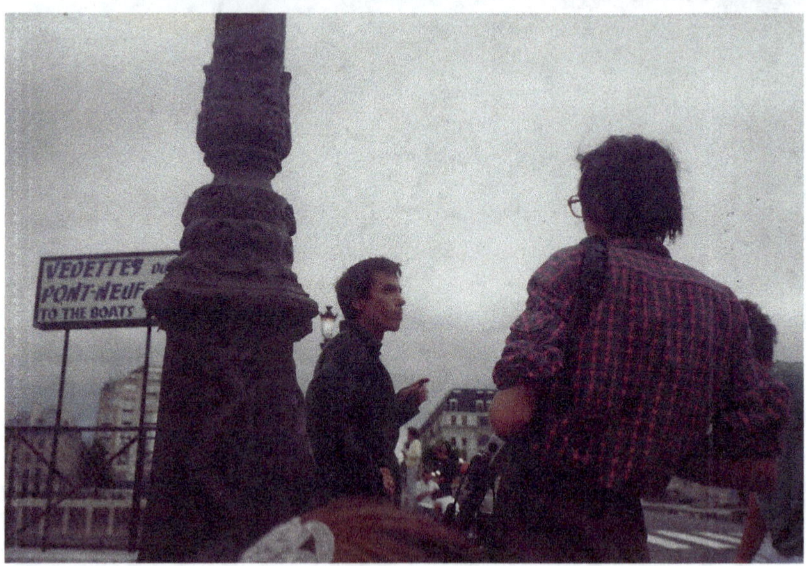

Vernice Klier and Jean-Yves Escoffier.

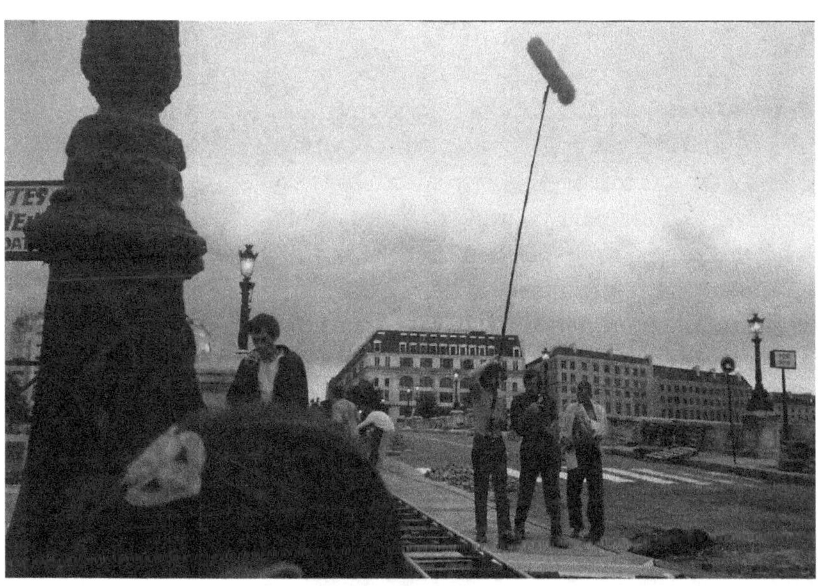

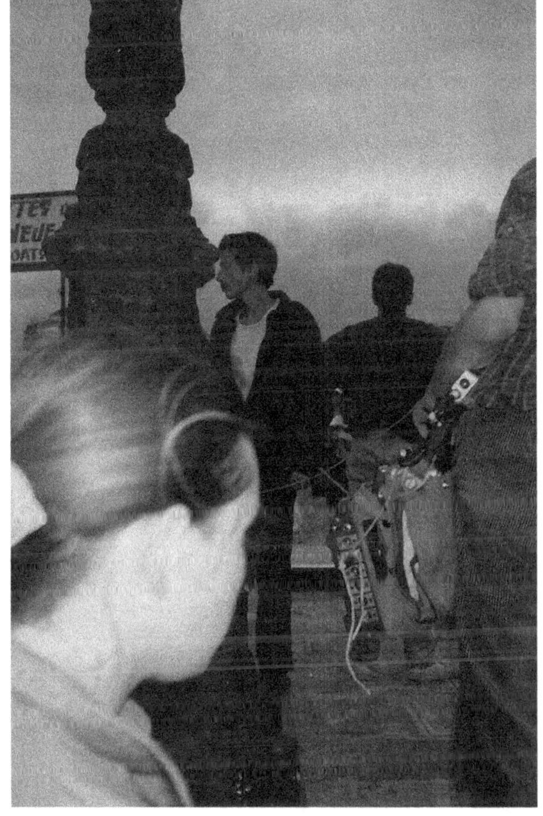

1.

You walk out of the canteen into a virtual shantytown: sand and mud. Under thin provisional roofs, construction equipment, cement mixer. A girl with tan legs splashed with cement pushing a wheelbarrow and whistling. Then a grassy space— a big white silo rears up and there's an immense squabbling sound: geese, a sustained racket. At dinner Leos explains that the sound occurs only during one particular hour near dusk, when the geese are fed. Funnels are forced down their throats, cornmeal poured in, to manufacture foie gras, which I have no interest in eating for the rest of my life.

They're filming here because it's flat. The set rests atop a level plane, the artifice unexposed by mountains, and there's a lot of sun.

The next morning, an active gray blue sky. Twenty-five takes for the elaborate tracking shot—Vernice diagrams it on a napkin—and during lunch they discover that the wrong filter was in the camera, effectively whiting out the sky. They do it again, several aborted takes. The lights are on and register sharply against the dim sky. They pause and wait for passing planes. The massive gate rattles as Denis runs past, though he's a good thirty feet away from it. I walk back through an open aperture in the set, past a construction spool the size of a car, down the slope: a splitting sound in the air and a sting-ray-shaped jet slashes by, a military plane.

They break about a half hour later, when rain lets loose. I scurry with Jean-Yves under a big navy umbrella.

2.

There's no evidence of a line producer or even assistant director in the standard American capacity. No one to watch the clock and bark at the crew. You spend a year thinking about the first day of shooting, Leos says, then that day comes, you do the shooting, you have to think about the next day. You think about it all night, you get to the set and you're exhausted. Then you see dailies, you have to sleep, you think about the day's shooting in the car on the way to the set.

Juliette smokes. There's something whittled, sharpened, in the line of her jaw, her cheekbones, sharp brown eyes.

Corrugated roofs over sheds. Broken stacks of bricks, cables, empty bottles.

Theo the little black and white dog follows him obediently, sits in his lap in restaurants. The authority, the boy in the big coat, like a comic book character. Mole-like concentration, wry, tolerant, cigarette in hand, a ready smile, hint of sunburn.

3.

Crates, stacked blocks, oversized spools. Apart from their size, the prop bottles and concrete slabs look indistinguishable from actual construction debris. [Juliette and Denis, shrinking when they get drunk, will cavort among these ruins.] Light wind ruffles the artificial Seine. Walking on the bridge, you can feel its hollowness—it's firm but feels fragile. Crossing it, you arrive at a wedge-shaped building whose lower bulk is plastered with a grayish photo collage. Beyond it, a marsh, muddy water, green grass, red emergency tape. On a grooved wooden track, a bus, slightly smaller than an actual bus, populated with mannequin busts rigged at window height. A driver and a dozen passengers.

Balmy air, dimming blue sky, the actors at their ease on the curb. Theo twitching around. Jean-Yves in a yellow sweater. Juliette smiling, delighted to display her ugly teeth. Denis in a sleeveless shirt, vest, gray-green pants, round-muscled and tan. His hair a close-cropped cap. Juliette in red sneakers, no socks, tan corduroys, navy sweater. I walk with them to the canteen, a large shack with orange metal chairs upended on arrayed tables. We rustle up an assortment of cheese from a round wooden container, yogurt, an orange.

For most of the past two weeks Juliette's been sleeping on the bridge with a pillow and blanket. Denis occasionally, too. This afternoon they're shooting more of a the scene involving carefully chosen extras seated at little tables, sipping drugged drinks, falling asleep so our heroes can rob them. A couple of the guest actors gave assent, took real sleeping pills and allowed themselves to be filmed nodding off. Juliette initially objected but as Jean-Yves recounts it she imitates one man—his enfeebled lifting of one finger as his head nods forward—and we all laugh. She offhandedly offers to let me stay in their apartment in Paris, and my unspoken surprise is proof that I've been living too long without friendship, with self-hatred and doubt.

I later learned that the drugged man was Leos's lawyer at the time. Another accommodating victim was played by Leos's father.

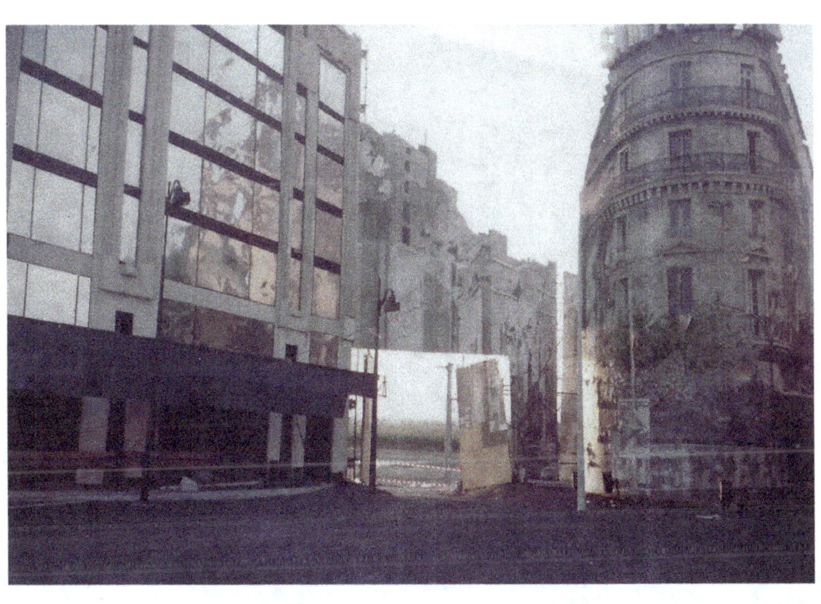

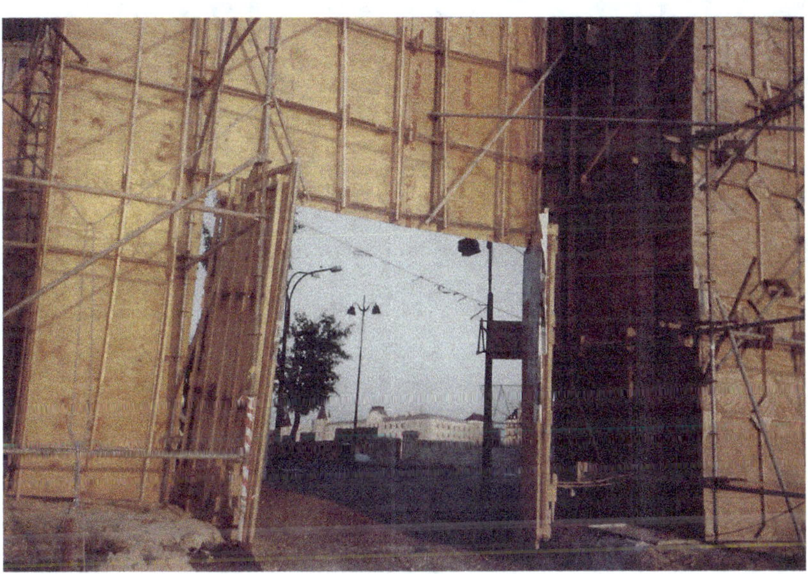

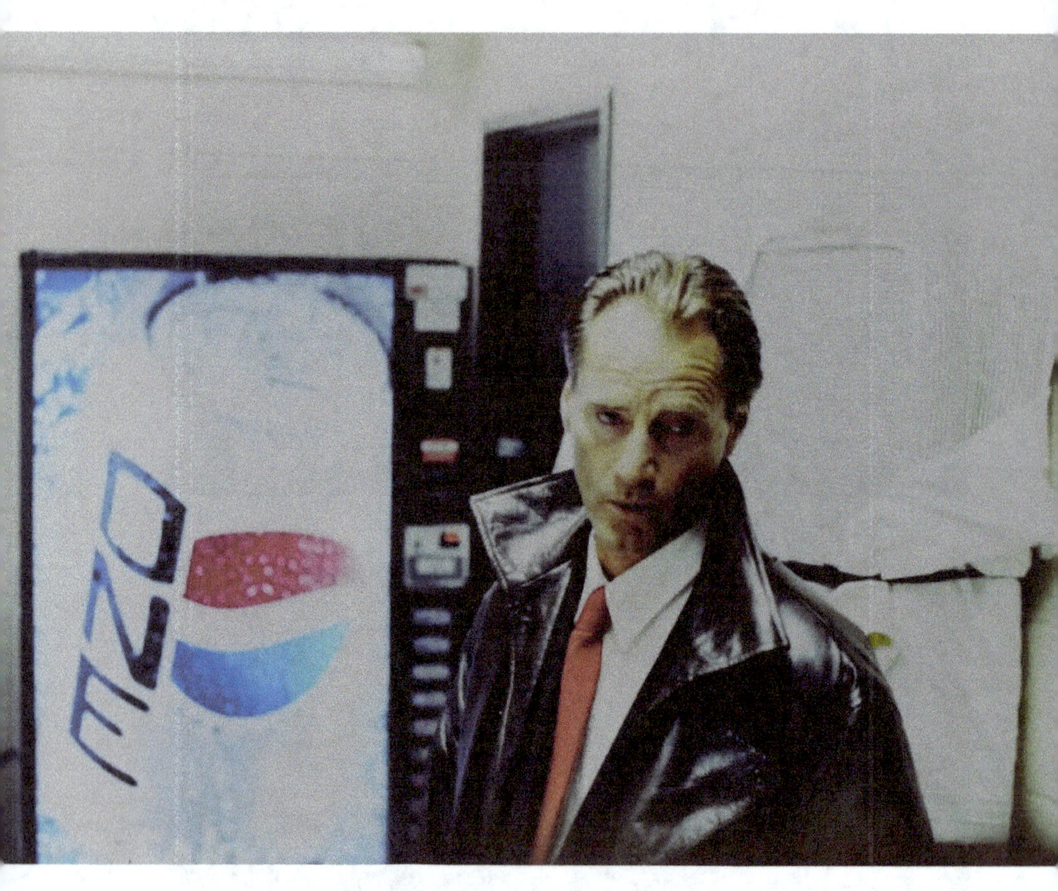

Sam Shepard in *Hamlet*, New York City, 1998. Photograph by Larry Riley.

Sam Shepard

Sundance

Park City, Utah. Sam Shepard mounts the stage of the Egyptian Theatre following the world premiere screening of his new film, *Silent Tongue* — a searing, strange hybrid of a Western/ghost story, playing out of competition at the Sundance Film Festival. Shepard, wearing worn blue jeans, a purple polo shirt and black vest, looks boyish, happy, ducks his head under a storm of applause, then sits — actually plonks himself down, elbows on knees — in a little stairwell cut into the apron of the stage. He then proceeds to name and thank and applaud every attending member of the cast and crew. None of the film's famous actors are present, but the audience dutifully applauds each name.

When this is over, Shepard takes questions, which are halting and uncomplicated. How long did it take to shoot the film? When did he finish it? What was the budget? Shepard's brief matter-of-fact responses are interrupted by voices shouting for him to talk louder. By the time a guy wrestles a standing mike on to the stage, Shepard confesses that he feels "incredibly awkward," thanks everyone for coming, springs to his feet and bounds out of the theatre. He's been up there for maybe four minutes. Well, as the Sufis will tell you, a candle does not illuminate itself.

A big voice

Sam Shepard is commonly, almost casually, regarded as the best playwright of his generation and, at 50, he remains one of the most vastly talented creative forces currently at large in America. "A big voice for a big place," as John Malkovich describes him. Shepard has been able to draw a bead on the national psyche while taking what may seem like a scattershot approach—colliding multiple sources from pop culture, vernacular poetry, bottomless visual metaphors. While keeping his stories and themes scaled within a distinctly private, personal terrain, he has managed, play by play, to describe something broad, deep and precise about America, to lift contemporary characters and events to an epic dimension.

If in recent years Shepard has appeared to be lying low, it's only because he's been less prolific than in the past (some 40 plays in 20 years) and this seems more or less inevitable. As does a darkening critical cloud, a backlash in the wake of Shepard's celebrity status and his relationship with Jessica Lange. His last play, *States of Shock*, received begrudging, dismissive reviews, while *Silent Tongue* ended up with a delayed US theatrical release at the same time that his new play, *Simpatico*, was scheduled to arrive on the New York stage.

Nightmare

Heaped in bright snow, with storybook icicles dripping from the eaves of reconstructed nineteenth-century storefronts, Park City, Utah, is basically a pricey ski resort doubling as America's most well-publicized showcase for independent film. If you show up at night, you see the slopes before anything else—a long double-laned zigzag of lights that seem to hover in the darkness, like a landing strip for extraterrestrials. The town proper is tidy, insistently quaint; the air is sharp and clear. But when you jostle through sidewalk traffic and hit Sundance headquarters, nestled among an arcade of cafés, bars and boutiques, it's hard to avoid the conclusion that you've entered a high-altitude Hollywood suburb. Because, simultaneous with its function as a festival, Sundance serves as a pressurized, semi-ecstatic arena for deal-making. You have to be in the thick of it and, just possibly, you have to have a film in the festival, to recognize the quality of cheerful desperation invading nearly every conversation.

A studio executive in his early twenties, newly promoted to scour the festival for possible acquisitions: "On a level playing field, all players being equal, the only thing separating you from the competition is a state of continuous, corrosive paranoia." A seasoned Hollywood producer: "Just sit back and think of a straight line going from the top of your head through your spine. People will think: 'He's so calm! What has he got that I don't have, and how can I buy it?'*

In the midst of this, Shepard's modesty and plainspokenness are almost unnerving. He remains affable, approachable, laconic. He laughs and smiles a lot. He happens to be one of the festival's true proofs of glamor—the recognizable movie star—and also, in this "authentic" Western setting, one of the few people in town who looks like he can actually ride a horse. "You can't cut yourself off from the—the nightmare," he laughs. "Otherwise you turn into some kind of hermit, spinning your wheels."

The film, it should be mentioned, is lush, magical, rich in detail and depth of feeling. The story centers on Prescott Roe (Richard Harris), whose son Talbot (River Phoenix) is crazed with grief over the death of his mixed-blood wife, Awbonnie (Sheila Tousey). When Roe, fearing for his son's sanity, kidnaps the dead woman's sister to provide Talbot with another wife, her father (Alan Bates) and his son take pursuit. Meanwhile Talbot, keeping Awbonnie's corpse trussed to the branches of a lone burial tree, has prevented her ghost from passing into the next world.

If this story, boiled down to essentials, sounds eccentric, that's because it is. Shepard's characters, all steered or strangled by blood ties, are galloping around on familiar thematic turf—the sins of the father visited upon sons and daughters alike—and familiar Shepard questions come into play: What is an identity? What separates identity from spirit? In a culture where everything is for sale, what remains beyond price?

Shepard, aided by Jack Conroy (cinematographer on *My Left Foot*), gets a lot of mileage out of the New Mexican prairie desert and continuous, endlessly watchable close-ups of Richard Harris. (Harris has aged the way you might wish Brando had; the years have sharpened his face and he seems able to just stand there—white-bearded, mouth half-open—radiating battered nobility and, in his eyes, controlled avalanches of emotion.)

From moment to moment, the film rolls along with a kind of concentrated poetic heft. You think of Noh drama, the way Shepard somehow charges single images—a fire, a tree, a man on a horse—with meanings that leap beyond themselves. Shepard's stunt team (the first unionized band of Native American stunt riders) supplies some of the most exciting horse stunt work in any film in recent memory. But *Silent Tongue*'s neatest visual spectacle and deepest sense of peril comes from Sheila

Tousey's performance as the unfriendly ghost. Tousey's presence—not merely her tribal/monster movie make-up, but the level of violence she unleashes in her voice—provides a special effect in itself.

At the film's finish, Shepard arrives at a basic message of rectitude, however bleak. One man's lies catch up with him; another's trueheartedness prevails. And it becomes clear, as the survivors watch the dead woman's corpse consumed in flames, that Shepard has delivered a bitter lament for a betrayed race and, within that, a love story between father and son.

High and low

What you might expect, although without being exactly prepared for it, is that Sam Shepard loves language, loves books. He recommends I read Webb's two-volume *History of the Plains*. He points out the derivation of the word "teamsters"—warped from a time when men drove teams of horses. And he praises Peter Handke, Walker Percy, Max Frisch, Richard Ford—particularly Handke for his ability to describe a feeling of aloneness ("aloneness even when you're not alone") before launching into a calm defense of existentialism. How is it, he wonders, that existentialism has been dropped like a kind of outmoded fashion when it seems to him still the appropriate, necessary framework for asking essential questions? Well, he says something like this. My tape recorder, choking on this patch of the conversation, translates his words into a low seashell roar, a seemingly infinite silence. The machine proves more receptive to Shepard's remarks about the issue at the heart of *Silent Tongue*.

"One of the amazing things to me about this clash of culture—the European and the Native American—is you have absolute opposite mentalities. The European wanted to acquire land, thought that God was in the sky somewhere, the lowly sinner had to aspire to heaven—completely foreign ideas for the Native American. For the Native American the land wasn't owned by anybody; the holy spirit moves through every animal, every plant, every living thing, including human beings. Those two mentalities could never see eye to eye. There was no hope of them ever seeing eye to eye. I think that's amazing.

"And now, of course, in our contemporary mess, what white Europeans would like more than anything is to feel a sense of belonging to the spirit world. That's why we've got these beaded vests and trinkets in the

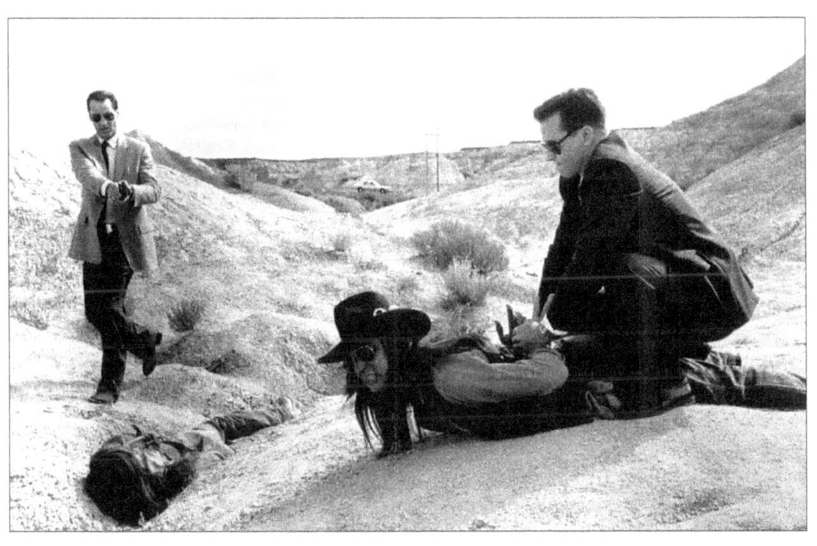

Sam Shepard, John Trudell and Val Kilmer in *Thunderheart*,
filmed in South Dakota's Black Hills in 1992.

windows out here. So people can put them on and feel like they're associated with the spirit world, which they're very far away from. Still, we're haunted by the Native American religiousness, the true religiousness of people who were in harmony with their environment, which we're completely not in harmony with. There's this starvation. Which is part of the reason this Native American thing is so popular. That and the fact that it's making money."

A pool game in Kadoka, South Dakota

Kadoka—the name, translated from Sioux, means "hole in the wall"—is just a few blocks of low buildings, a central water tower, big sky. I stay at the Cocklebur Motel, visiting friends working on *Thunderheart*, in which Shepard appears as a homespun FBI agent who turns out to be a bad guy. The invading film crew has given the place a shot of adrenaline, but there is no effacing the town's true backwater innocence. It is an innocence mixed with an essentially unnamable quality, a feeling of stark mystery somehow connected to the lavish changeable sky and to Native American tribal territory a few miles out: the Bad Lands, astonishing ranges and bluffs of red and brown rock. *Thunderheart*, a mildly likeable, mediocre thriller, offers glimpses of this, but Shepard mentions another movie to evoke the place for a third party: "You ever see *Bad Day at Black Rock* with Spencer Tracy? It's like that—not really malevolent, but one of those unbelievable outposts on the edge of nowhere, 90 miles from Rapid City, right on the edge of the Pine Ridge reservation, and it has this incredible cross-cultural mystery to it. I fell in love with it." I buy a pair of Redwing boots and stay a week longer than I'd intended. Shepard, settling in for the film, is much more thoroughly seduced. He buys a horse (named Kadoka—"really fat now"— and fills a couple of hundred notebook pages with a long running start for a novel—his first—which sounds something like an Antonioni film transposed to South Dakota.

"It's about a couple travelling through the South to celebrate the anniversary of their wedding in Rapid City, and in the course of things the wife has a little panic, she goes into a kind of panic, not really explained too thoroughly, and they're forced to stop in Kadoka [laughs]. And then she disappears."

Shepard is finishing his last few days of shooting when I show up. The place is tiny and I see him around, hawk-faced in a Stetson, hanging out mainly with stuntmen and local ranchers. Everybody in town appears to like Sam; he is open to everyone, fits right in. And I note one stray, incidentally haunting remark, delivered one night during a late loopy pool game in which multiple players are crisscrossing between the table and the bar.

Nobody can quite remember whose turn it is, whether they are shooting solids or stripes. At one point Shepard leans in on his cue, with something hard and final in his eyes, saying: "Personality is not the man."

He's talking to local stunt-double/painter/poet Marty Cuny—an elegantly world-weary man in his late thirties, three-quarters Sioux. I remember Marty's kind eyes, ponytail, earring stud. Shepard doesn't blink, and his voice remains emphatic. "Personality," he says, "is the opposite of the man."

A bunch of actors standing around

"He carried no baggage as a director," recalls Stephen Rea, who performed with Bob Hoskins in Shepard's first stint at directing his own work, *Geography of a Horse Dreamer*, at London's Royal Court Theatre (seating capacity: 75) in 1974. "I remember thinking it was very special, but it wasn't particularly acknowledged as special by anyone around," says Rea, "Sam was very good at letting people do what they could do… It felt like a very easy experience I don't mean that it was sloppy, but everybody was in tune with everybody else. We played a lot of poker. There was a lot of spare time because we were on top of it. He brought in records that suited the characters. For my character it was Hank Williams." Shepard has since directed six productions of his own plays, and two films, and the testimony of other actors gives a corresponding picture of relaxation, freedom and trust. But anyone who's seen Shepard directed by Shepard can attest to the ferocity and precision of these productions, their startling go-for-broke physicality. These productions are shaped around language and performance but they feel tightly wound, urgent, passionate, and their emotional power includes   probably depends on—stretches of wild breakaway humor. They defy Holden Caulfield's demolition of most theatre as "a bunch of actors standing around."

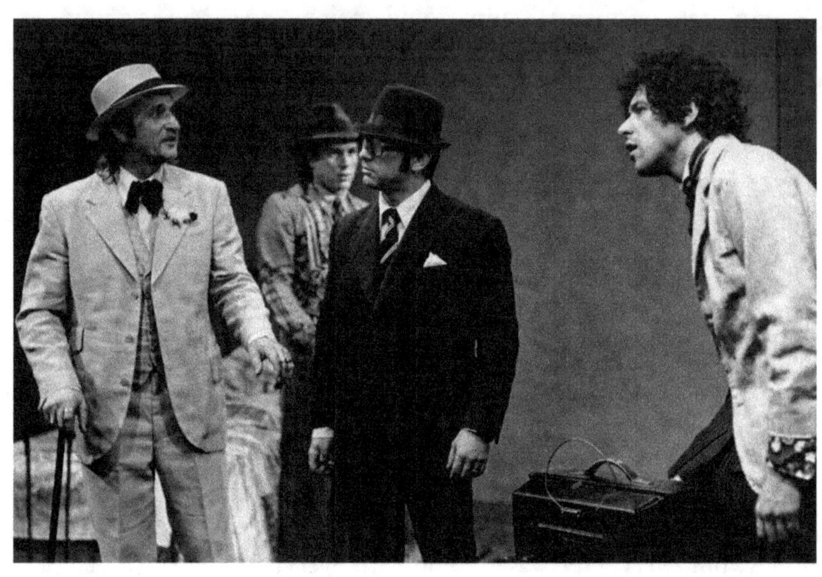

Bob Hoskins (center) and Stephen Rea (right)
in the 1974 Royal Court Theatre production of
Sam Shepard's *Geography of a Horse Dreamer.*

Stephen Rea: "The people are all dislocated and strange in Sam's plays. It's all about this kind of terror, the horror that's outside, that undefined outside world. Unseen terror suddenly striking." "If you don't understand that about Sam's plays," Rea continues, "then you can't do them."

Amanda Plummer: "He's very trusting of his actors... He spoke differently to everyone. He can communicate with you in your dilapidated way, and it won't be a dilapidation. There wasn't one way to do it, in life; let alone in theatre. So, he was very agile. Not to get a result necessarily. There was a warmth. It wasn't question/answer, ever. More of an image—image talk."

John Malkovich: "The plays are very dreamlike but also very lifelike. Very exalted—or naked... The big challenge of it in my experience is the incredible amount of energy it takes. After *True West*, I was tired for about a year after it. *States of Shock* was the same. So many nights I was saying, 'Jesus, am I going to be able to make this?' But it needs to be on that kind of exalted cartoon mythic plane. Which doesn't mean it doesn't have real fury and real rage... All of his work is so American: about the size of the country, the terror we feel, what liars we are. But also about how we exist in spite of it all. And how entertaining we are."

The recorded history of ghosts

"To me," Shepard says of directing, "it all comes out of language. You can't talk about action and movement and physicality as separate things. They're always, particularly in theatre, connected impulses." These impulses seemed to have seized up in Shepard's first film, *Far North*, a warm, small-scaled domestic comedy. The picture was notable for its gentleness, for sparks of bitter humor involving the shooting of a horse, and for a delicate, riveting performance by Jessica Lange. Wim Wenders likes the picture for what he calls its "innocence"—a generous way of describing Shepard's initial limitations as a film director. The plain fact is the film showed little of the intensity or resourcefulness of Shepard's work as a stage director.

"In *Far North*," Shepard admits, "I was really frustrated by interiors. I hate interiors. For some reason whenever I got inside four walls I felt paralyzed. I felt absolutely stupefied. I mean I could do it—mathematically you figure it out. But as soon as I got outdoors it immediately presented itself: where to put the camera, how to move the camera, what to include in the frame.

"So," he concludes, laughing, "in this film I only had one interior. I wanted to do everything outdoors. Without walls."

As it happens, *Silent Tongue's* longest indoor scene—in a covered wagon, where Richard Harris almost shyly reveals his wish to buy a new daughter-in-law—is among the best in the picture, stamping the film with an assurance sustained even as the story becomes flat-out strange. This is, after all, a ghost story, owing more to Japanese ghost movies than to anything inherited from John Ford, and a crucial sense of weirdness emerges from the sheer matter-of-factness of Shepard's approach. As he presents her, the ghost is solidly in the world, alternately watchful or exploding into action. And her bitterness, her fury, registers as a mythic, racial rage.

When I try to ask about this, Shepard doesn't quite catch my drift. "One of the most interesting things about the ghost to me," he says, "is that it's on the fence. It's between two worlds, the living and the dead. It's in purgatory, in a state of frustration.

"In most accounts of ghosts, they're agitated. They want out of this predicament. It's very common in the recorded history of ghosts that they're agitated. They're not content. They're not sitting there smoking a pipe."

The Z-Place

I try to retrieve the "personality is not the man" remark from the pool table in Kadoka—it had somehow burned its way into my brain—but Shepard is hard-pressed to remember. He lights a cigarette, offers a game snaggle-tooth smile: "Don't you have the feeling that we all develop masks," he says, "layers of masks, and these masks make up a personality, a persona, and if you stripped these away what you come down to would be something completely different? An essence. Something more pure—or nothing at all."

"Yeah," I say, "but some personas—personae—are more authentic than others."

We're sitting now at a table squared to the balcony overlooking the central floor of the Z-Place—a ballroom-sized saloon converted into a hospitality lounge for certified Sundance attendants: journalists, distributors, agents and, here and there, actors and filmmakers.

"Nobody down there," Sam says, "wants to think they're inauthentic." He catches my eye, and isn't about to crown me, or himself, with some notion of superiority. "Nobody," he repeats, "thinks they're inauthentic."

Art in America

On the way to Park City, after fixing a flat tire somewhere outside Lyman, Wyoming, I stagger dazed with cold into the nearest truck stop, go straight to the counter, and order coffee. When I look up I see my travelling companion, a young woman from Belfast, walking towards me with a wild grin on her face. She's holding a carved bas-relief figure, about three feet tall—a goddess sitting cross-legged, arms crossed, serenely smiling. Dozens of these carvings, I now see, are mounted or stacked along the wall—male and female figures, a full population of divinities, angels and demons, suffering mortals. We tramp around the diner, looking at them all. Some are painted, others left raw. Whoever made them, I think, has a violent imagination and a terrific sense of fun.

We scrape together all our cash and pay the waitress $40 for four small figures—plus money for coffee and French fries.

"Who made these?" I want to know. "Who is this guy?"

The waitress indicates a red-faced man in a heavy green coat, sitting hunched at the counter about two feet away.

"Thanks for buying my stuff," he says. His name is Gary Hegal. Like the philosopher? I didn't ask. We shake hands. My friend tells him how much she likes his work. We are all keyed up but he is taking it in his stride. He tells us the figures are carved out of pine, mostly. I ask how we could reach him in the future.

"Well," Gary Hegal says, "you can always reach me here. This is where I live. In this chair."

Not fooling around

When I catch up with Sam Shepard at Sundance, two days later, I can't resist the impression that I'd already met his unworldly double on the road. The fact is, I'd never interviewed anybody before and it was just odd, talking with half a mind bent on getting the promotional goods while pretending to carry on a casual conversation.

There is a point when I realize 1 am losing him, I am glazing over and Shepard seems to be de-materializing as he speaks. Entirely my fault, as I have resorted to asking simple fan-ish questions:

Q: "Who are your favorite film directors?"

A: "Buñuel. Although he's dead."

Q: "What music have you been listening to lately?"

A: "I was listening to Bach the other day. One of those organ pieces on the bottom end of the keyboard. He's pretty incredible. I mean, that guy was not fooling around."

It hits me that there is only so much you can discuss over a tape recorder at 9am in the upper reaches of the Z-Place. The famously elusive man answered my polite questions and amiably, casually, effort-lessly—eluded me. Why not trust that Sam Shepard's truest self is in his work, where he is not fooling around. His work, after all, remains alive and kicking, and hitting his half-century hasn't fazed him. "Forty was tough," he has observed, "Fifty, you're already cruisin'. You better be. There ain't no way to stop it..."

It was a pleasure to hear his easy laugh.

Excerpted from *Empire* magazine, January, 1995.
(The piece had been cut adrift following an
editorial changeover at *Esquire*.)

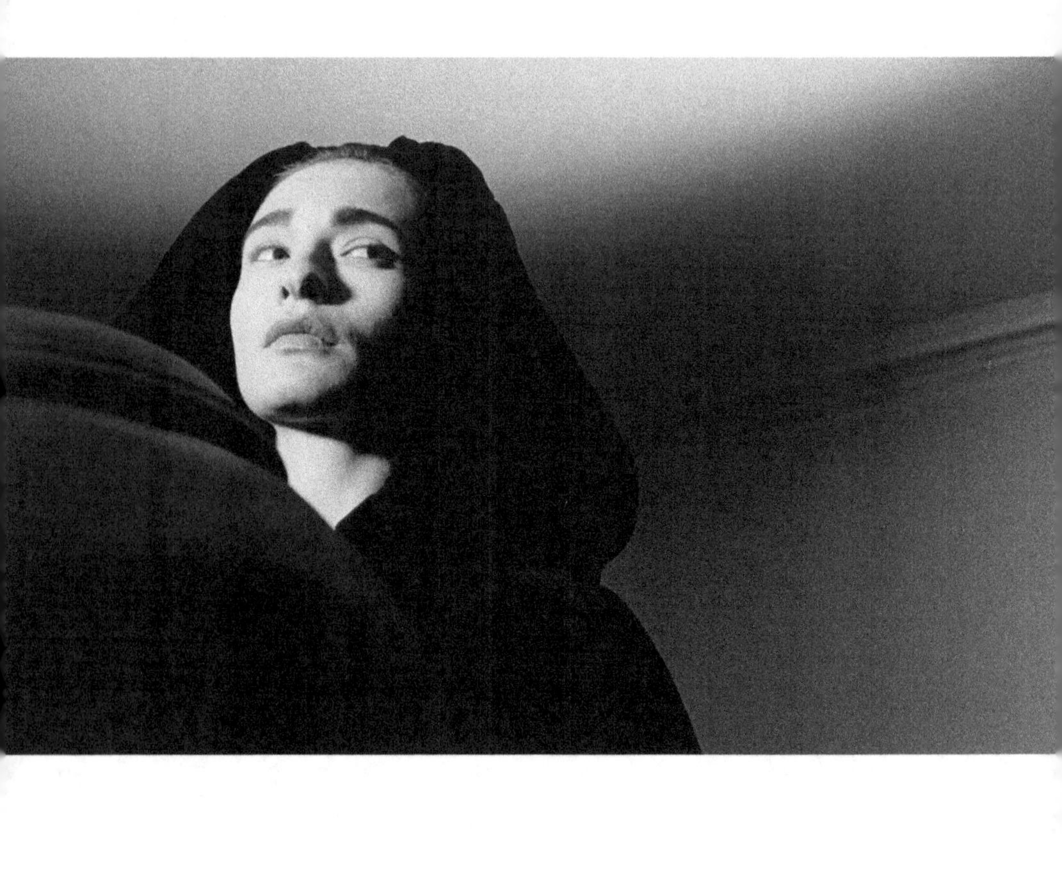

She is older than the rocks among which she sits; like the vampire, she has been dead many times, and learned the secrets of the grave...

— Walter Pater, on the *Mona Lisa* (1893)

Then her eyelids close and reopen very quickly, as when you find yourself in the presence of someone you haven't seen in a long time, or that you never expected to see again, as if to signify that you "don't believe your eyes." A certain struggle seems to be raging in her, but suddenly she lets herself go, shuts her eyes completely, offers her lips.

— André Breton, *Nadja*

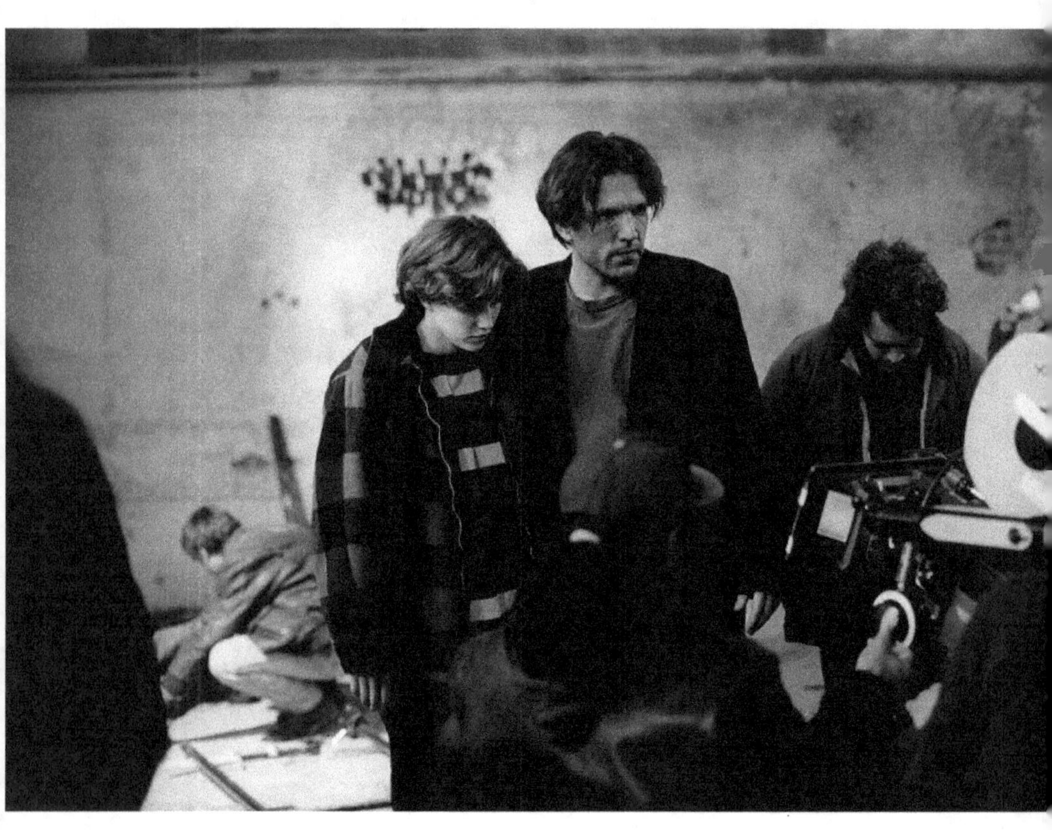

Galaxy Craze as Lucy, Martin Donovan as Jim,
and the director, on the right, apparently fixated on the video monitor.
New York City. Photograph by Susan Shacter.

NADJA (1994)

35mm & Pixelvision / B&W / 90 minutes
CAST: Suzy Amis, Martin Donovan, Peter Fonda, Karl Geary, Jared Harris, Elina Löwensohn, David Lynch.
Camera: Jim Denault; Editor: David Leonard
Producers: Mary Sweeney and Amy Hobby
Associate Producer: Andrew Fierberg
Executive Producer: David Lynch

Ramin Bahrani: You are working here for the first time in a "genre" which to no surprise you have wonderfully made your own. A vampire film seems suited to themes in your first two films: fate, free will, (in)ability to change, love and death. (Lucy's brother's suicide. Nadja's father's death.) Can you talk about what it was like to work in genre?

Michael Almereyda: It felt open-ended at the time—rather than restrictive. I was looking at all kinds of vampire predecessors, and reading early vampire stories, and recognized how thoroughly this particular genre speaks to human nature, as a metaphor for fundamental needs and fears. It's a pretty unique genre, isn't it? Both wider and wilder than almost any other I can think of. I remember reading that Scorsese screened every boxing picture in existence when he set out to make *Raging Bull*. I tried to watch every vampire movie but soon realized I didn't have time, there are too many of them; I could never catch up, and just had to jump into the torrent. Sink or swim.

RB: And, it also seems obvious, yet it took your vision, to bring this genre into the contemporary world of bars, the Village Copier, and the old Tower Records in the East Village. It is an approach you later re-employ with *Hamlet*. Can you talk about how this came about and why? The "cartoon" reality of the first two films seems to have gained a more solid, subtle and haunting footing here. Do you agree?

MA: Vampires are eternal, and there's a glut of them. It doesn't take much (or any) imagination to bring them into contemporary culture. *The Hunger*, Tony Scott's first film, covers this territory better than you might expect, and it was preceded by *Vampire's Kiss*, a faux vampire farce with a delirious performance by Nicholas Cage. And then, Abel Ferarra made *The Addiction*, a contemporary female vampire movie in black and white, shortly after we shot *Nadja*. That same year saw up-to-the-moment female vampires from John Landis and Larry Fessenden, plus an Eddie Murphy vampire movie, and of course *Interview with the Vampire*, the biggest and most conventional of the bunch, has a modern-day frame. It was a busy year for vampires.

All the same, my guiding light for *Nadja* and in fact for most of my movies has been Godard, who always updates everything, always recognizes the present as the essential terrain to explore, even or especially if you're talking about history, playing with genres, invoking older traditions, forms and ideas. (It's also a blunt fact that you can shoot much more cheaply if you embrace things as they are, here and now.)

RB: Can you talk about the arresting image of the stunning Elina Löwensohn (Nadja) walking and smoking with the rear-screen background behind her. How did this come about? It is one of your most memorable visual designs in all your films.

MA: The street and the running figures were shot in slow motion from the bed of a pickup truck, then re-photographed as a rear-screen projection with Elina walking in place in the foreground. It's meant to embody the feeling of pursuing something unattainable. The harder you run, the more remote the goal. As in André Breton's book, Nadja, in her relations with other people, is something of a mirage, a point in the distance. Even for herself, she can be like a ghost trying to solidify.

RB: Later, when Nadja and Lucy are reunited in Transylvania, Nadja says, "It's no good to resist... You have to accept things... It's not so bad," to which Lucy replies "But love is voluntary." I know we have talked about fate and free will, but can you discuss more specifically how you "love" affects your characters?

MA: I don't think there's anything schematic about love, in these movies or outside of them. Love is by its nature unpredictable, elusive, uncontrollable, and it manifests itself in different ways. But clearly the movie is about that—and vampirism is an obvious metaphor for it. Not just sex, but kinds of yearning, need, stealth and power inspired by love.

RB: Where did you shoot the final scenes that take place in Transylvania?

MA: It's all in the upper reaches of Central Park. At night, in black and white, the park is Transylvanian. The long tunnel leading into the castle was under the Central Park reservoir. It seems remarkable, now, that we were allowed to shoot there. For the castle, we cleared out a former cancer ward that hadn't been inhabited for several decades. There was yellow tape everywhere, demarcating where you could safely walk. Karl Geary ventured out past the tape, to smoke a cigarette. In the dark, he flicked his match and watched the light travel far past his feet—there was no floor; he was lucky he hadn't taken another step. He turned around and managed to survive the movie.

LUCY
I think about death a lot, actually...I feel
like, feel that -- everything is slipping
away. All the time. All kinds of little
deaths every day. There's no traction in
my life. I'm twenty-six and I haven't done
anything. Mary Shelly was nineteen
when she wrote "Frankenstein."

NADJA
Don't compare yourself. Mary Shelly was
a slut.

LUCY
She wrote a great book. Nineteen years
old. What have I done? A few bullshit
stories. Poems. Only three poems that
are any good.

NADJA
Don't compare yourself. That leads
nowhere.

The bartender brings two new drinks.

BARTENDER
These are from the guys down there.
With their compliments.

Lucy flicks a glance towards the other end of the bar.

LUCY
Tell them thanks, but we're not interested.

NADJA
We're lesbians.

Smiling, Nadja takes the drink, drains it down.

LUCY
Yeah. We're man-hating muff-diving
lesbians. If they know what's good for
them, they'll stay away.

A page from the *Nadja* screenplay,
featuring dialogue entirely jettisoned when the film was edited.

"VAMPIRE GIRL"
December 21, 1993

Executive Producer: David Lynch
Producer: Mary Sweeney
Director: Michael Almereyda

LOCATION: New York
SHOOT: 30 Days

Acct #	Category Title	Page	*(handwritten)*	Total
1100	STORY & CONTINUITY	1	450	850
1200	PRODUCERS	1		0
1300	DIRECTION	1	2,100	4,700
1400	CAST	1	28,000	31,223
1500	TRAVEL & LIVING	2	4,000	6,550
	Total Fringes		4,955	5,431
	TOTAL ABOVE-THE-LINE		40,220	48,754
2000	PRODUCTION STAFF	2	7,950	8,350
2100	EXTRA TALENT	3	1,050	300
2200	ART DEPARTMENT	3	14,630	15,530
2400	PROPERTY	4	2,100	2,100
2800	SPECIAL EFFECTS	4	800	800
2900	WARDROBE	5	5,900	6,300
3000	MAKE-UP & HAIRDRESSING	5	2,300	2,300
3100	GRIP & ELECTRIC	5	15,850	16,300
3200	CAMERA	6	9,275	10,175
3300	PRODUCTION PIXEL	6	2,978	2,978
3400	PRODUCTION SOUND	6	3,870	4,920
3500	TRANSPORTATION	6	5,933	7,058
3600	LOCATION	7	13,850	15,500
3700	PRODUCTION FILM & LAB	8	8,742	9,339
	Total Fringes			0
	TOTAL PRODUCTION		95,228	101,950
4500	EDITING	8	9,900	17,400
4600	MUSIC	9	8,000	8,000
4700	POST PRODUCTION SOUND	9	25,000	25,000
4800	POST PRODUCTION LAB	9	48,300	48,300
5000	MAIN & END TITLES	10	1,500	1,500
	Total Fringes			0
	TOTAL POST PRODUCTION		92,700	100,200
6800	MISCELLANEOUS	10		0
7500	FEES & CHARGES	10		0
	Total Fringes			0
	TOTAL OTHER			0
	Total Below-The-Line		187,928	202,150
	Total Above and Below-The-Line		228,148	250,904

Movie Magic — MB134m-3863 — Tue. Dec 21. 1993 4:58:38 PM

Amy Hobby's preliminary budget for *Nadja*, initially titled *Vampire Girl*.

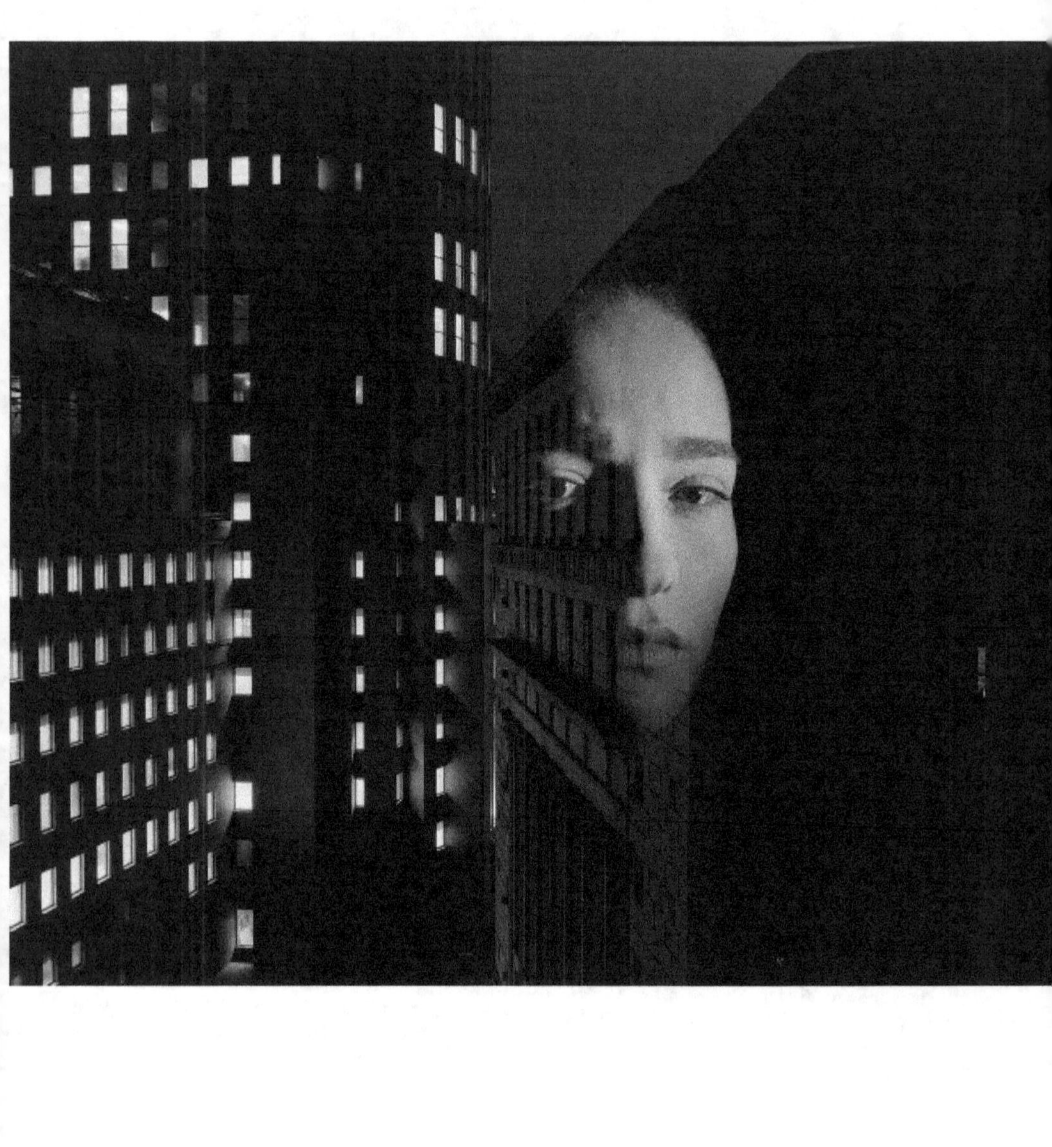

NADJA photo gallery

Susan Shacter and Tim Davis were our on-set still photographers on random days, occasionally overlapping. Tim rustled through his archive to share previously unpublished images, making up the following sequence, with one exception.

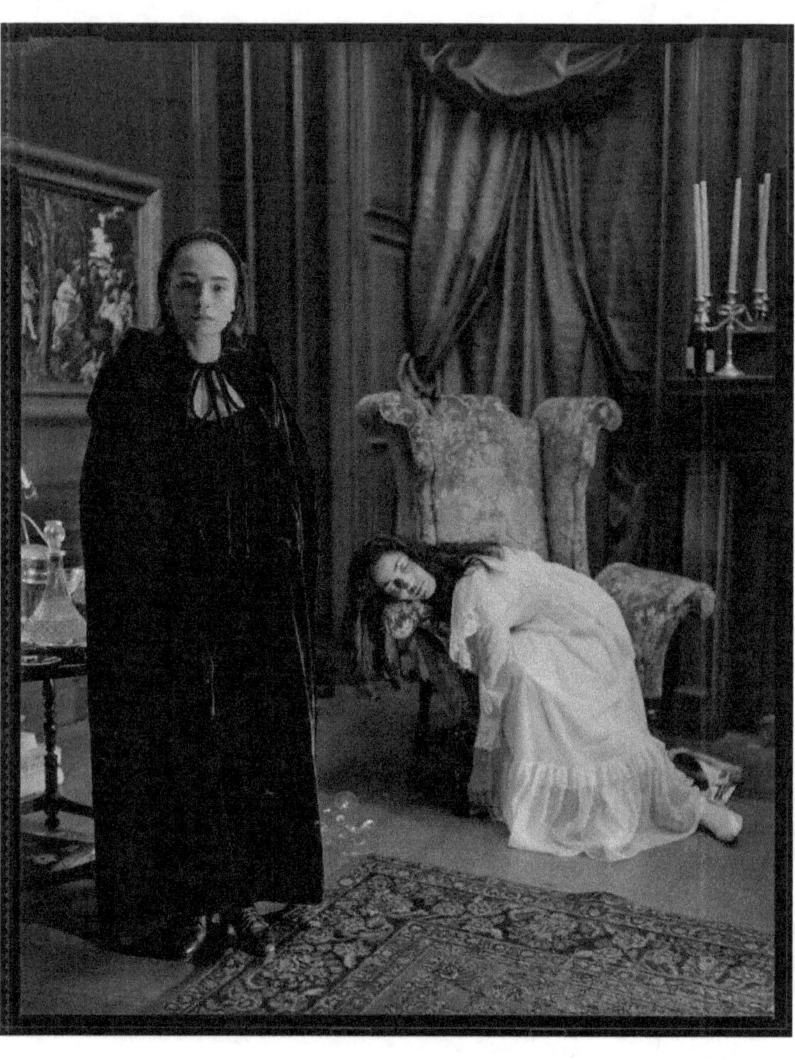

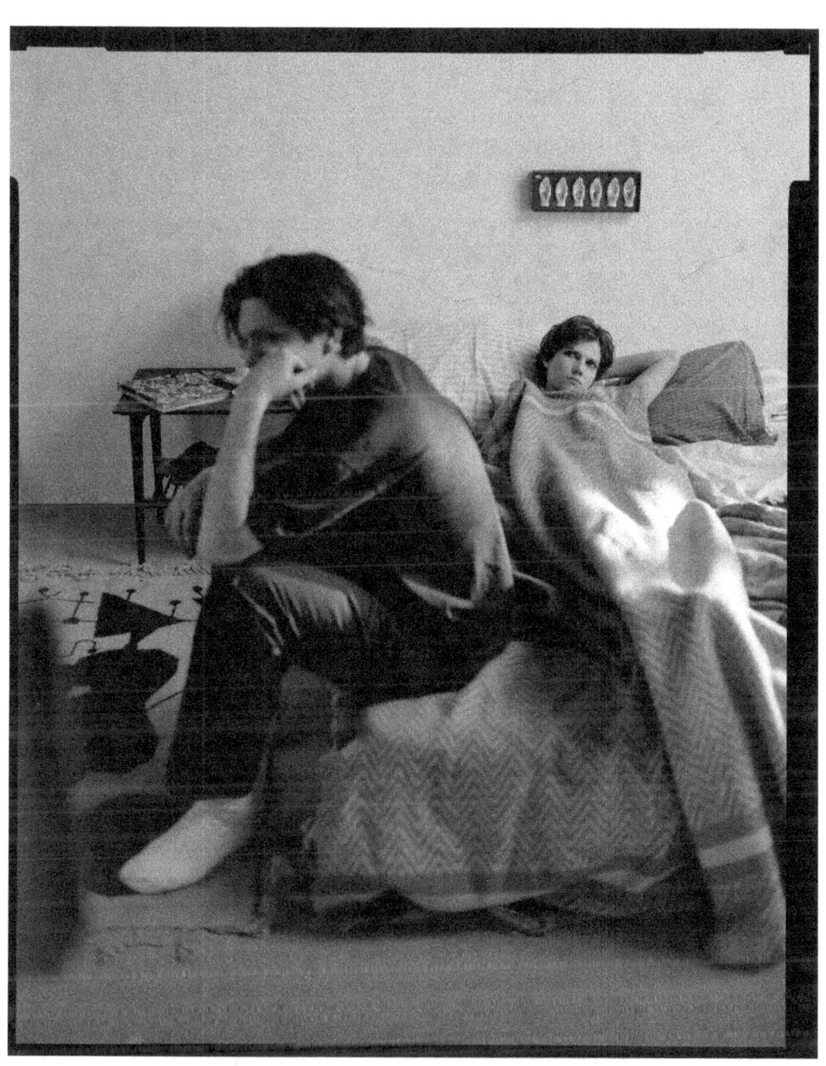

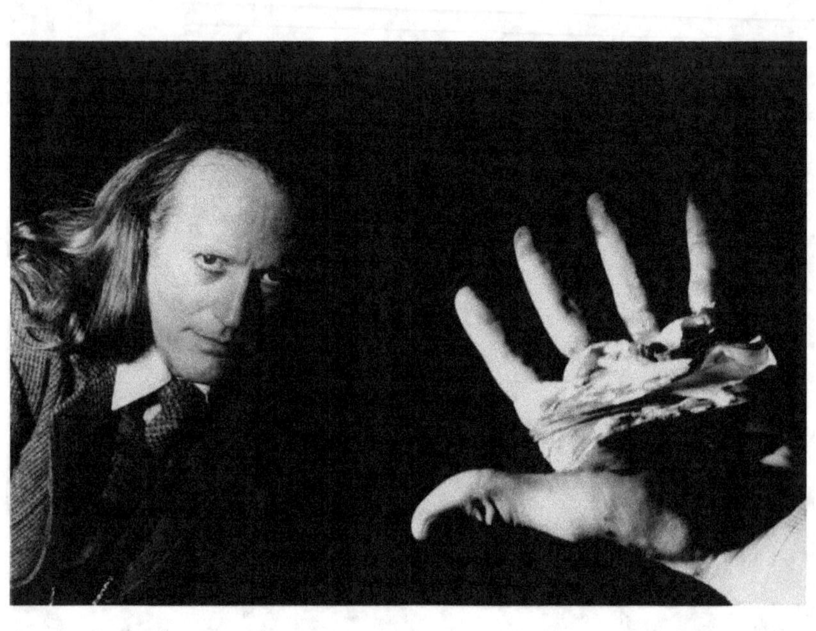

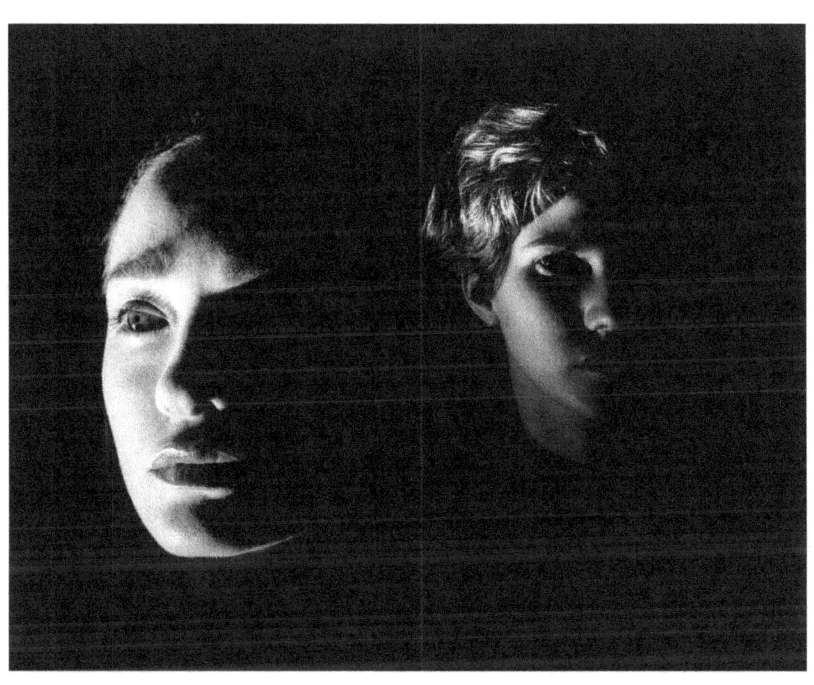

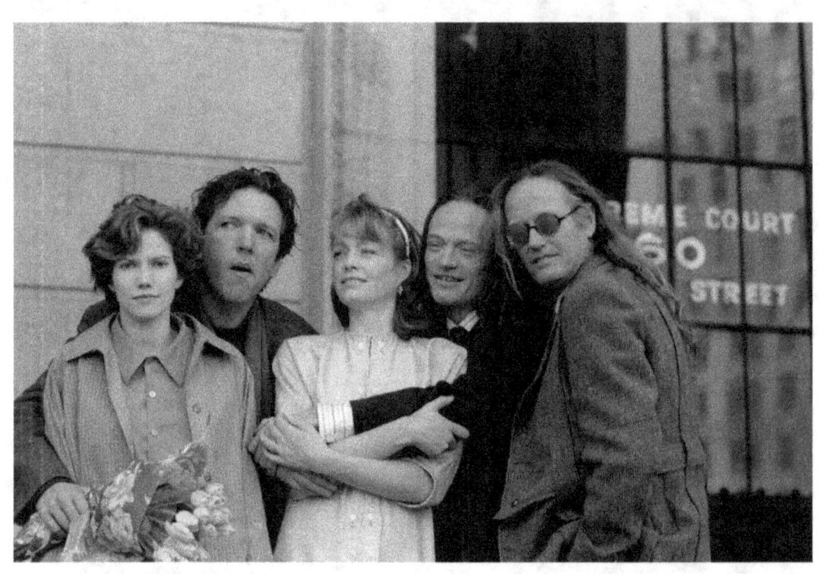

Galaxy Craze, Martin Donovan, Suzy Amis, Jared Harris, Peter Fonda. A wedding caps the story—nominal proof that the movie is a comedy. Photograph by Susan Shacter.

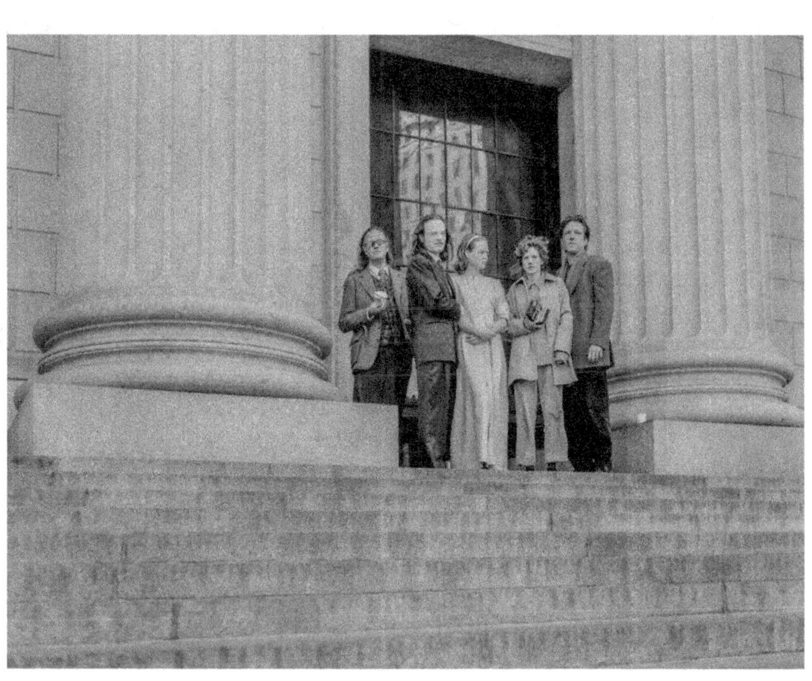

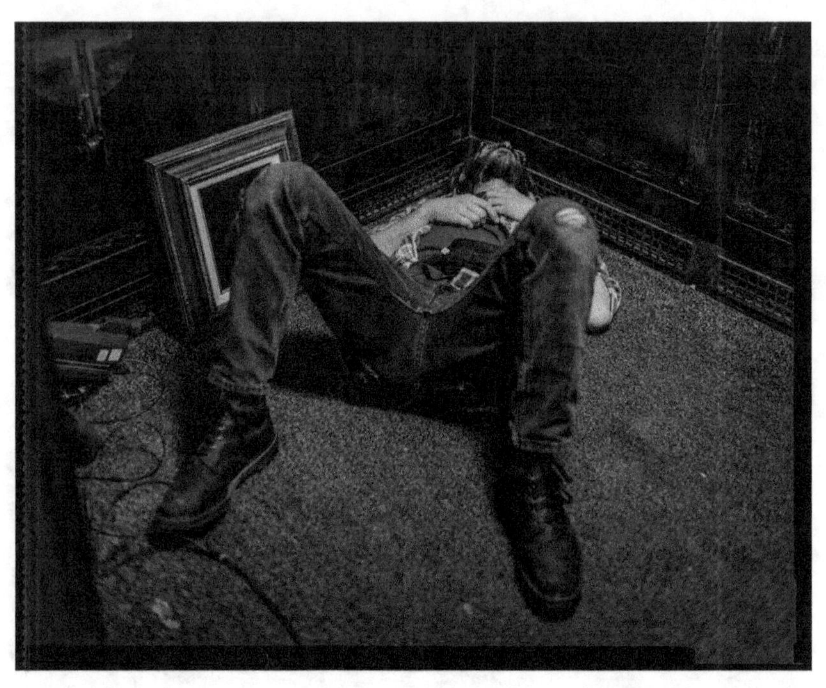

Nadja cinematographer Jim Denault.

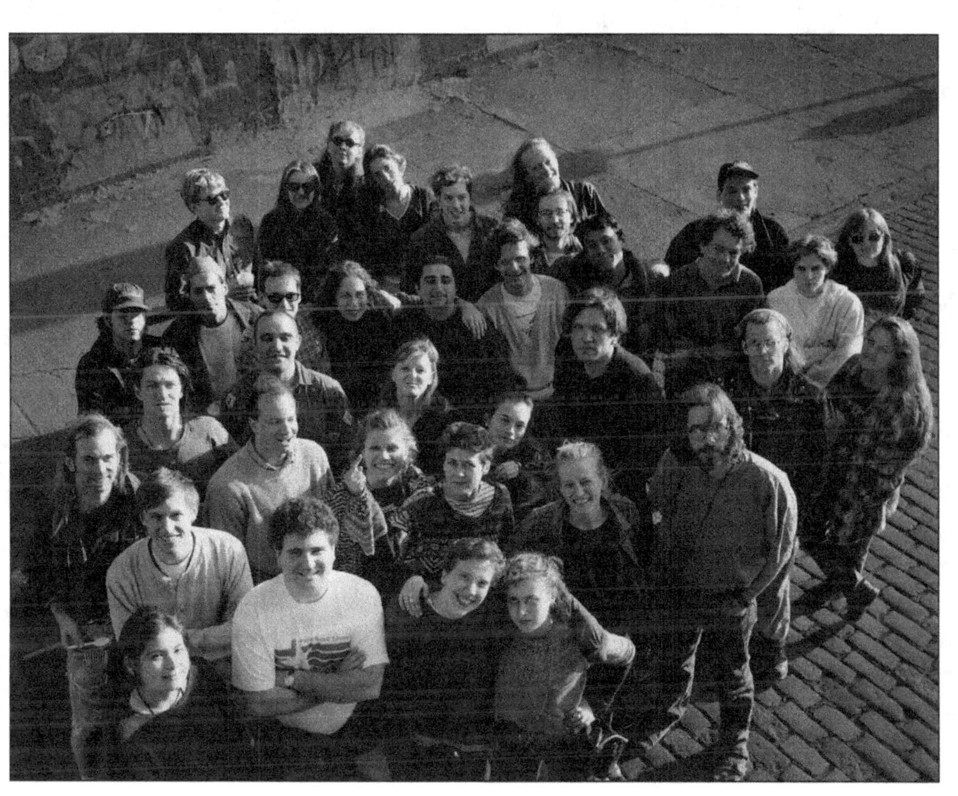

Nadja's official cast and crew photo.

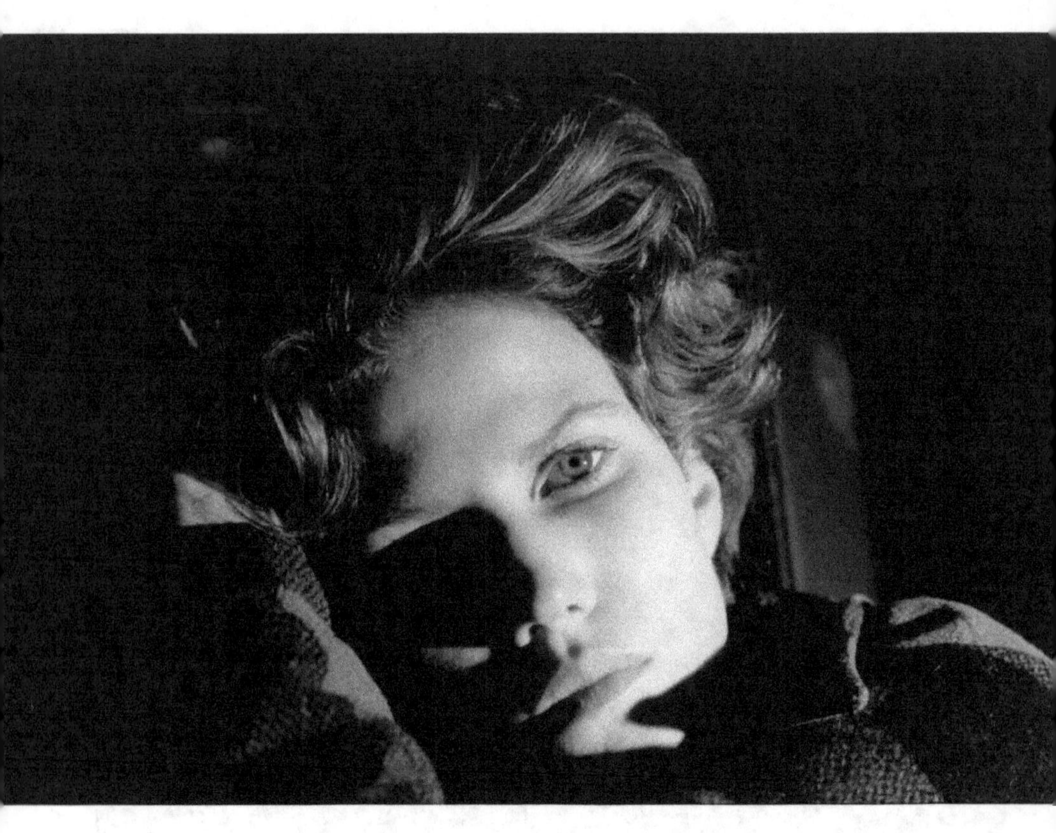

Galaxy Craze photographed by Susan Shacter.

Five Found Objects (a partial list)

1.

While flipping through an issue of *Interview*, Amy Hobby and I paused over a Bruce Webber photograph of Galaxy Craze, identified as a promising writer on the evidence of an award-winning short story. "This," I said, "is what Lucy should look like." Our casting director didn't disagree, knowing that Galaxy was also an actress. (She can be glimpsed in Woody Allen's *Husbands and Wives*.) When I met with her, gliding on instinct, I felt she could fill the contours of the part. Galaxy was quick to point out that her name, given to her at birth, didn't really suit her. Her English father had cut Mick Jagger's hair in the 60s; her American mother split from him when Galaxy was eight and raised her in a hippie commune in Florida. Galaxy had, and still has, a quality of unsettled, uninhibited restlessness, inseparable from the qualities I was looking for in Lucy. She provided a sharp visual contrast to Elina. And she allowed me to splice in bits of her own writing to enhance the script. ("She keeps getting that late Sunday afternoon depression, every day," is Galaxy's contribution. And these lines: "Monday I ate half a bagel, hot tea and a can of Coke. Tuesday I ate two diet Cokes and a piece of pizza. Today I had a bag of M&Ms, but I didn't eat the yellow ones.")

Galaxy also resembled Nan Gray, who played Lili, the prototype for Lucy, in *Dracula's Daughter*—a sacrificial victim, killed halfway through the movie. I recycled her death in the script's first draft, but after Galaxy showed up, it felt appropriate to allow the character to live, albeit caught between waking life and a lovelorn zombie state, restored only when Nadja's spell is broken with a stake in the heart.

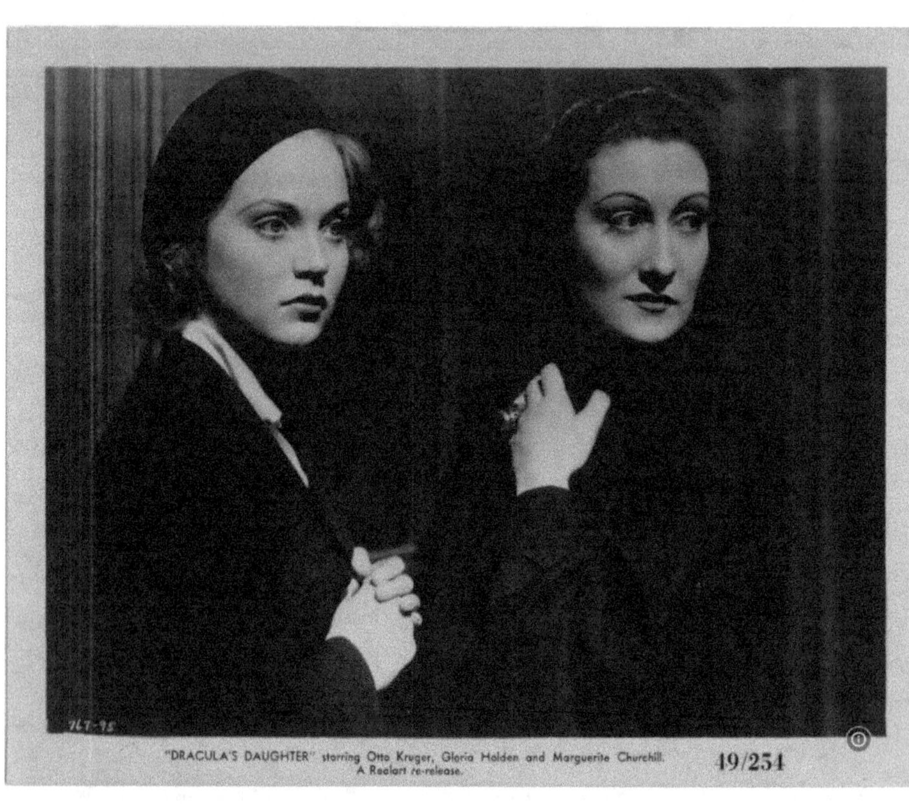

Nan Grey as Lily and Gloria Holden as Countess Marya Zaleska in *Dracula's Daughter*, 1936.

2.

"It's true, life is full of pain. But the only pain I feel is the pain of fleeting joy." Nadja's monologue, declaimed beside a gleaming jukebox and parroted by Lucy in a later scene, provides the movie with its most memorable catch-phrase, and it was lifted, with permission, from *Blaming Mom*, a comic stage play written by the critic David Edelstein, one of my rare friends from college. I'd read an early draft of the play and offered encouragement. There was plenty of strong stuff in it, I recall, but this particular block of dialogue offered itself up as a fitting *cri de coeur* for a poor little rich girl who happens to be a vampire. David was gracious enough to let me take what I needed, vampirically, nearly word for word.

3.

What are the odds of meeting a woman in a bar who brings you back to her apartment and introduces you to her pet tarantula? This is essentially the scenario that unfolded when I met Bob Gosse (the guy in coveralls who suffers a bloody death in the garage scene) in a bar on 17th Street, the neighborhood watering hole for a brassy blonde William Morris agent who learned I was looking for a tarantula and, after a few drinks, escorted me to her place to audition Sean, her friendly arachnid, darkly gleaming in his murky terrarium. At the time, I insisted I'd never ask an actor to do anything I wouldn't do, so I held the tarantula in my cupped hand, to be able to assure Elina there was nothing to fear. The creature was surprisingly light, lighter it seemed, than if he were made out of paper.

4.

Does anyone notice, or care, that the plaid coat worn by Elina Löwensohn in *Another Girl Another Planet* also appears in *Nadja*, worn by Galaxy Craze? The coat was left in a closet in the home of my friend Susan Kismaric, who handed it over one cold night when I was notably underdressed. It had been left there, Susan explained, over a dozen years ago, by a charming pot dealer named Bill Shapiro. "Handsome," she remembers now. "Hair as dark as the black in the coat. Light and funny as a person. Ex-beau of Lynn Schneider, former communications minister for the White Panther Party out of Wisconsin. I knew both of them in the late '60s, early '70s." I wore that coat for years.

5.

Nadja's sound mix was done at Baby Monster Studios on West 14th Street, where a young Englishman named Royston served as a kind of studio manager, easing our way through the process and literally sweeping floors at night. When he mentioned he was in a band about to release their first album, I was happy to listen to the cassette tape he handed over—and even happier when I genuinely liked the music. After considering various options, we inserted one track over the film's final credits, giving the ending an extra jolt of energy. The band was Space Hog and the song was "In the Meantime," a massive hit, soon enough, playing from car radios coasting along the street—I can attest to it—the week *Nadja* was released.

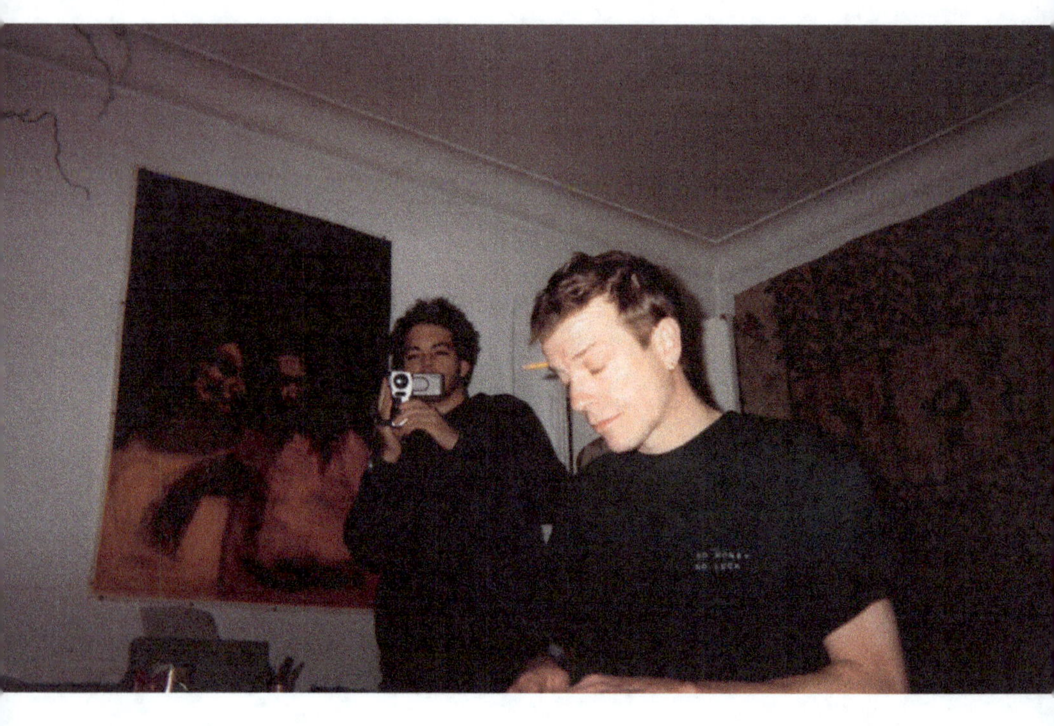

Simon Fisher Turner, Michael Almereyda with camera
in London. Photograph by Amy Hobby.

SFT

In August of 1993, Derek Jarman's *Blue* was screened at the Edinburgh International Film Festival. I was there (flown in for *Another Girl Another Planet*) and not alone in finding *Blue* the highlight of the festival. It was given the Michael Powell Award for Best British Feature Film. I'm not convinced it's necessary to mention the award, or to declare the film a masterpiece, as *Blue*, by the nature of Jarman's defiance in making it, is continually pitching itself beyond common standards and measures, bathing you, its audience, in unchanging blue while activating your imagination, your direct participation, the way waves can activate a swimmer. A key component in what makes *Blue* such a mesmerizing experience is Simon Fisher Turner's score: music, sound collage, *soundscape*.

I shared a car with Simon in Edinburgh, going to or from some festival event. He was, I remember, very modest, even reserved. His hair was cut short, like a monk's. I told him I'd like to work with him—*Nadja* was just gestating. In October I met Derek Jarman, briefly, in New York. He died in a London Hospital in the new year, February 19, age 52. A few months later Simon was in New York, in a delirium of sorts, as I remember him, energized and gabby, recording local sounds and voices into his mini DAT recorder, integrating them into his score for *Nadja*, composing as we were shooting, an integral collaborator on what became, I strongly feel, *our* movie.

Simon's label, Mute Records, released the soundtrack album, eight tracks assigned titles by SFT, including "The Dead Travel Fast" (a line lifted from Bram Stoker) and "Love, Death, Avoid It."

A frame from Derek Jarman's limitless *Blue*, 1993.

Notes on Derek Jarman

Watching *The Last of England* for the first time felt something like being caught in a lightning storm. The film moved in bursts, surges and jolts, leaping from one inspiration to the next. At least half the scenes featured bonfires and flares, and the whole picture unspooled with a continuous flickering, flashing and hissing quality.

As a portrait of a ruined empire, an anguished political cartoon, a howl of conscience and rage, the film invited its viewers to feel fairly grim, but you couldn't doubt that the director was furiously in love with the world, and Jarman's ecstatic formal energy outshouted the declaration of doom. I was amazed to see such momentum, emotion and life sustained in a film that turned its back on conventional storytelling. I left the theatre feeling exhilarated.

Someone from the New York Film Festival supplied me with Jarman's number and I called him a few days later. I was back in Los Angeles, in post-production on my first feature, fighting with the producer and editor, men fifteen years older than me who found my intentions incomprehensible. I could see I was in for a rough ride, I was looking for guidance, and I wanted to make another movie, fast and cheap. Jarman, of course, was the same age as my unhappy collaborators, but I sensed a kindred spirit. His work had opened a window in my head.

He called back without having any idea who I was. I told him I liked *The Last of England*—that seemed to be enough to warrant his goodwill, and we talked for more than twenty minutes. He explained he'd made the film with three or four Nizo 8mm cameras, venturing out on weekends with friends for improvised shooting sprees. He was patient and specific, detailing his technical processes and decisions, and at the end of this he invited me to London to visit and possibly work on his impending *War Requiem*. I got the impression, later, that such offhand openness and generosity were characteristic of him, and I came to feel a lingering regret that I wasn't quite foolhardy enough to leap at his invitation. But I did buy two 8 mm cameras—a handsome old Nizo (a product of West Germany, as sturdy as a Volkswagen Beetle and just as defunct) and an expensive Beaulieu with multiple lenses—though it shouldn't have taken much thought to recognize the simple differences between Jarman's situation and my own. He was shooting without scripts, without dialogue, without sync sound, using slow, rich Kodachrome film in natural sunlight. The movies I wanted to make involved scripted stories with night scenes and torrents of talk.

All the same, in the ensuing year, working with friends in New York, I shot a series of Super 8 tests before someone, late one winter night, broke into my apartment and made off with every camera I owned. It took a while for me to get back to work, but Jarman's voice was still in my ear when I wrote new scripts, still intent on following his lead.

Jarman was original and willful enough to make films that were intrinsically uneven, unclassifiable, imperfect. He had his obsessions and could be counted on to toss in at least one stridently kitschy dance number per picture. But you didn't have to share his passionate interest in flowers, crucifixes or half-dressed young men to feel shaken and moved by his work, to receive his images as gifts. And all his films reliably lift off the ground for long stretches, usually when Tilda Swinton shows up and when Jarman flings in footage of water and sky, his specialty being Turneresque red and yellow sunsets, radioactive clouds rushing in reverse at high speed.

As his health became more embattled, the emotions in his films, it seems to me, became sharper, increasingly pressurized, and his description of the world became both more convincing and more private, moving from the apocalyptic commotion of *The Last of England* and *War Requiem* to a quieter, more piercing turmoil in *The Garden*. In that film, as in the others, depictions of innocence and wholeness jostle against scenes of humiliation and horror, but Jarman was now literally bringing it all home, filming in and around his cottage on the coast of Kent, peeling back his sense of allegory to a diaristic core.

What he conjured there, in his own backyard, was often blazingly simple. Tilda Swinton, looking like a ghost haunting her own life, lights a candle, watches the flame, and abruptly screams. Jarman himself lies curled naked in bed. The bed's on the beach, ringed by men and women carrying flares. By the film's end, all panic and rage seem to have burned away. Swinton and a young boy and a pair of apotheosized young men sit together at a table and raptly watch burning paper lift and float in the air like disembodied spirits.

Clearly enough these images are about AIDS, mortality, mourning and loss.

Also about yearning, acceptance, transcendence. But this doesn't say enough; or rather, it says too much. You just have to experience them.

I met him once, four months before he died. Sat through a meal in a New York coffee shop. He was in town for *Blue*, riding the last festival wave. He had an impressive, oracular voice. He was unguarded, theatrical in a dry, dapper way, advising me to take a walking tour of the British countryside, then discussing, with the same fervour, the virtues of *home* fries versus *French* fries. The ravages of his illness registered on his face like a sort of irrelevant horror movie make-up, but I thought I could recognize, outside my own feelings of sentimental awe, that he was at peace and unafraid.

Back at his room in the Chelsea Hotel, amidst an entourage of old friends, he took off his shoes—revealing bright blue socks!—and sat on the edge of the bed, ignoring a sitcom on TV. "I've become an invalid," he said calmly. "Old before my time."

"At least you can get round on your own,' somebody said."

"That's true. At least I'm not like—" He named a friend's mother. "She calls him *Doris*. Her mind's gone and as far as I can tell mine's not."

He lay on his back, fully dressed, knees up, hands on his chest. We variously said goodnight, goodbye, but hovered another half-hour, mostly listening as Derek held forth, focused and funny, his voice creating a slow aural whirlpool of declamation and gossip.

Earlier, like a dutiful acolyte, I had presented him with a handful of gifts gathered from my apartment before I rushed out the door. Postcards of paintings, and a box of Chinese sparklers. "These," I said of the sparklers, "are for the plane ride back."

He took them solemnly and looked at me, it seemed, for the first time.

"I love sparklers," Derek Jarman said.

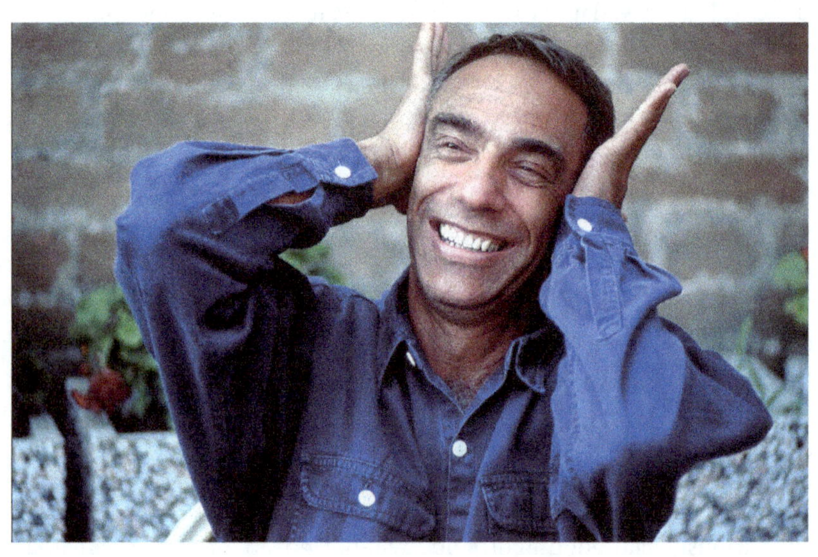

Derek Jarman at the Venice Film Festival, 1991.

His films remain, among other things, anthems for freedom of all kinds. They refuse to settle down in my mind. As a routinely impoverished filmmaker, watching Jarman's work, glimpsing his life, I read an immensely basic message, sharp as a shout: the world is open. Don't let your life escape you, or allow your work to detach itself from your deepest feelings. Get on with it. Hurry. *Now*.

From *Projections* 4½, 1995

Fresh Blood
by Amy Taubin

Michael Almereyda is girding himself for the opening of *Nadja*, his now-from-New York female vampire film that has more to do with such historic (and hysteric) maps of the unconscious as Dreyer's *Vampyr* and André Breton's surrealist novel *Nadja* than with Anne Rice. Almereyda's previous films — *Twister*, his windswept comedy of Midwestern l'amour fou, and *Another Girl Another Planet*, his pixelvision transposition of Godardian romance to the East Village — were never released theatrically, although they generated lots of press on the festival circuit. Some critics, including yours truly, think he's one of the most exciting young directors around. Others have reservations.

Scarfing down a sandwich in the Time Cafe, Almereyda is trying to focus on things about *Nadja* that make him happy. There's the MPAA's explanation of why they gave *Nadja* an R rating. "They said it was for 'scenes of bizarre vampire sexuality,'" he says, looking, as usual, like a bizarre vampire himself — although more morose than rapacious. I guess the scene where Elina Löwensohn (as Dracula's daughter or maybe just your average East Village exotic) goes down on Galaxy Craze (who plays the Lucy character, or maybe just a restless young married) and drinks her menstrual blood was a bit upsetting to them. But since this particular scene is shot in pixelvision — which, when transferred to 35mm, has the blown-out but sharp-edged quality of ancient black-and-white nitrate stock — its sensuousness is more abstract than specific. *Nadja* plays like a dream: the sex is all in your head, which doesn't mean you don't feel it in your body.

He's also happy that *Nadja* is the first fiction film that David Lynch has produced (outside his own). Lynch had gotten Propaganda Films involved in financing *Nadja*. But when Almereyda lost his "name" actor shortly before shooting was scheduled to begin last summer, Propaganda withdrew, and Lynch, unwilling to see the film go down the tubes, stepped in with his own money. Though the budget was only a few hundred thousand dollars, *Nadja* is as elegant a film as it is economical in both conception and execution. Its rapturously tatty look has to do with the combination of 35mm and pixelvision. When Almereyda cuts to a pixel vision image, it's as if the world were sliced open and we see from the inside out.

"I never thought of pixelvision as a gimmick," he says. "It's allowed me, as a filmmaker, to survive, so I tend to think of it as an enchanted, lifesaving medium. And I just like fooling around with the camera, using it as a sketchbook. But I wouldn't mind putting it away if I could get on to other things." (He's currently wrapping up postproduction on a pixel-vision documentary shot at and about Sundance.)

Almereyda hardly expected, when he dropped out of Harvard to jump start his filmmaking career, that a decade later he'd be known as the prince of pixelvision. "I was intent on making Hollywood movies, large scale spectacles. I had something in mind like Fritz Lang's German films, or the kind of thing Tim Burton pulled off recently. But my old ambitions have collapsed and I'm ready to accept Roger Corman as the guiding light. With any luck, I can hit the ground running and make a few rapid-fire genre movies, movies that are urgent and tossed off, like pop songs."

Among the genre pictures he has on his agenda are an adaptation of *The Mummy*. Trimark, an indie company looking to upgrade its profile, came to him with the idea. "It would be a female mummy, of course." Also in the planning stages are a film about Amelia Earhart and a beach party picture called *Satellite Beach* that the Shooting Gallery is committed to producing although they haven't raised the money for it yet. "It would have big surfing scenes," he says, and then, as if sensing my disbelief, "and it would have some other things that would make it stranger" And he would still like to make the film about Edgar Allan Poe that he's been working on for years. Some elements of the Poe project bled into *Nadja*, particularly the idea of the doppelgänger.

"I don't want the movie to be seen just as an AIDS metaphor. It's about a more general fear of death or separation. Talking about vampires is a way of talking about how people need and use each other. One of the main subjects in Breton's *Nadja* is identity—the book's first sentence is

'Who am I?'—and he's great at describing the particular feeling of cities, the feeling of walking down the street and being alternately lost and found. It's not standard alienation he's describing, but a more jangled up, thrilling sense of possibility. The feeling that life is open, irrational, magical. A search. That, at any rate, is how a vampire might see it. Cities are places where vampires can convince themselves they're alive and well."

While waiting to see how *Nadja* performs in theaters (which will determine how fast he can get his next film off the ground), Almereyda's gone back to his "day job" of writing scripts for other directors. He's currently working on a script for Tim Burton, a small film that he plans to make after he's finished *Mars Attack*. Of all Hollywood directors, Burton is probably the one to whose sensibility Almereyda is closest. I get the feeling that Almereyda is trying to figure out how Burton manages to be weird and commercial at the same time. "I'm looking forward to making heaps of money for people," he says. "I just haven't gotten around to it yet."

From *The Village Voice*, 29 August, 1995.

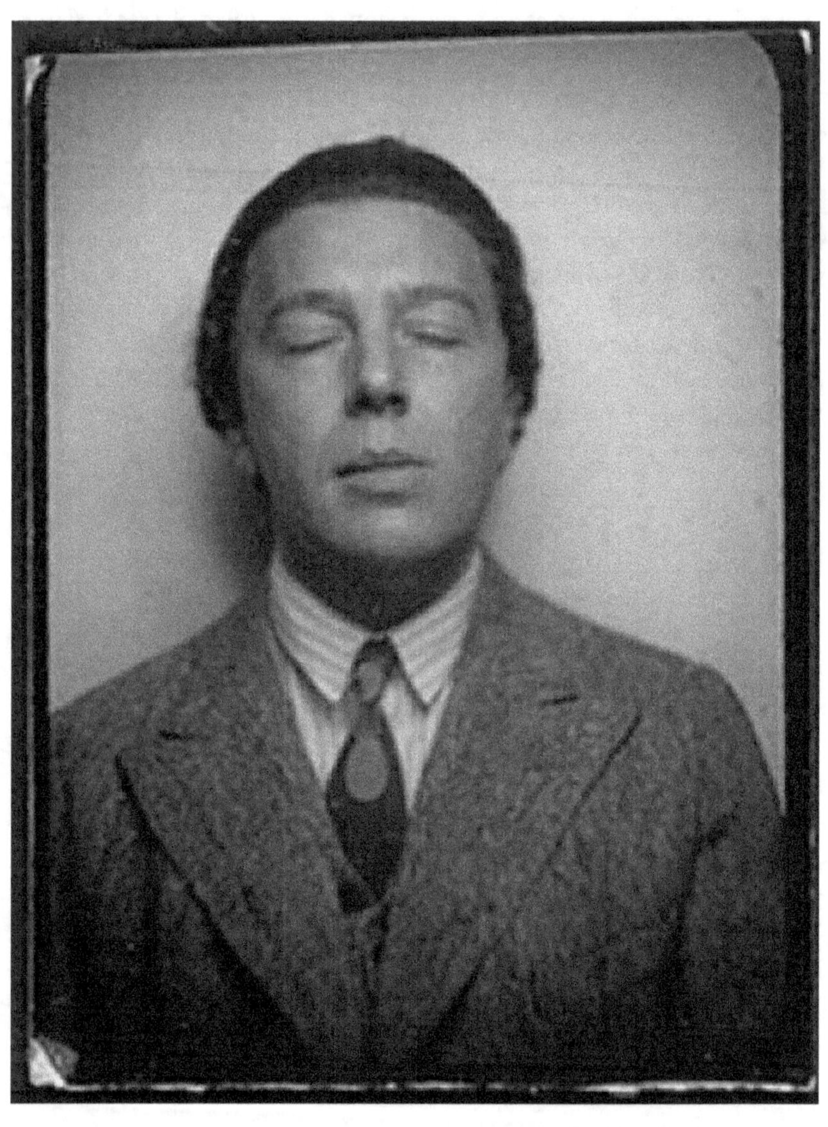

Photobooth portrait of André Breton, 1928. His *Nadja* was published the same year the automatic camera booth was introduced in Paris.

On Chris Marker and André Breton

I happened to be in the audience when Chris Marker presented *The Last Bolshevik* at the San Francisco International Film Festival in 1993. I knew of Marker's identification with cats and owls—evasive, predatory creatures—and his aversion to being photographed (he can be glimpsed in a sake bar, hiding behind a napkin, in Wim Wenders's *Tokyo Ga*). It was a surprise to see Chris Marker in the flesh, an impish figure, unaffected and even comical, with a quick stammering voice and a giddy air of agitation—a Gallic Woody Allen. I hovered in the small crowd gathered around him after the screening. As if his shyness protected him from close scrutiny, I remember his hands better than his face. He was clutching his video camera, one of the earliest compact models, which he confessed to love and take with him everywhere. At one point he set it on a table (his knobby knuckles never far away) and, grinning, compared the camera to a cat. I wondered then—and still wonder, up to a point—why he chose to entrust the narration of his films to people with calm, neutral voices. The films would be so different if he narrated them himself! But maybe he considers his work already brimful with his own personality. Maybe he has a dream of himself as an objective, lucid, level-headed observer. Maybe he simply prefers to hear his words spoken by Alexandra Stewart. In any case, plainly enough, Marker is intent on rejecting the false authority of routine documentary voiceover, trading standard (masculine) assurance for something quieter, more questioning and, not incidentally, more poetic.

While we're somewhere near the subject, I find it curious that Marker, in his new movie, salutes André Breton as a connoisseur of visual images ("He had a perfect eye, as some have perfect pitch") and quotes him at length, but never gets around to confessing an appreciation of Breton as a conscience for his generation, a voice combining moral imagination with lyrical impulses, a poet pushing the boundaries of everything he undertook. Who other than Chris Marker, on his own idiosyncratic terms, has carried this voice into filmmaking and into the current, perilous century? Taking in even his simplest movie—crammed with inklings, warnings, and recognitions—it's impossible not to feel a rush of gratitude.

> Abridged from a review of *Remembrance of Things to Come* (*Souvenir d'un avenir*), directed by Chris Marker and Yannick Bellon. From *Film Comment*, May/June, 2003.

Breton keeps surfacing in these pages, and in my thoughts, like a Hitchcockian silhouette, half comic, half sinister, but also endearing, the way a principled provocateur can present you with vital, unsettling questions. Read through his work and you will find a proud, searching and sometimes self-effacing man, a linguistic acrobat yet also a romantic who can recognize a kindred soul in the older Symbolist writer Saint-Pol-Roux, who, Breton tells us, posted a formal note on the door to his house, every night before he went to bed: "THE POET IS WORKING."

Breton's coiling sentences ride on a tone that's at once speculative, excitable and precise, whether describing an emotion or a landscape—emotions, for that matter, become landscapes, as physical details flexibly flow into metaphysical musings. And (like most good or great poets) he rustles up metaphors as if jangling loose change in his pockets. I'll offer one random glittering example, from *Mad Love* (*L'Amore Fou*; 1937) which Mary Ann Cawes, Breton's translator, considers his masterpiece. Describing a clump of cacti, he writes:

> Nothing keeps the thought of misery more alive than these plants, exposed as they are to all the affronts and disposing of such an amazing power to scar over—here a hundred-branch chandelier of a spurge with a stem as thick as your arm but three times longer, which, hit by a stone, bleeds abundantly white and stains.

Elsewhere, and often, throughout the book, he luxuriates in calibrated dream logic, as if writing a screenplay for his American descendant, David Lynch:

> You ascend by an elevator for several hours, your heart switching unnoticed to a white-red, your eyes closing at the series of landing stages.

Breton's current reputation, I've noticed, has been fogged over by an aura of disapproval, due to his quaint lyrical loftiness, perhaps, his collection of female muses, or maybe his autocratic conduct, early on, while maintaining control over a movement dedicated to imagination and freedom. I'm aware of Shana Lutker's project, "The Nose, The Cane, The Broken Left Arm" (2013–2016), cataloguing young Breton's habit of getting into fistfights, outright brawls, giving and receiving physical damage to defend his stake in the Surrealist game. In *My Last Sigh*, Luis Buñuel confirms that Breton "seemed the perfect gentleman, ever courteous and forever kissing women's hands... Neither his serenity nor his beauty nor his excellent taste, however, kept him from sudden violent explosions of temper." The Pope of Surrealism (surely more than a little sarcasm went into this self-description) expelled an impressive list of artists from his church—Salvador Dali, Antonin Artaud, Max Ernst, Joan Miró, Robert Desnos, George Bataille—most of them condemned because they were caught pursuing ventures and venues that Breton considered too commercial, too impure, the Pope insisting that a true Surrealist can't be bought and sold. It's amazing that all these guys were once along for the ride, for more than a minute, and it's even more amazing when you tally the names of figures who were not thrown from Breton's bus, who stayed on for years, not only Buñuel but Louis Aragon, Paul Eluard, Rene Magritte, Hans Arp, Francis Picabia, Alberto Giacometti, Man Ray, Marcel Duchamp, and Méret Oppenheim. (Duchamp was never "officially" a Surrealist, but he was a close and durable Breton ally, designing the International Surrealist Exhibition in Paris in 1938. And yes, the fact that Oppenheim is the lone woman in this roster is a problem, reflecting an imbalance hardly limited to the Surrealists, the global art scene, or the 20th century.)

Buñuel, in his memoir, concedes the limitations of Breton's movement while also insisting that "most Surrealist intuitions were correct," singling out, in particular, "their attack on the notion of work, that cornerstone of bourgeois civilization," contending that salaried labor can be "fundamentally humiliating." The Surrealists, he continues, "were the first to sense that the work ethic had begun to tremble on its fragile foundations. Today... people everywhere are asking if they were born merely to work." All the same, Breton valued *workers*. Heated disagreements erupted from his insistence, in his *Second Manifesto* (1929/30), that Surrealism should be aligned with Communist and Marxist principles. It's worth pausing to consider

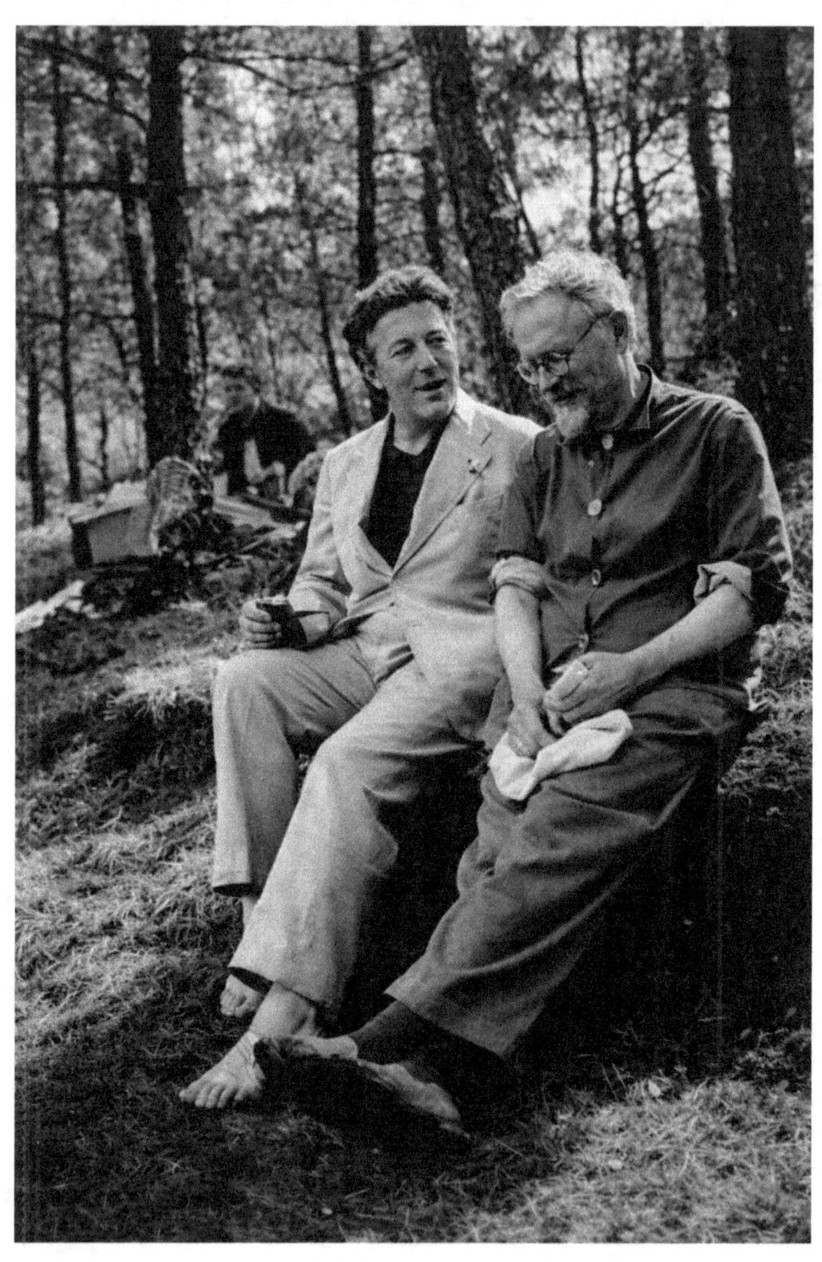

André Breton and Leon Trotsky in Coyoacán, Mexico, 1938.

this—to recognize the dreamer's engagement with the material world. Political struggle was not necessarily his subject (as it was sometimes central, for instance, for Chris Marker), but Breton's thinking was grounded by political awareness. In *Nadja*, André first encounters his elusive heroine after turning from a bookstore stall where he'd just purchased "Trotsky's latest work." A few years later, Breton became one of the first and most prominent public intellectuals to renounce the Soviet show trials, vehemently calling out Stalin's betrayal of the revolution. Just ahead of WWII, in 1938, hosted by Frida Kahlo and Diego Rivera, Breton traveled to Mexico for seven months with his second wife, the artist Jaqueline Lamba, and their two-year-old daughter. He spent time with the exiled Trotsky—they took walks and went fishing. The photo of a barefoot Breton looking chummy with a sandal-shod Trotsky allows us to picture more precisely the unlikely alliance that resulted, with the mediation of a translator, in their *Manifesto for an Independent Revolutionary Art*, co-authored by Breton and his new pal, though Trotsky insisted the document should be credited to an artist. (Diego Rivera lent his name to the published text.)

The tract proved to be inessential. Kahlo and Rivera soon stopped supporting the movement Trotsky was straining to establish in exile, as their convictions convinced them that Stalin's regime provided the best bet for a unified Communist front. It's worth noting, in the thick of personal entanglements and betrayals and ideological reversals, that Breton's contact with Frida Kahlo turned out to be consequential. As an early champion of her art—"a ribbon around a bomb" was his famous catchphrase—he helped arrange the first exhibitions of her paintings in New York (in November of 1938) and in Paris (in March, 1939). The work didn't sell particularly well—people with money were jittery about the impending war—but the Louvre purchased *The Frame*, a 1938 self-portrait layered onto a sheet of aluminum acquired in an Oaxaca street market, anonymously painted with flowers and birds, an inspired collage. This was the museum's first acquisition of a work by a Mexican artist and also—is this possible?—the institution's first painting by a living female artist.

Kahlo scorned the Surrealist label—"I never painted dreams. I painted my own reality"—but it doesn't require Freudian insight, or Bretonian condescension, to note that some people's reality opens out into extended displays of wonder and horror, pleasure and pain, dream logic prevailing while their eyes are wide open.

Kahlo, in any case, became thoroughly disenchanted with Breton and his cadre. He had borrowed "200 bucks" from her to restore a group of 19th

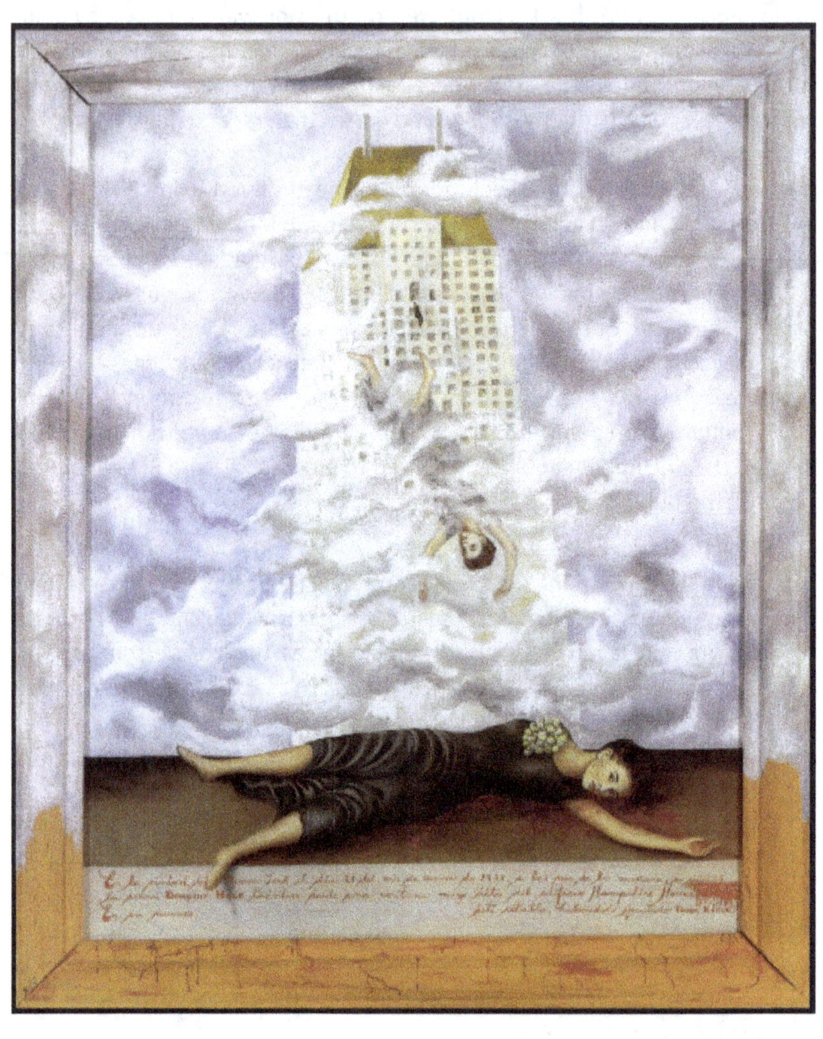

The Suicide of Dorothy Hale, painting by Frida Kahlo, 1938.
(A commissioned memorial portrait, so disturbing it was given away
and kept out of sight instead of being gifted to the dead woman's mother.)

century-paintings he wanted to display with her work, after neglecting to clear her paintings in customs. "You have no idea the kind of bitches these people are, they make me vomit," she wrote in a letter, in fluent English, spiked with madcap invective. "They are so damn 'intelectual' and rotten that I can't stand them any more... [I'd] rather sit on the floor in the market of Toluca and sell tortillas, than to have any thing to do with those 'artistic' bitches of Paris."

Breton was forty-three when WWII broke out, France fell to the Germans and the Vichy government banned his work. He shipped out to New York, exiled from his native culture and language, and lived in Manhattan for five years, until 1946. He was poor, neglected to learn English, and his marriage frayed apart, but he managed to scrape by, organizing art exhibitions, writing articles and essays. In 1943, he noticed, and introduced himself to, a woman in a restaurant—Chilean-born Elisa Bindhoff Enet—and she became his third wife. He writes to her in *Arcanum 17*, composed the next year: "When fate has brought you to meet me, the greatest shadow was in me, and I can say that it is in me that this window has been opened."

I think of him as man standing half in shadow, in thresholds, in laby-rinths and libraries, cautiously and impulsively opening windows and doors—always primed for the next chance encounter.

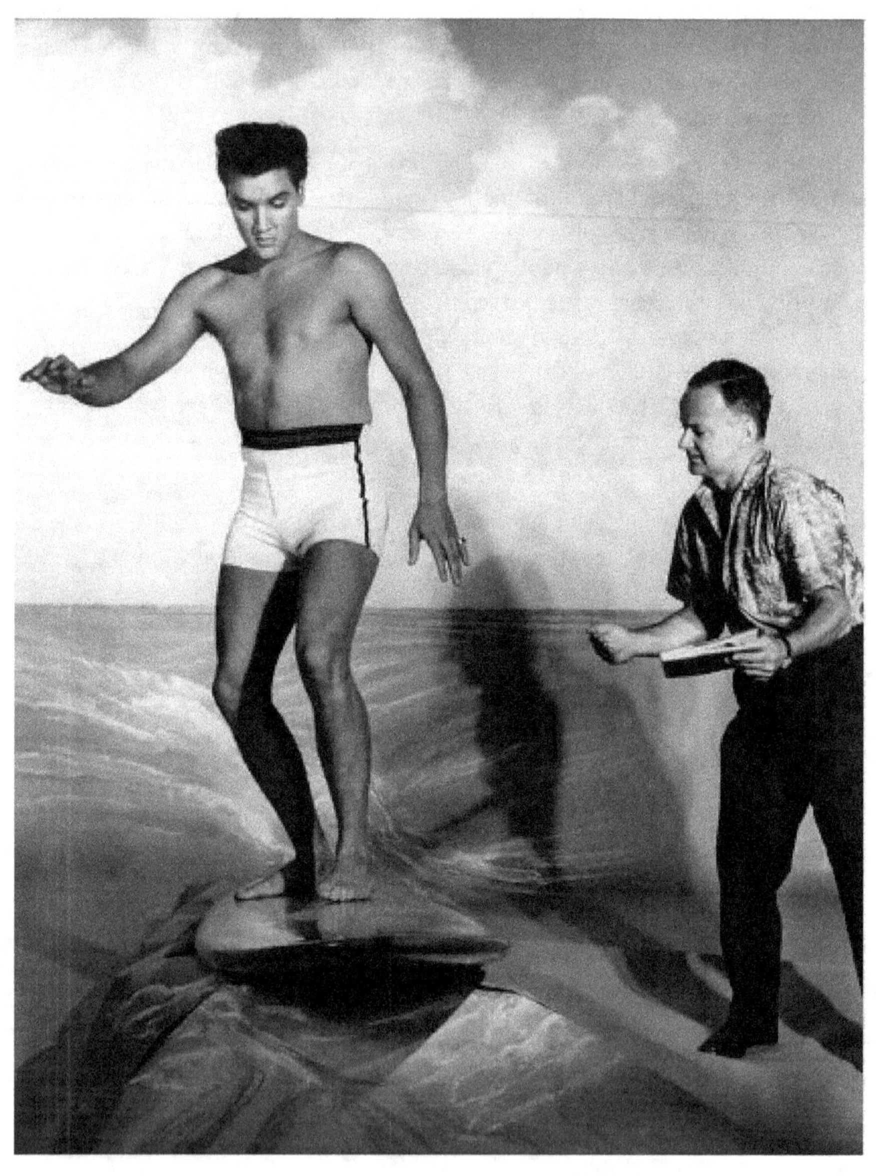

Surf's up for Elvis Presley in *Blue Hawaii*, 1961.

Satellite Beach (another footnote)

"I climbed out of the production office window, onto the roof, and watched the sky go deep dark red..."

Amy Hobby invited me to step out of the *Ed Wood* office/warehouse window for a better view of the flaming and dimming sky. It wasn't a chance encounter. She was working with Michael Flynn, *Ed Wood*'s co-producer, who recommended her as a line producer for *Nadja*. Amy was twenty-six, and her lone previous producing credit was on a striking 16mm black-and-white indie film, *Bad Apples*, for which she also served as cinematographer. I was impressed—anyone could tell Amy was remarkably sharp and bright and ready for anything—and *Nadja*'s sovereign producer, Mary Sweeney, echoed my opinion and gave her the job. Soon enough, Amy tapped Andrew Fierberg—a caustic, can-do character, a suave former plumber—to serve as associate producer. Together Amy and Andy formed Double A Films, putting their stamp on a series of exceptional independent films over the next eight or nine years. Our *Hamlet*, shot in 1998, released in 2000, was a kind of apotheosis for me. Double A scored a bigger critical and commercial hit with Steven Shainberg's *Secretary*, released in 2002.

I sentimentally tell myself that the lurid sunset, viewed from a slightly unsafe vantage, colored our path forward, or rather, our uncharted non-path, as if Amy and I were kids standing on the rim of a volcano, preparing to jump. With Double A's assistance, I aimed to follow *Nadja* with *Satellite Beach*, another comedy concerning the estranged children of confused parents, though it was conceived as an antidote to *Nadja*, an escape from the vanity, dejection and late-night habits of vampires, as if we could melt through a mirror and arrive on the other side to make a dazzling *beach movie* shot in broad daylight and in color.

The script was co-written with Jim Robison, whose knowledge of surfing and Florida ran much deeper than mine. Dostoevsky, Poe and Breton were not consciously invoked, but William Burroughs was, and a fair bit of pop-cultural strip-mining came into play. What if the married couples at the center of symmetrical 60s TV shows—*Bewitched* and *I Dream of Jeannie*—were neighbors in a cozy beach town near Cape Canaveral and their offspring, in late adolescence, felt the tug of latent, inherited super powers, more or less synonymous with the kind of sexual awakening that beach movies simultaneously celebrated and suppressed? I imagined Patricia Arquette putting a spin on Sandra Dee's Gidget, playing identical twins, the good girl and the bad girl, and Johnny Depp in the Elvis part, trying to tell them apart, or determine which he liked better. This was, it belatedly occurs to me, probably my most Lynchian screenplay, and perhaps the most plainly *fun*, steeped in an idea of American delirium and self-belief, innocence and wantonness, drunk on pure sunlight. I told Amy Hobby I'd learn how to surf if we could find the money to make the movie.

At Cannes—I hasten to say *Nadja* was not invited to the festival proper; the film screened in the international market—Amy, Elina, Mary Sweeney, Peter Fonda, and Simon Fisher Turner joined me in what was intended as a kind of charm offensive to lure potential distributors to take on the movie, though I mostly recall being wedged in the corner of a reception for Jim Jarmusch's *Dead Man*, glancing across the room at Johnny Depp while Martin Landau held my wrist in a vise-like grip, insisting I make eye contact as we discussed an urgent matter that has escaped my memory. On another night, I tried to find Patricia Arquette at a party in a house reached by spiraling up a steep mountain road. I was told, upon arrival, that she'd left twenty minutes earlier. These are the kinds of situations, suspenseful and delusional, by which dream projects remain dreams.

Need I add that Satellite Beach is an actual city on the eastern coast of Florida? Though I suspect the real thing can't compare with the place still burning in my imagination.

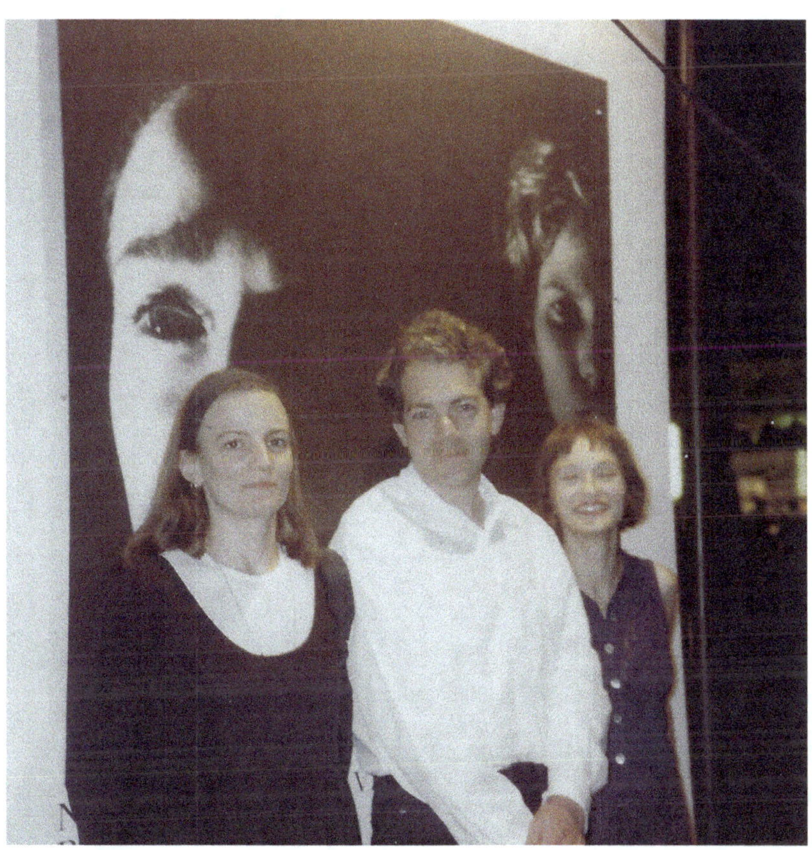

Flanked by Amy Hobby (left) and Elina Löwensohn (right) in Cannes, 1995.

I Bet You Think This Dream Is About You

During these years, outside the amateur activity documented in this book, the self-financed films undertaken without a salary, I was occasionally scoring professional screenwriting jobs, resulting in a series of screenplays that, I'd like to think, display as much resourcefulness and care as any of the scripts I wrote for myself. But to list these and entertain you with kiss-and-tell accounts of what went wrong is not an appealing assignment. I'll limit my remarks to one quick case study.

In 1990, Rachel Talalay persuaded me she wanted to do something different, and extraordinary, for her directorial debut, the sixth install-ment of the *Nightmare on Elm Street* franchise. She'd worked her way up from assistant roles to full producer on the first four *Nightmares*, and she'd also produced John Waters's *Hairspray* (1988), a commercial crossover for Waters. Rachel told me she aimed to deliver a movie that would break free of formulas and clichés, that would allow the characters a degree of psycholog-ical complexity while setting them loose in a maze of shifting realities. I was interested. I was primed. It sounded like fun. Defining and defying the distance between dreaming and waking, with death waiting like a wake-up call, is a central storytelling challenge in these movies. My memory's not precise, but I recall that Rachel and I agreed on a basic framework, essential plot points, and I holed up in upstate New York, in the summer place of a friend teaching at Bard College, and hammered out a script. It was *"the best first draft ever,"* according to the New Line Cinema executive assigned to the picture. I was naïve enough to believe he meant it.

I was flown to LA to discuss the next steps. I remember being led into a room with a sizable table outfitted with notepads and a canister lightly packed with pencils with sharp points. It was a room of smiling strangers, people I'd never met, and more than I'd anticipated. No one, as I recall, took up a pencil or made a note. Rachel, the director, said hardly a word. The charming executive who had lavished me with praise on the phone was now telling me, with a dazzling grin and impressive confidence, that the script was far from perfect, that we really did need to adhere to certain audience expectations, that the rules of the game really had to be followed and fulfilled, and so of course it would be necessarily to make extensive revisions.

I glided out of the West Hollywood office in a rental car, driving directly to Santa Monica, to an unassuming warehouse where the Coen Brothers were filming *Barton Fink*. (Joel and Ethan and I, in those days, were casual friends. I'd met them when they were outside the Nuart Theater passing out photocopied handbills for a movie called *Blood Simple*.) In Santa Monica they'd constructed two identical hotel hallways, fitted side by side. One hall was fireproofed yet artificially flammable; flames would leap up from the floors and walls with the turn of a dial. I watched John Goodman run down this hallway with a blazing shotgun while screaming *"I'll show you the life of the mind!"* I watched this for about twenty minutes—I thought it was really interesting—then found my way to a payphone within the building and called my agent at William Morris and asked him to extricate me from the *Nightmare* job. I said I realized I'd be sacrificing a lot of money, but I didn't want to continue with it. I didn't ask him for advice, and I wasn't interested in talking with Rachel. I was, I now realize, a bit of a brat. A little later, a mutual friend mentioned that the character Barton Fink may have been based, at least a little, on me. I refused to believe it, though I never asked the brothers outright. They'd told me, after all, that Barton was based on Clifford Odets. But the *hair*, maybe...? Or perhaps it was the air of becalmed humiliation and stifled rage—but isn't that common to every high-minded, hardworking, self-deluding screenwriter?

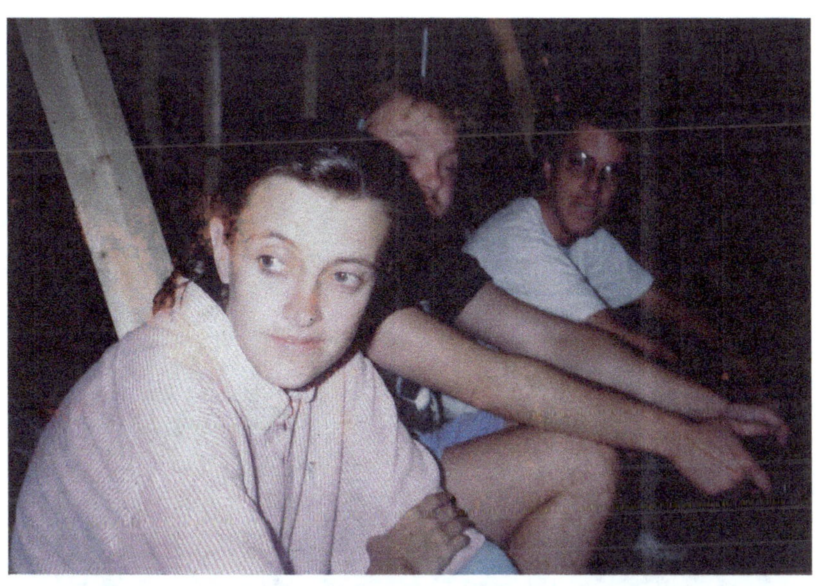

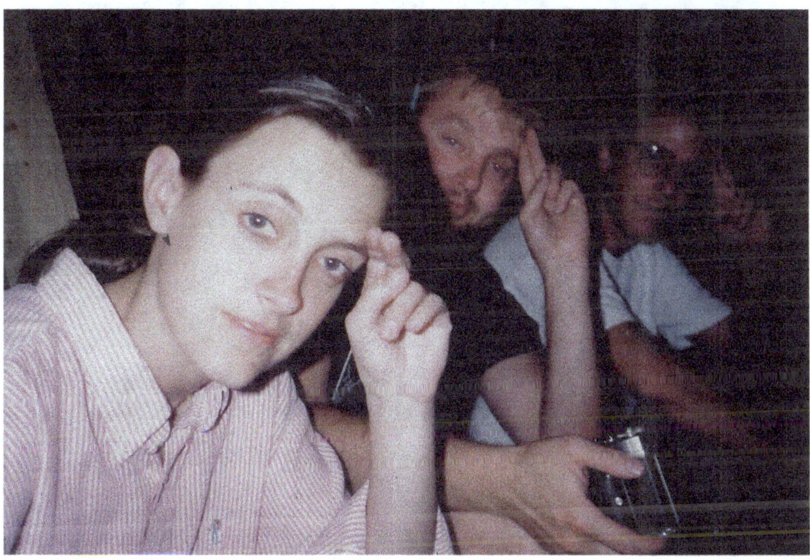

Tricia Cook, J. Todd Anderson and Ethan Coen
on the set of *Barton Fink*, 1990.

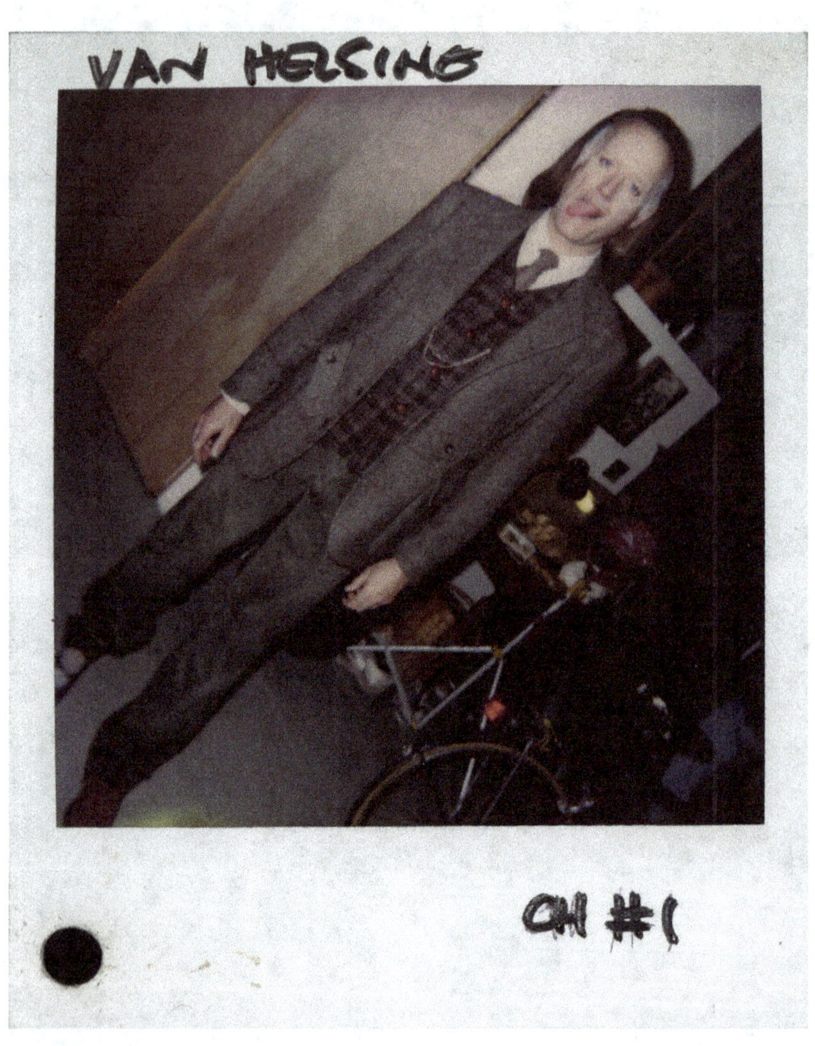

Van Helsing's wardrobe Polaroid. New York, 1994.

Peter Fonda in the Rearview Mirror

We were shooting a vampire movie in New York, working nights, keeping vampire hours. Just about everyone in the cast and crew was under 35, but Peter Fonda was irrepressibly, indisputably, the youngest person on the set—the most high-spirited, open-hearted, *inexhaustible*. I'd cast him as Dr. Van Helsing and outfitted him in a tweed suit, one pant leg rolled and bound with a rubber band as evidence of his prowess as a bicyclist. When I think of him, he's always grinning, showing his teeth, his gums, gleeful. He was at a low ebb in his career, I guess, and happy to be working, happy to trade in his cowboy boots, denim, and designer glasses for Van Helsing's tweed.

His one stipulation for taking on the role was that he would not cut his hair. "Let my freak-flag fly"—this, as best I can remember, was delivered by fax, the most urgent form of written communication at that time, the time being March 1994.

Amy Hobby, one of the film's primary producers, recalled in a text, "My first memory of meeting him was in the production office and Prudence asked him if he would try something on and he just dropped his pants on the spot and had no underwear on!" (Prudence, an unfazable Australian, was the costume designer.)

Peter often brought wine bottles to the set, fitted snugly in Van Helsing's satchel—a prop satchel containing superb red wine, uncorked and poured out to other actors at the conclusion of a day's work at sunrise.

His wife was there at least part of the time—Becky, a tiny woman with a huge smile. He seemed absolutely devoted to her; they were giddy in each other's company.

I find myself thinking and writing about him at a run-on clip because, as anyone who knew him can attest, this was his rhythm, his personal velocity, *the man could not stop talking*. He was an excellent listener but a better talker. Much of the talk was rehearsed and recycled but still charged with a level of high excitement, absolute conviction.

He was sympathetic to the strictures of making a low-budget movie: He flew in from Montana and put himself up in his Tribeca apartment; he agreed to work for Screen Actor's Guild minimum wage, without complaint, the same as everyone else in the movie; and he contentedly shared the single hair and makeup trailer where other actors tended to wait between takes, huddling against the cold, listening to him hold forth.

Part of the proof of his undervalued skill as an actor was his effectiveness in playing silent or taciturn characters. There were the early toughs in biker films, but I think with particular fondness of the self-doubting young man in *Lilith*, in which Jean Seberg's playful cruelty drives Peter's character to kill himself. In reality, of course, Peter Fonda was gallantly extroverted—a boundlessly democratic, uniquely American aristocrat. He'd explain that he was born famous, bathed in the light reflected off his famous father and famous sister, and he'd be quick to confide the unexpected anguish of that privilege—his father's impenetrability, his mother's violent suicide. His talk was river-like, rhapsodic and, not incidentally, overwhelming. I loved him for it, even if I might have been guilty of steering clear of him some days when I needed to keep my head down and make a movie.

Unlike some of *Nadja*'s future critics, Peter recognized that the film was a comedy, but he approached his role with the utmost seriousness. His script was covered with dense handwritten notations detailing every pause, stammer, and fumble he inserted into Van Helsing's elaborate dialogue.

John Cale had agreed to play Dracula, but at some point a scheduling issue interfered and we had to find another actor. Peter was pleased to take on the double role: Van Helsing, the assassin, and Dracula, the assassinated. I don't think the completed scene—shot in glary Pixelvision—quite conveys the audacity and intensity of Peter's performance. He staggered and moaned convincingly, claw-like hands outstretched, wearing the outrageous cape in a blizzard of artificial snow. In interviews afterward, he was pleased to recount, "I got to stake myself."

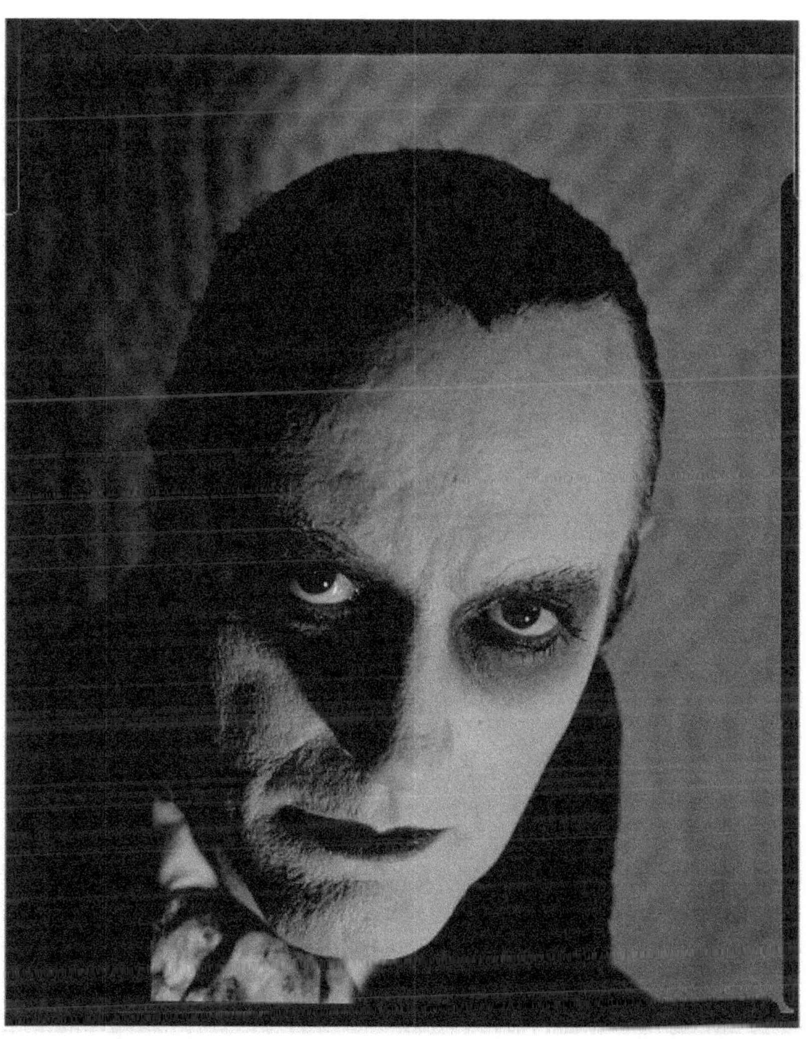

Peter Fonda as Dracula. Photograph by Tim Davis.

Karl Geary, who played Renfield, was part of the ensemble that traveled with the movie to the Sitges Film Festival in 1995. Karl just unearthed the above photo and supplied this caption: "Peter was given a special award that night. He was mostly concerned with an issue with his cowboy boots, and all throughout the festival, people would drop by his room to smoke and he'd sit at the first laptop I'd ever seen and instead of writing his autobiography, he'd tell the stories."

When Peter received an Academy Award nomination for *Ulee's Gold* in 1997, I was touched to see how much it meant to him. During his Oscar push, after an appearance on *The Rosie O'Donnell Show*, we met in the dimly glittering lobby of the Four Seasons hotel and drank our way through a series of dimly glittering martinis. He thanked me profusely, gratuitously, for recommending him to Victor Nuñez, *Ulee's* writer-director, and for casting him in *Nadja*, and he started reciting Van Helsing's lines, leaning across the table and racing through the sidewinding monologues, in character and with total recall, although we had shot the movie three years earlier. Through the blur of alcohol, I could appreciate that this hallucination was something akin to seeing a drunken race car driver madly weaving through pylons in the rain at 100 mph, without hitting anything or spinning out.

I was grateful that he found space in his autobiography to mention *Nadja*, naming me as "our fearless leader." But Peter was the fearless one, the unhesitating resistor of complacency and clichés. Skimming through his obituaries, I see without surprise that the films he directed go unmentioned or are only glancingly referred to. But *The Hired Hand* and *Idaho Transfer* are singular accomplishments, rapturous and death-haunted, formally adventurous and controlled, telling stories with dire outcomes, not just trippy but tragic. His sunny disposition didn't prevent him from reaching into darker corners of experience and history. (And though he skidded into triviality on *Wanda Nevada*, his third film as a director, it allowed him a chance to connect with his father.)

Can it be that the last time I saw him was at his ranch in Livingston, Montana, in the winter of 2006? The place was surprisingly modest, surrounded by a vast amount of snow. He was back in his jeans and cowboy boots and wearing a red T-shirt, his hair in a ponytail. We sat together near a cast-iron wood-burning stove. There was an American flag stretched across one wall.

One of Peter's favorite, insistent sayings was "Do not back up — severe tire damage!"

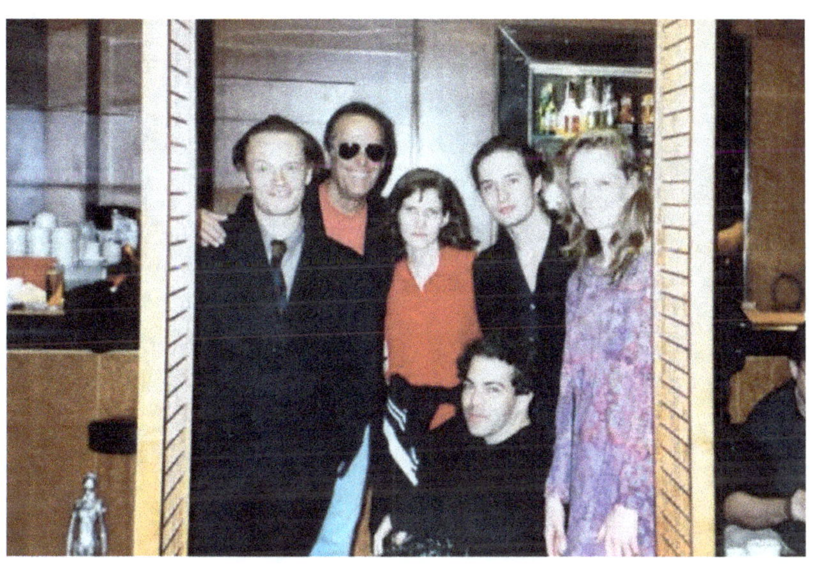

Jared Harris, Peter Fonda, Galaxy Craze, Michael Almereyda, Karl Geary and
Suzy Amis at the International Fantastic Film Festival of Catalonia,
in Sitges, Spain, 1995.

Time floods past, and I'm bereft, wondering how we lost touch over the past ten years. Why didn't he direct more films? Why didn't we make more films together? I was going to reach out, to offer congratulations on *Easy Rider's* 50th birthday. But Peter's achievement, and his spirit, radiate beyond that one phenomenal flash point. He was, in my book, Whitmanesque, a supreme celebrator of the self, irreversibly optimistic in the gloom, an embodiment of generosity and joy.

Originally titled "The Eternal Light of Peter Fonda," published in *New York* magazine, August 19, 2019.

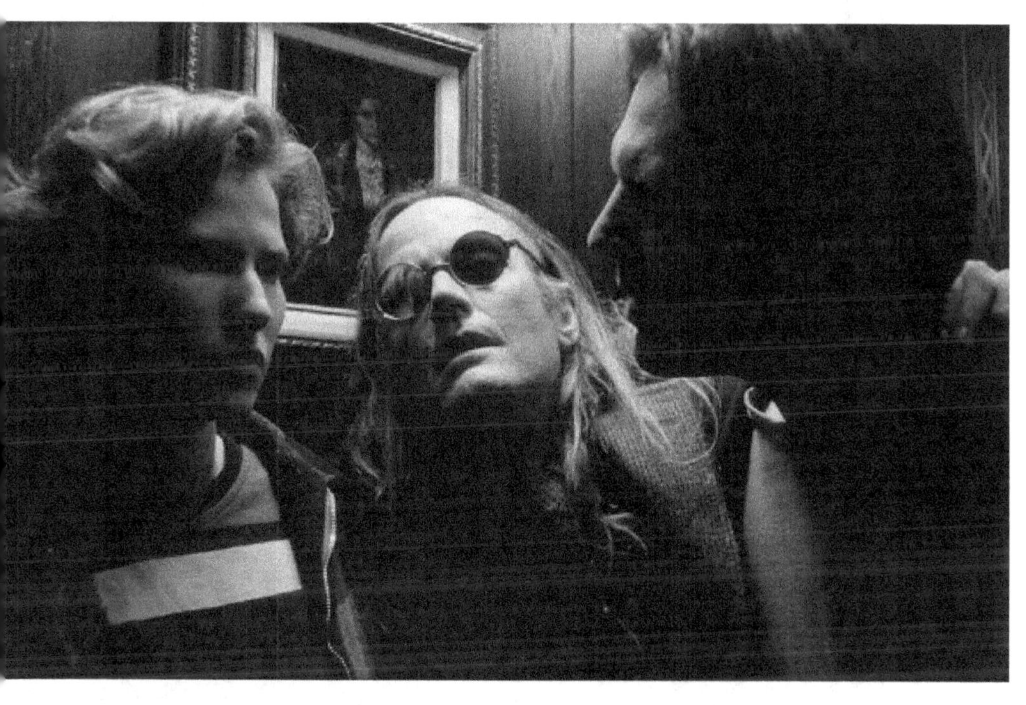

Galaxy Craze, Peter Fonda, and Martin Donovan ride an elevator in *Nadja*.

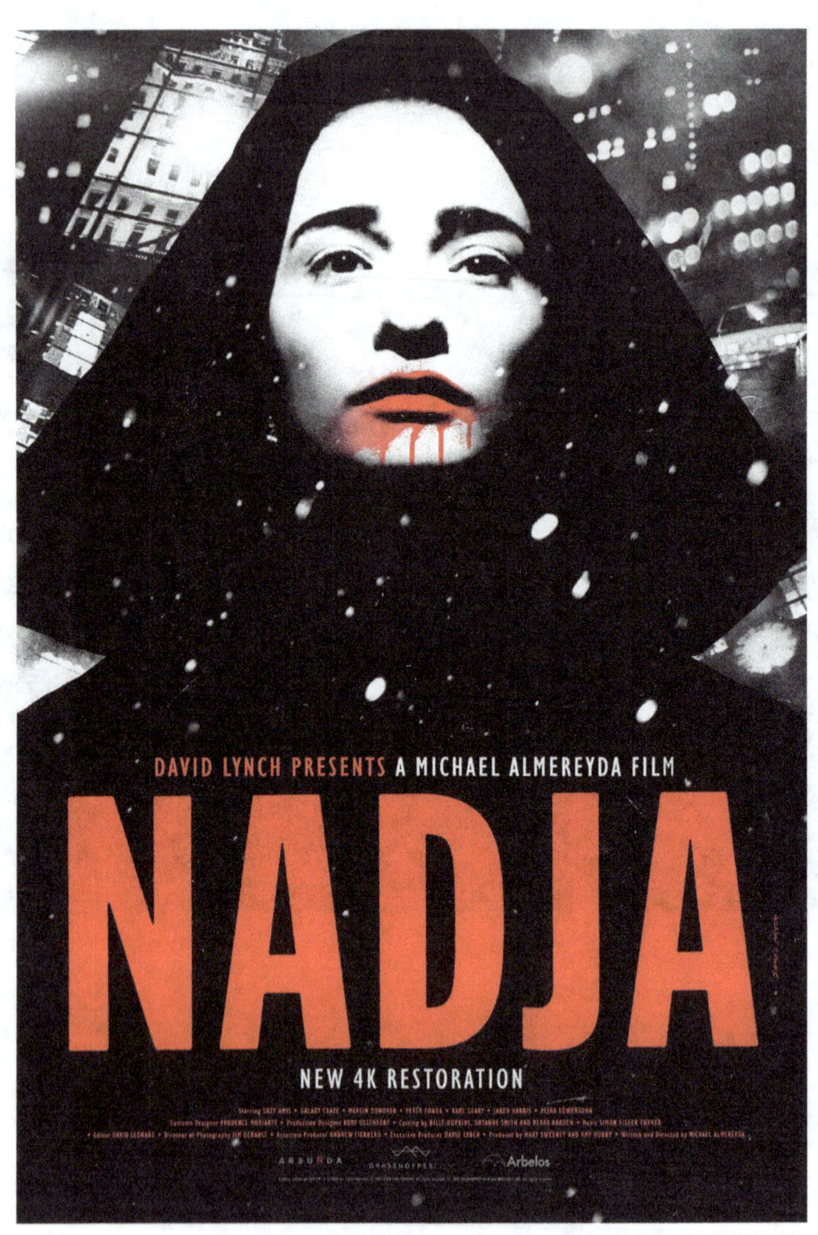

Nadja's new poster, designed by Sam Smith, 2025.

Afterlife

I re-watched *Nadja* to assist with the restoration, remembering just about every frame with some precision, though I found myself unsettled by the film's mix of sincerity and irony, and I was a bit taken aback by how much of the dialogue was brazenly stitched from disparate sources—a newspaper clipping, a line from a surrealist poem, an interview with Sinead O'Connor, and stories, some of them quite intimate, from scattered friends.

Identity, disillusion, mortality, the ephemeral nature of our feelings and our lifespans—these aren't topical or temporary concerns; and so, as the film resurfaces, I've come to resist commentary that attempts to pin *Nadja* to the 90s, regarding it like a ship in a bottle, a quaint cult item providing a window into "shoe-gaze" sentiment and the spectacle of indoor smoking. I'd rather think of the film, and its relationship to you, dear reader/viewer, as something more mysterious and visceral, seductive and haunting. A resurrected vampire, after all, an undead, uninhibited creature on the prowl in the moonlight—should be a force to be reckoned with.

I was particularly surprised when Edgar/Jared Harris makes a desperate declaration from his sickbed, before his sister feeds him blood dripping from her wrist. "I can no longer bear this miracle," he says, then continues:

> ...knowing nothing of this world—to have *nothing*—but to love things, and to eat them alive, and to listen to their farewells as the hours strike in the distance.

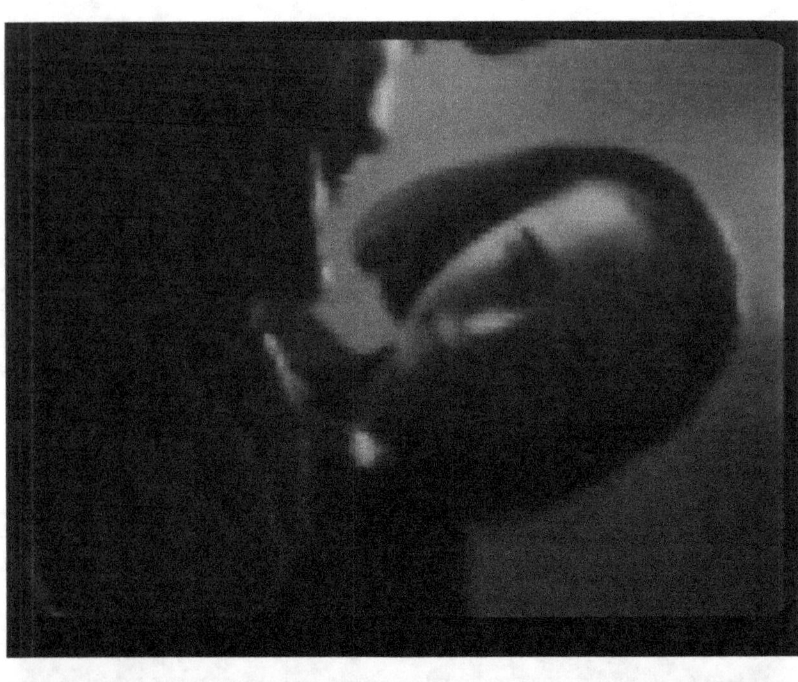

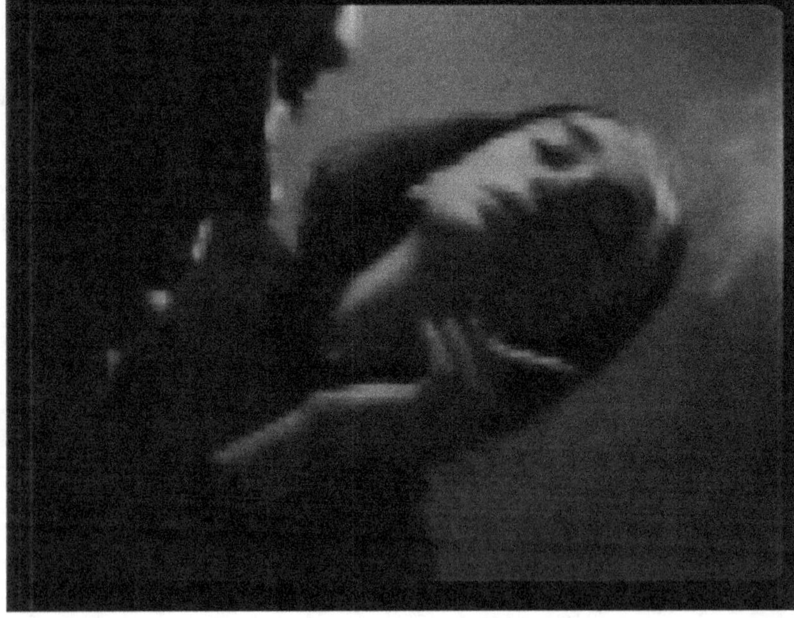

Jared recites these words as if they're being pulled from his chest, and they sound conspicuously collaged from an outside source, though I can't confidently trace them. The words strike me, at any rate, as a fitting credo for a tormented artist/vampire eager to embrace the world, to "love things" even as he unrepentantly devours them. I wouldn't want this on my tombstone, but then again, I have no intention of being buried. And it may be fair to say, after all, that each of my films is a tombstone, outlasting all the wishful thinking that went into them.

DAVID LYNCH
AMERICAN HIEROGLYPHICS
AND VIOLENT COMEDIES

4-25 FEBRUARY 1989

LEO CASTELLI
578 BROADWAY NEW YORK

1989 gallery notice for David Lynch's first and only show at
Castelli in NYC, shortly before the debut of *Twin Peaks.*

Remembering David Lynch

Someone slipped me the script for *Blue Velvet* long before David went into production with it. I was excited just to picture the movie he would make from it, and in 1985 Dennis Hopper acted in my first film, *A Hero of Our Time*, during a break in his *Blue Velvet* shooting schedule. ("It's funny," Dennis said to me, "You're always telling me '*Less. Less.*' And David's always telling me '*More. More.*'") So I felt a proximity to Lynch for many years and even, presumptuously, a kinship with him. I remember meeting him and Isabella Rossellini, glancingly, at his Castelli show in 1989, but David and I didn't talk privately, one-to-one, until October 31, 1993, a meeting arranged by Mary Sweeney after he'd read a ten-page treatment for *Nadja*.

David and Mary understood that the movie was intended as a rough-and-ready collage, and we agreed that the idea was to follow a Roger Corman production model, to make it fast and cheap. Low as the budget was, we lost financing a few weeks before our start date when Eric Stoltz fell out due to his mother's illness. (Martin Donovan was his worthy replacement.) That's when David bravely decided to pay for the film out of his own pocket—an act of generosity that still startles me.

I have a terrific book of his paintings, drawings and incidental texts, *Images*, published in 1994. When I recently revisited the inscribed title page I found a sheet of paper folded in quarters, a letter written in pencil, signed "your friend, David." I'm not quite vain enough to quote the inscription or the letter, but you can be sure these are cherished souvenirs.

In financing *Nadja*, David owned it, but I had no other obligations to him. I was grateful to be able to return the favor, in some small measure, when he tasked me with rewriting his script for *Fantomas*, adapted from the venerable French serial. He liked my idea of updating the story to the late 1920s, intersecting with the world of the French surrealists, and I recruited

                    CATHERINE
          I love you, but I feel bad luck
          coming at us like a storm.

EXT.   CAFE DE LA PAIX - NIGHT

Juve and Catherine, holding hands and nuzzling like
schoolchildren, walk out into the Place de L'Opera.

Juve seems to see something out of the corner of his eye,
pulls Catherine closer and tries to hustle her away, but she
looks back for an instant and gasps--

HER POV - FANTOMAS

A giant figure, one hundred feet tall, wearing a black top
hat, a domino mask, a white scarf, white gloves and long
black overcoat, rests one foot on top of the Palais Garner,
one elbow on his knee, smoking a cigarette as he looks out
complacently over the city.

                    JUVE
          Don't look back. Don't let him
          know we've seen him.

But Catherine can't resist one last look. And the figure
catches her eye, smiles slowly, tosses his cigarette in the
direction of the Madeleine, takes his foot off the top of the
opera house and starts to walk slowly south.

Juve, sensing this, glances back, and he and Catherine start
running.

EXT.   THE PONT NEUF - NIGHT

Juve and Catherine, exhausted, driven by horror, run like
bats out of hell over the old bridge. Behind them, the
gigantic figure casually strolls towards them. He doesn't
have to hurry, his stride is so long.

EXT   THE LEFT BANK - NIGHT

Juve and Catherine race across the bridge and head into a
maze of streets.

                    JUVE
          Here! His shoes are too big for
          those streets.

But it's too late. The figure has waded the Seine and
reaches down to grasp Catherine in his delicate gloved hand.
Juve tries to hold onto her.

my friend Lloyd Fonvielle to help with the twisting plot. At one point David called to supply a clue for the story, a single sentence imparted in a dream, involving the country house where part of the mystery unfolded. A sentence that taps on the glass, as Breton would say—though not quite as memorably as "Dick Laurent is dead." What Lloyd and I came up with may be the best script I ever concocted for another filmmaker, and we delivered it with impressive speed, but by the time it arrived David had moved on. Mary Sweeney told me David had become interested in telling stories set in the present—and this turned out to be true for the rest of his life.

Despite his countless interviews and public appearances, the sweet sincerity conveyed in the *Art Life* documentary, and of course *his weather reports*—I still hold onto my impression, from when I first met him, that David Lynch was actually very shy. No one was more fun than Lynch in party mode, a glass of red wine in one hand and a cigarette in the other, but I was aware that he wasn't always comfortable around people, that the ease he projected publicly was in fact a skill and probably came at a cost. He had built a compound for himself, after all, a domestic space fused with multiple studios and work spaces, and it wasn't an easy thing for him to venture outside of it. His celebrity played a part in this, but that was hardly the whole story. There's no need for me to guess or project; he gave plenty of testimony on the subject: David was someone very comfortable operating by strict rules and routines and living largely in his head.

There's no question of the depth of David's influence and inspiration sweeping through generations of filmmakers, so it may be more revealing for me to acknowledge a few very specific things I learned from him.

Sound & Image

David told me that for movies sound and image are equally important—exactly fifty percent each. Then he qualified this: with video, the percentage shifts, sound is slightly more important, 51 percent. He didn't offer any further justification, but I immediately accepted his conviction as true.

Casting

I was privy to early production details of *Lost Highway* and remember hearing that the role of Bill Pullman's unknowing doppelganger, Pete the mechanic, was offered to Brad Pitt and Johnny Depp before Balthazar Getty accepted the part. One of the agents softened the rejection by suggesting that this "wasn't the right one. Maybe next time." It was illuminating to think about how the feel and meaning of the movie (and its box-office reception) might have been dramatically different if Pete was played by Brad or Johnny, measured against the relatively seedy, slouching simulation of bad boy beauty captured by Balthazar; but now, of course, the mismatch feels exactly right, and it's folly to imagine it any other way.

Moving on to new projects, about a year later, David described, with a strange glow of delight, how he and Harry Dean Stanton had gone to Marlon Brando's house to court him to play opposite Harry Dean in *Dream of the Bovine*, an outright comedy co-written by Bob Engels—a delirious Van Nuys version of *Dumb and Dumber*, with the film's ending delivering on the film's title: the two main characters are simply a couple of cows projecting them-selves into human form as they dream. Brando, wearing a robe and appar-ently nothing else, made a big deal out of serving them homemade cookies and had to be prodded by Harry Dean, who finally asked if Marlon had read the script. (David was too nervous and polite to bring it up.) Brando said yes, he had read the script—and he announced that it was *"completely hollow."* The meeting didn't last much longer. Upon hearing the tale, I recommended Tommy Lee Jones for the role Brando rejected, and I was flattered when David took my advice and offered it to Jones—who also turned it down. The film was never made, though sequences from the script still play in my memory and make me smile. The moral: Great actors can make not-great decisions, and even David Lynch gets turned down by movie stars.

Final Cut

Upon seeing *Nadja* at Sundance, the head of Trimark Pictures asked if I wanted to adapt a Bram Stoker mummy story. (Actually, he said "Bram Stroker," but I knew what he meant.) I had an idea, wrote a script and shared it with David, who was on board to executive produce. When he learned Trimark wouldn't give me final cut, he suggested that they could grant him, David, that privilege, assuring me I'd retain control. But Trimark declared they'd never given final cut to any filmmaker; they couldn't do it. David said "I have a bad feeling about this" and sweetly stepped aside. I believed Trimark's assurances—one of the worst decisions I ever made. Since then, I've adhered to David's belief that it's better to stay home and not make the movie than to be unprotected from the whims and worries of other people, no matter how much optimism is flooding the air at the outset.

I should qualify this by saying I got to know him during what Dennis Lim calls Lynch's "black cloud period" when commercial success eluded him and he was facing various uncertainties, and it's disheartening to think that our

David and Riley Lynch in their Hollywood home, circa 1994.

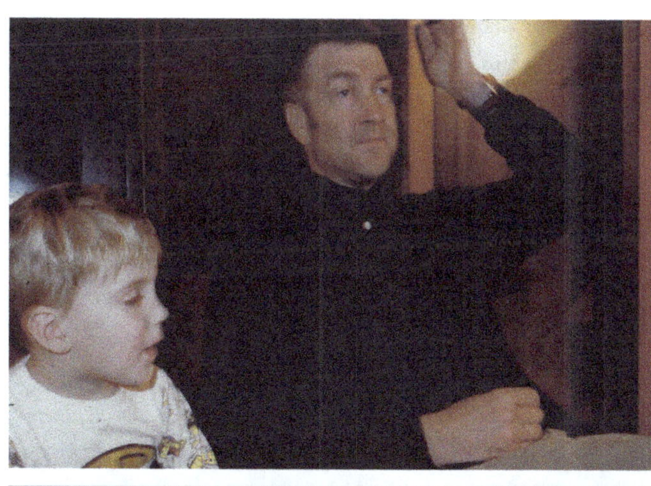

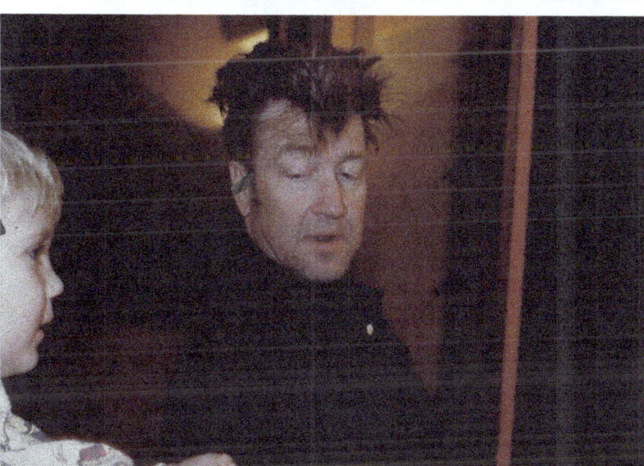

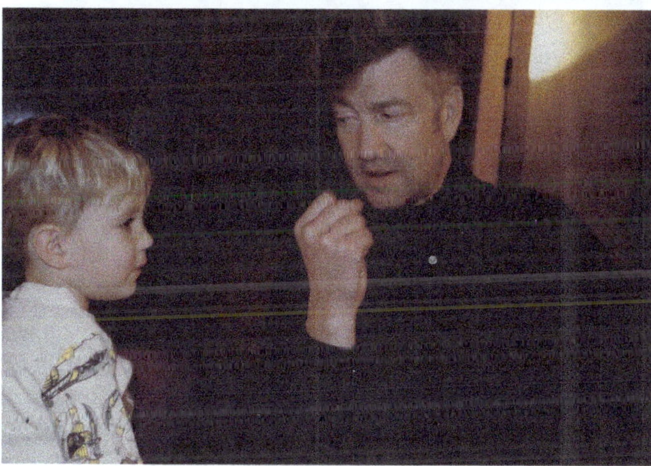

little vampire movie might be considered part of the enveloping cloud. David didn't participate in the publicity for *Nadja*—that was never the plan—but there was enough buzz and fanfare following our debut screenings at the Toronto International Film Festival for Mary Sweeney to receive an appealing offer from the Samuel Goldwyn Company, a deal that would have more than doubled David's investment.

I remember being a bit amazed that David and Mary agreed to a test screening of the film in Santa Monica, organized by the Goldwyn people, before the deal was signed. I wasn't present for that, but flew in from New York for a post-screening debriefing with Goldwyn executives. Mary must have been with us, but in my memory it's just me and David riding up the Century City elevator and being greeted in the sleek sunstruck office tower, getting the royal treatment, assistants hopping to bring coffee, people saying how *honored* they were to have David in the room, men in suits oozing a vibe of smiling deceitfulness. I remember David, unshaven, wearing a shirt buttoned to his neck, no jacket, looking unusually unpolished and unsure while mutely paging through a sheaf of papers they presented to us, the execs talking brightly while the ash on David's cigarette got longer and longer, a thin stream of smoke twisting up into the air and dissolving in sunlight just as the deal eventually twisted and dissolved.

When I think of the scene in *Mulholland Drive* where Angelo Badalamenti spits a mouthful of coffee into a cloth napkin—a scene that takes place, you may recall, in a Century City office building—I think of our encounter with the suave Goldwyn executives, though I'm sure David had plenty of other memories and meetings to draw on, to come up with that particular objective correlative.

David remained a cheerleader for *Nadja*, with Mary acting as intermediary and translator for all further business discussions, and as an assured editor she guided the film through a fast revision, an attempt to appease our Santa Monica critics. (A few shots were quickened and trimmed and Portishead songs were layered in over patches of Simon Fisher Turner's score.) This version, shorter by just three or four minutes, screened at Sundance In January of 1995, at which point Bingham Ray of October Films came to the rescue with a less lucrative but acceptable distribution deal, a bridge enabling Bingham to develop a strong relationship with Mary and David, leading to the domestic distribution of *Lost Highway* two years later. This turn of events allows me to assure myself, to this day, that in practical terms *Nadja* was not entirely a black stain or lost cause for David Lynch.

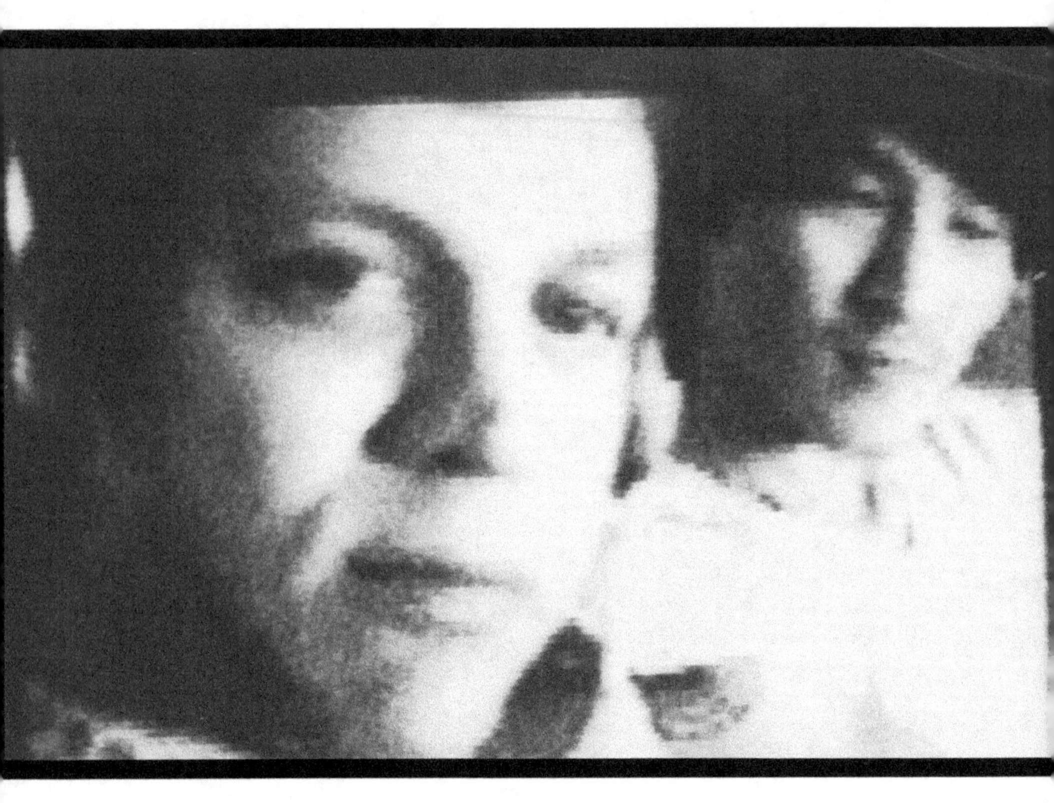

Todd Haynes and Greg Araki in *At Sundance*, 1995.

AT SUNDANCE (1995)

Co-directed with Amy Hobby
Pixelvision / B&W / 75 minutes
Interviews with Robert Redford, John Turturro, Atom Egoyan, Danny Boyle, Tod Haynes, Greg Araki, Abel Ferrara, Rebecca Miller, Richard Linklater, Ethan Hawke, Whit Stillman, Haskell Wexler, etc.
Camera: Michael Almereyda and Amy Hobby; Editor: Kristina Boden

Ramin Bahrani: You began *At Sundance* in flight, not with a train crashing across the screen, but a plane flying in the sky, shot with your toy camera. We hear a baby crying. Was using the toy camera a way to return to the simple, exhilarating moments of recording images for the first time?

Michael Almereyda: The film was co-directed by Amy Hobby, who produced *Nadja* — we handed the camera back and forth; the person not holding the camera took care of the sound. We wanted to invoke that history, sure, and catch that exhilaration. The landscape shots that punctuate the interviews, particularly the long ski lift shot, which is Amy's gift to the film — I never considered these incidental or extra, they're part of the dialogue. At any rate, I knew from experience how difficult it is to actually talk to other filmmakers at Sundance, and this was a calculated way to get around that.

RB: Robert Redford is the first (film/festival) director who appears. He is optimistic because of more distribution channels being open to filmmakers. This was before YouTube, iTunes, Netflix, and other forms of Internet distribution, which we are just embarking upon now. Have these modes of distribution made any significant difference to you or other independent filmmakers you know?

MA: *At Sundance* was conceived with the future in mind, as a time capsule. We wanted to present a rogue's gallery, a group portrait of people making independent films at that moment. And of course it's significant that there were few women or people of color. Robert Redford was our host—we couldn't have made the movie without his blessing. He was also the only person who couldn't come to my hotel room—we had to go to him. He shared his skill in delivering sound bites; he was gracious and smart. So we put him forward as the first voice, the valedictory optimist, before allowing some admissions of doubt and dismay. (As at most festivals, everyone at Sundance is trying very hard to be optimistic.) But, to leap to your question—which I think you can answer better than me—distribution for truly independent work remains achingly difficult. We're in a transition now, everyone's been saying for at least three years. As ever, filmmakers need to find the right person at the right company to fall in love with their work. There's a degree of necessary luck, as with every other kind of love.

RB: Ethan Hawke and Richard Linklater appear together. Hawke was pessimistic about appearing in *White Fang* while Linklater was optimistic about the breakthrough of digital technology. Larry Gross was also optimistic about new technology, embracing video as a medium of change. As you know, all three of my films were shot on HD and I am personally tired of "nostalgia" for film. I know you have also been using digital recently. Has technology brought us to a point that "film versus digital" is a dead subject?

MA: It's not a dead subject, but it's a lot less lively than other questions. I'll admit that my optimism—about technology and storytelling, the audience and the paths to finding the audience—is guarded. You have to be an optimist to make movies, to justify the effort, to face the long odds. But after a while, if not immediately, you recognize the routine injustice—you see the good films that get sidelined or ignored, bad films that are considered triumphs. I take comfort in Rick Linklater's quote from Truffaut, recognizing film as an open form, a personal form, and I've long been fond of something Godard said years ago. We may be at the end of cinema, he insisted, but the end can be a good time, like sunset, when lovers walk along the beach hand in hand. If this is the end, let's take that walk.

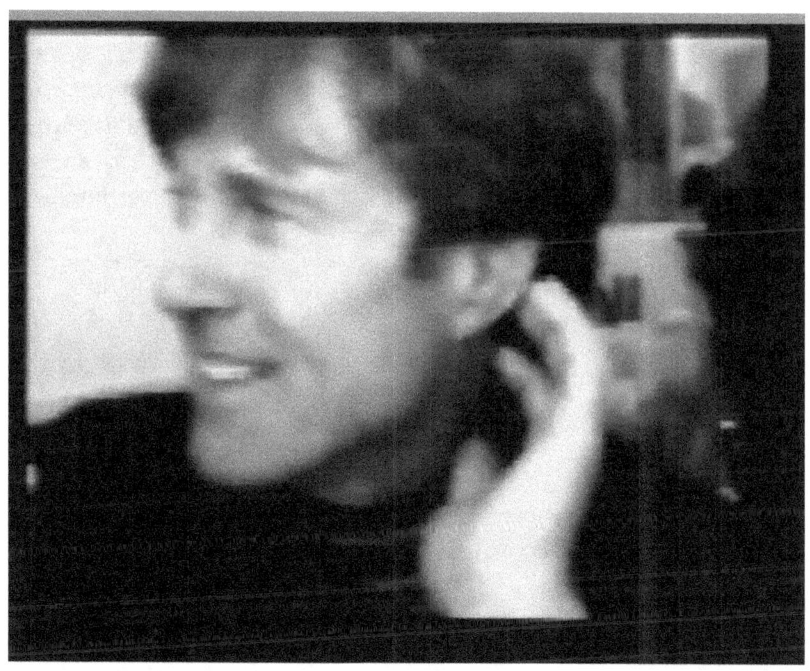

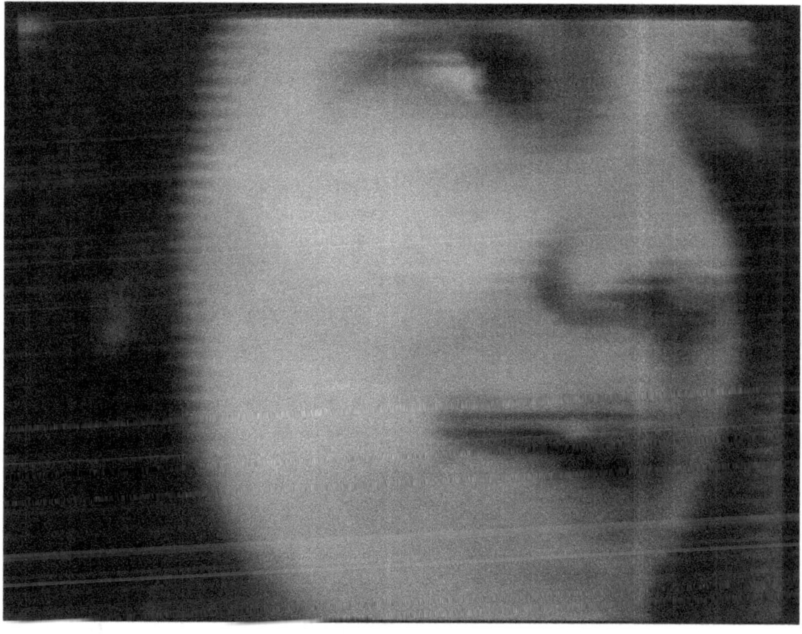

Robert Redford and Amy Hobby in *At Sundance*, 1995.

As the Sundance festival currently un-tethers itself from its home base in Park City, declaring the end of an era, the documentary now offers its fair share of nostalgia and prescience. In the editing room, the film was a jigsaw puzzle, the ordering of interviews constantly shifting as we attempted a balance of faces and voices, self-promotional banter alternating with occasional displays of selfless insight. I remain impressed by Haskell Wexler's blunt pessimism:

> The future of film is tied in with the future of every other thing in this country and in the world. Am I optimistic about it? I'm not optimistic about the condition of our country and of the world *for most people*. I think that for some people, it's worthy of optimism, but for the vast underground of citizens and not consumers—I notice they always call us consumers now instead of citizens—it's tough times. It'll be tough times for the arts and tough times for filmmakers and it'll challenge their courage to see if better and more meaningful things will come out.

Thirty years later, it's revealing to re-watch David Salle, on the scene to debut his first and (so far) only feature film, *Search and Destroy*, offering a cogent overview of cinema at the crossroads, placing *Blue Velvet* and David Lynch at the center, an assessment that seems both personal and farseeing:

> I remember maybe ten years ago, thinking with relief that no one had to worry about movies anymore because they basically had come to an end. And that Hollywood had killed off movies, and it was just a form that had run its course. Glorious as it had been, it wasn't infinitely renewable. And it was fine and you know, people think that, feel that way about painting, rightly or wrongly. So it just seemed like an historical fact and then *Blue Velvet* came out, and it's funny how one film can galvanize for a whole generation the sense of possibility and optimism. I think that David Lynch gave voice to a generation whose sensibility had been influenced if not formed by concerns that were typically found in art school, and what David proved was that the sensibility of art school, in the best sense, rhymes with a sensibility in the culture. And heretofore people assumed that they were irreconcilable. That was a legitimately optimistic moment in the history of cinema.

Despite the volatility of the edit, our decision to end *At Sundance* with Rick Linklater and Ethan Hawke was firmly settled early on. Perhaps, consciously or not, I saw Rick as a cheerful surrogate. Without seeming

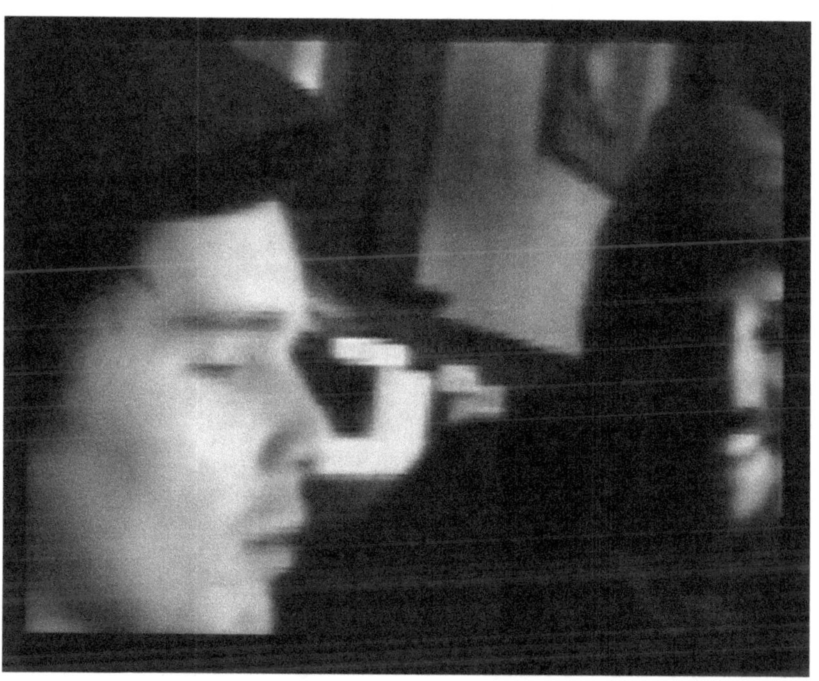

Ethan Hawke and Richard Linklater in *At Sundance*, 1995.

strident or bitter, he echoes Haskell Wexler: "The reasons to be pessimistic are the reasons to be pessimistic about our society, or just money, or what motivates us as people... It goes into a political dimension. I think all that is affecting current cinema and our, you know, commodity-based consumer culture, the way movies are just a part of that."

Ethan Hawke, twenty-four years old, another (future) surrogate, responds: "I think there will always be people interested in telling the truth and making something that's, for lack of a better word, *beautiful.*"

As mentioned above, Rick flipped open a book at the session's start, quoting a Truffaut essay from 1957, a paragraph that helped define the French New Wave and set it in motion.

Let's end with that beginning:

> The film of tomorrow seems to me as even more personal than an individual and autobiographical novel, like a confession, or a diary. The young filmmakers will express themselves in the first person and will relate what has happened to them. It may be the story of their first love, or rather, their most recent. Or their political awakening, the story of a trip, a sickness, their military service, their marriage, their last vacation. And it will be enjoyable because it will be true and new... The film of tomorrow will be an act of love.

Thank you to everyone named, pictured or quoted in these pages; to Jessica Almereyda and Jim Robison for reviewing rough-and-tumble drafts, and Spencer Kayden for coming through in the home stretch; to Mary Sweeney, for believing in me early on, through good weather and bad; to Walter Donohue for instigating three previously published pieces ("My Stunning Future…," "Hollywood Halloween," "Notes on Derek Jarman"); to Will Blythe for commissioning the Sam Shepard interview and Gavin Smith for inviting me to write about Chris Marker; to Fairfax Dorn and Ralph McKay for bringing me and my films to Marfa; to Jim Stark for making introductions; to Ryan Krivoshey of Grasshopper Films and David Marriott and Ei Toshinari of Arbelos Films, for exhuming *Nadja* from the crypt with the blessing of Sabrina Sutherland and the David Lynch Estate.

The book wouldn't exist without the reckless and patient support of Paul Cronin, who fully embraced the idea, steered the course, and set the type.

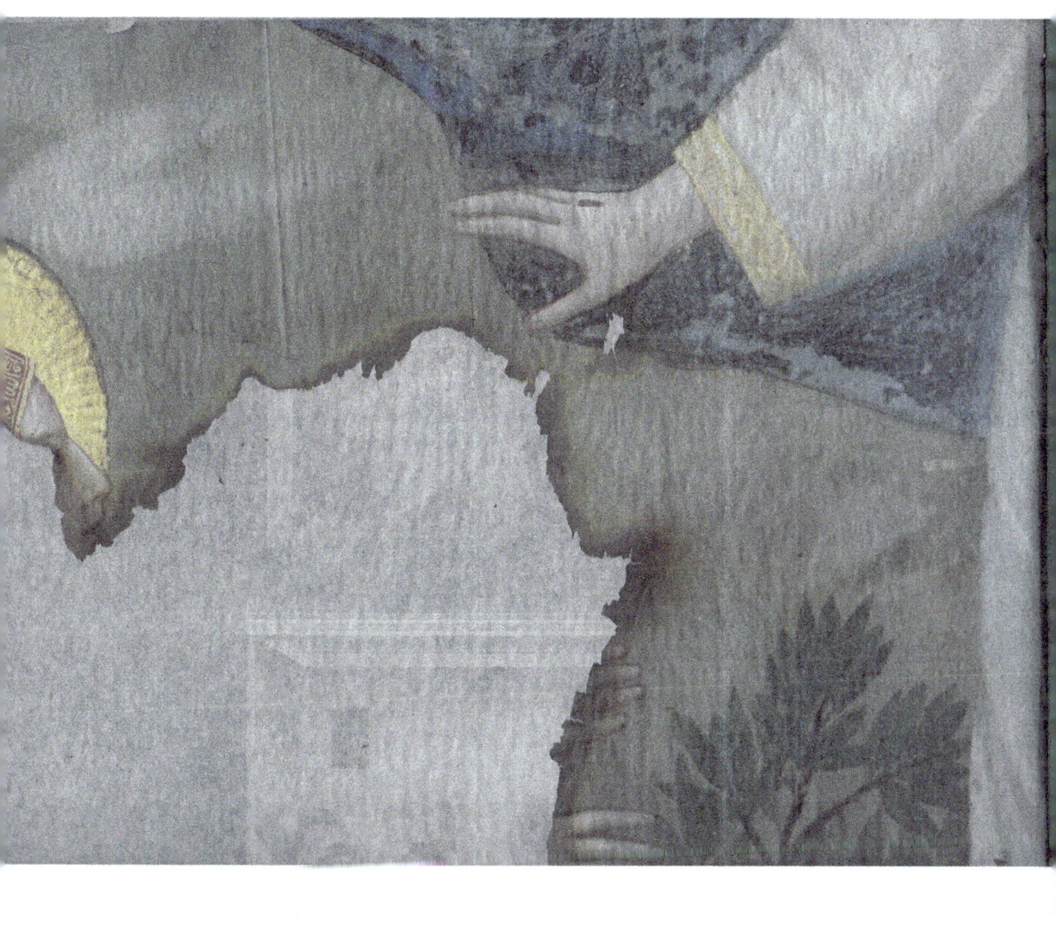